A
Resource Allocation
Decision System
For Education

Program Budgeting

(PPBS)

Stephen J. Knezevich

University of Wisconsin

McCutchan Publishing Corporation
2526 Grove Street
Berkeley, California 94704

Library of Congress Catalog Card Number: 72-5703
International Standard Book Number: 0-8211-1014-4

To six tall men in the field of educational administration who influenced my thinking and shaped my professional career:

> *Forrest E. Conner,* Executive
> Secretary Emeritus, AASA
>
> *Glen G. Eye,* Professor, University of
> Wisconsin, Madison
>
> *John Guy Fowlkes,* Professor
> Emeritus, University of Wisconsin,
> Madison
>
> *Russell T. Gregg,* Professor Emeritus,
> University of Wisconsin, Madison
>
> *Elmer T. Peterson,* Dean Emeritus,
> University of Iowa, Iowa City
>
> *Mode L. Stone,* Dean Emeritus,
> Florida State University, Tallahassee

Contents

Foreword   vii
Michael W. Kirst

Preface   ix

1.   Program budgeting and its many acronyms   1

2.   History and development of program budgeting   14

3.   The planning dimension of program budgeting   29

4.   Generating the quality and types of objectives needed to operate in the PPBS mode   39

5.   PPBS and its relationship to management by objectives (MBO) and accountability   52

6.   Programming and generating programmatic formats for educational institutions   71

7.   Budgeting and the budget document   109

8.   Budgeting in transition: evolution of performance and program budgeting   123

9. Cost accounting and unit cost analysis in education:
    additional fiscal dimensions of PPBS   147

10. Analysis dimension in program budgeting: generating
    alternatives and preliminary thought on systems
    analysis   171

11. Analytic procedures and procedures in program
    budgeting   182

12. PPBS as decision technology and its impact on the
    political process   224

13. The total system: appraisal and state of the art   236

14. Strategies for implementation and operation of PPBS   252

15. Problems and promises after years of trying: why it
    doesn't always work   272

    Appendix A. Bulletin 66-3   283

    Appendix B. Supplement to Bulletin 66-3   301

    Appendix C. Bulletin 68-2   310

    PPBS and systems management glossary   325

    Index   331

Foreword

Several years have elapsed since PPBS and MBO were added to the lexicon of educational administrators. The concepts began to spread in the mid-sixties from the federal government (primarily the Department of Defense) to state and local public agencies. Educators have made many modifications in the original formulations to better fit the particular circumstances of educational organizations. Consequently, this book is especially timely. We have passed through the stage of overly simplistic transfers from defense to education. Now we must guard against discarding the underlying validity and usefulness of these management tools.

Professor Knezevich has something new to say about a topic that has been widely discussed and debated for many years. His service as Director of AASA's National Academy for School Executives has provided many insights on adapting PPBS to the peculiarities of education. For instance, his concluding section analyzes "why it doesn't always work." He cuts through the euphoria and negativism that earlier surrounded PPBS for education to the core techniques for implementation. This book does not analyze all PPBS issues and concepts in depth, but it does provide the practitioner with some concrete courses of action that have withstood the testing period. While the term PPBS may ultimately be replaced by something else, the essence of Professor Knezevich's book will live on.

Michael W. Kirst
Series Editor

Stanford, California

Preface

Perhaps the first sharply focused document on program budgeting was a collection of papers edited by David Novick and published as part of a study sponsored by RAND Corporation in 1964. The number of articles on PPB proliferated thereafter. I have been able to identify over 300 articles related to some aspect of PPB; by the late 1960s, many articles and one book on PPB in education came off the presses. By the early 1970s, writings about PPB in education appeared with regularity, but most were journal articles describing efforts to implement it in a school or university.

There is considerable variation in the literature focusing on education as to the precise meaning and application of the PPB system. In this book PPBS is perceived as a decision system whose time has come. It is more than a new approach to budgeting, even though the format of the budget document may be different in schools operating in the PPBS mode. Most of the book is dedicated to describing in considerable detail how much more than the fiscal dimensions of educational operations will be affected by the decision system.

PPBS took its rise in the federal government a little over a decade ago and then slowly spread to other agencies. What happened during this first decade is now history. There appears to be less rhetoric surrounding the idea and more realistic appraisal of what PPBS can and cannot do for an organization. The critics are less timid in attacking those who promised more than could be delivered. The literature in educational administration is replete with exhortations to school systems to "get going with PPBS." Nonetheless, experience with PPBS in education remains limited. It is difficult to identify a significant and well documented experience of a sophisticated PPB system that is fully operational in an educational institution.

After a decade of experience in the federal government, the completion of a significant PPB experiment in education and the further conceptual development of PPB makes the time ripe for a more realistic description and appraisal of that promising technology called PPBS. Oversimplifications of the substance and operations of PPBS, typical in most popular magazine accounts, have been found wanting. There is a need for a more disciplined analysis of what PPBS is all about as well as what it can and cannot do in educational organizations. PPB is a complex system. Those who would seek to implement it need more than sketchy details or recitations of its potential.

This book is addressed to those concerned with the management of educational institutions. The target population is present and future administrators of schools and universities, those at the top echelons and those in operational divisions. It begins with an analysis of the basic concepts, reveals some semantic problems, and then describes and illustrates the many dimensions of that complex decision technology called PPBS. It is pictured as a system; no one element can stand alone, nor can a single dimension be assumed to be the sum and substance of it all. Furthermore, it is seen as a means to an end. It isn't worth the time and effort to implement PPBS unless it helps an administrator do something he couldn't do otherwise. From the point of view of this writer, PPBS will help the administrator make more prudent resource allocation decisions.

The pressures to inaugurate the PPB system in education are likely to intensify rather than diminish during the 1970s. The book, therefore, reviews many of the problems and issues in implementation. PPBS is a difficult system to manage. Those who would seek to enjoy its benefits must be aware of the credibility gap that develops when more is promised than can be delivered. PPBS is not magic, but it does have real power. It may not be installed instantaneously nor easily, but it is worth the extra effort and patience to get the job done.

The book was written with the practitioner in mind, whether he is perceived as the administrator at the elementary-secondary school level, in a vocational-technical institute, a junior college, or a major university. It is more than a primer on PPBS. It seeks to establish the rationale necessary to support all "how to" directions. Publication was delayed about three years to accumulate practical applications and illustrations of PPBS in education. Much remains to be done, but the illustrations do represent a significant start. The built-in redundancy is worthy of mention. There are recurrent themes that are repeated in chapters. It is assumed that this volume is likely to be read one chapter at a time over an extended period rather than completely at one sitting.

The volume will be useful as well to the graduate student or administrative trainee in education. The ideas and organization of material are based on more than a decade of study of the pioneer efforts and observations of practices in many different kinds of agencies. They were tested with school administrators attending the AASA National Academy of School Executives' PPBS clinics during 1969, 1970, and 1971. At least three classes of graduate students at the University of Wisconsin, Madison, have had opportunities to react to the substance of the ideas presented as well as the illustrations. That the writer was strongly influenced by the early developers of PPBS and economic thought in general will be evident throughout this volume.

Aside from the men to whom this book is dedicated, thanks are due to Cleo H. Coenen for her devoted and tireless efforts in typing and retyping the manuscript. Cleo's contributions in preparing this document for publication are worthy of special recognition. Deserving acknowledgment as well are my graduate assistants David Lewein of Milwaukee, Wisconsin, Wen Dar Lin of Taiwan, and Bal K. Thaper of India. The art work of Janice V. Gruenwald so necessary in translating rough ideas on cost-effectiveness curves into meaningful diagrams deserves to be acknowledged as well. I acknowledge the many kindnesses and professional courtesies extended to me by Dr. William H. Curtis, Director of RC-ASBO PPBES project, and Dr. Charles W. Foster, Executive Secretary of ASBO, in making available to me and my university classes the many excellent ideas and materials produced during their "PPBES Project." These ideas and materials were utilized in and influenced the preparation of this book as well. Lastly, acknowledgment is made of the assistance of an understanding wife during manuscript preparation and particularly in the production of the index.

Stephen J. Knezevich

University of Wisconsin
Madison

1. Program budgeting and
its many acronyms

The overwhelming popularity of the term *program budgeting* and the acronym **PPBS** is evident from the literature on the subject. In this book, the popular term and its most common acronym (both defined more precisely later in this chapter) will be considered synonymous, unless specific statements are made to the contrary. **PPBS** is not, however, the only acronym around, nor should it be assumed that the most frequently used ways of identifying a management decision system are the most precise.

The consensus of informed opinion during much of the 1960s was that **PPBS** was, indeed, a revolutionary development in the science of management and that primarily good would flow from the practical application of its concepts and techniques. The excitement intensified after October 1965, when President Lyndon Johnson directed that "an integrated planning, programming, budgeting system" be installed in all federal executive departments and establishments. The spread of the idea was described by one source in these terms: "PPB, introduced in 1961, had become epidemic by 1968."[1]

After about a decade of writing by proponents who preached the power of program budgeting and exhorted one and all to implement the system, critics appeared to increase in number and become bolder in their declarations. The writers who found that **PPBS** had become an "epidemic" declared that they did not intend to project negativism, but rather were "reacting against what seems to us to be

an over-abundance of laudatory and superficial discussions of PPB."[2]
As a result it is less difficult now to find writings on the shortcomings and complexities of operating in the PPB mode. This is not
to suggest that program budgeting has run its course—far from it!

At this point in the history and development of program budgeting more balanced and realistic appraisals of its promise and pitfalls
are evident. The practical problems likely to confront organizations
seeking implementation are not as likely to be swept under the rug.
Specialists from a number of disciplines had a hand in generating the
concepts and outlining the practical applications of program budgeting. Economists, more than any others, led the revolution and
deserve recognition as its originators and developers. Political scientists, government officials, and business managers were involved to
lesser degrees. The first to criticize the overzealous rhetoric were
political scientists, not economists. More recently, educational
administrators have begun adapting its concepts and techniques to
the unique challenges confronting educational institutions.

Analysis of the Acronyms

We live in the day of acronyms, those unusual words formed from
the initial letters of more complex sets of words. Some acronyms,
such as radar and PERT, are pronounced. Others, such as PPBS and
CPM, are recited letter by letter. Within the past decade a number of
firms have adopted acronyms, pronounced letter by letter, as official
corporate titles. Acronyms are not new. The federal government
informally identified emergency relief programs in this manner during the depression of the 1930s. It was popular then to refer to the
WPA and the NRA. The ability to coin and banter about acronyms
remains the "in" thing. An acronym is like a nickname, an efficient
communication model that identifies and projects the image of a
complex idea.

The derivation of acronyms related to program budgeting is in-
triguing. Industries prefer three-letter acronyms as corporate titles. In
contrast, PPBS is a four-letter word, although the fourth letter is
sometimes omitted. The acronym is derived from a set of processes
within the system: "planning, programming, budgeting system." The
S suggests that all the elements are interrelated; it is not another
process like the first three. More writers of late speak of PPB or the
PPB system. An analysis and further interpretation of what is meant
by each element will be made later in this chapter.

In the field of education a closely related acronym, PPBES,

gathered some popularity during the late 1960s. The E meant "evaluating," a fourth process. The originator and popularizer of this acronym was the Research Corporation of the Association of School Business Officials (RC–ASBO) during the early part of its project. When its final report was published, however, it indicated a preference for another acronym, ERMS, derived from "educational resources management system." At one time in its development, this was called "educational resource management design" (ERMD).[3] These two acronyms convey meanings that are in harmony with the spirit and substance of this book.

Another group put the E as the first letter, standing for "education," and coined EPPBS, to suggest the field to which the system was applied. This acronym never gained much currency.

The most popular acronym, PPBS, can be criticized as an inaccurate and unfortunate representation of the decision system for various reasons. A title should help convey the purpose of the management system. PPBS is a mission-oriented approach, namely, a disciplined way of relating activities, or inputs, to objectives. Processes and procedures are relevant only insofar as they contribute to attainment of stated goals. Instead of stressing outcomes, the acronym PPBS emphasizes what the technique seeks to avoid, namely, processes. Planning, programming, and budgeting are not ends but means for reaching a goal. The outcome or purposes of the management system are not implied in either the acronym PPBS or the term *program budgeting.*

Another criticism is that PPBS is an incomplete abbreviation, for it identifies only a few processes. It fails to recognize some that are most important in achieving the full potential of the system. For example, the step of analyzing the alternative approaches for reaching a goal is not mentioned; nor are evaluating, deciding, and recycling listed. The failure of PPBS to identify many important processes exacerbates the search for its full meaning and increases the probability that some may focus, inadvertently or otherwise, on one element rather than on the total system. In the field of education the most familiar element is budgeting. Many, therefore, erroneously conclude that PPBS is simply an approach to budgeting. This one process may be so fixed in the minds of some that they will make only passing reference to planning and programming, and will practically ignore other important processes.

These criticisms have brought the author to recommend two alternative acronyms for the decision system. The first, PPBADERS, seeks to overcome the incompleteness of the acronym PPBS by identifying all the processes: "planning, programing, budgeting, analyzing, deciding, evaluating, and recycling system." The PPBADERS cycle of activities is illustrated in figure 1-1. Obviously, it is a more cumbersome acronym. Perhaps it was the penchant to make PPBS a four-letter word that accounts for the incomplete designation. PPBADERS is suggested primarily to reveal all processes, rather than as a handy way to communicate the system.

Although expanding the number of letters in the acronym increases its accuracy (and thereby detracts from the ease of communicating its concepts to others), it does not correct a more fundamental oversight; the acronym fails to suggest its reason for being: a disciplined emphasis on missions to be accomplished. For this reason, the author generated a new four-letter acronym, RADS, meaning

Figure 1-1. The PPBADERS cycle of activities

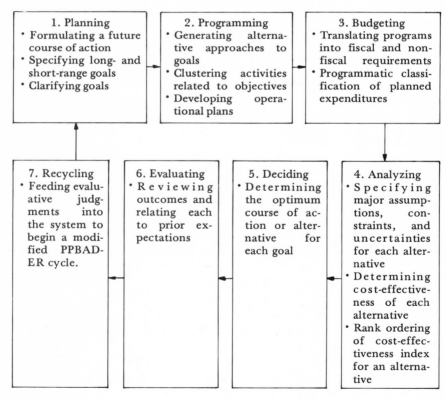

"resource allocation decision system." This was proposed in a 1969 publication but failed to get much attention or many converts.[4] The system was designed to improve "federal decision making about resource allocation."[5] The acronym RADS stresses that improved decision making is what program budgeting or PPBS seeks to accomplish. It enables the administrator to enhance his capabilities in making specific kinds of decisions, namely, decisions relating to allocating resources among the competing purposes or objectives of an organization. Whereas PPBS suggests processes, RADS focuses on the mission or outcomes hoped for, namely, improved resource allocation decisions. This is the point of view that pervades this book. A resource management system will be described that the author hopes will give administrators a more rational basis for selecting one course of action (or expenditure of school funds) as opposed to another. RADS and RC—ASBO's ERMS are very similar in spirit.

PPBS and Program Budgeting as Words, Not Descriptions

Although the author's preference for RADS is obvious, he is more interested in conveying the concepts and skills necessary to implement a mission-oriented management systems than in gaining converts to a better acronym. PPBS will be used in this book because of its popularity and not because it makes the best sense. The reader is asked to think of it as a "word" that conveys the image of the management system. Simplistic efforts to define PPBS in terms of what P, P, B, and S mean are to be avoided. Such activities will confuse more than help in conveying the substance and full potential of this decision system. Again, much more than "planning, programming, and budgeting" is involved, and these processes are not ends in themselves.

What about the other "word," program budgeting? Economist David Novick was among the pioneers in the RAND Corporation who made a special study of resource allocation decisions in the federal government, particularly in the Department of Defense. A more complete history of his contributions is presented in chapter 2. Novick's distinct preference for the term *program budgeting* is evident in his many writings. In the author's opinion program budgeting fails to overcome the semantic pitfalls of PPBS. It, too, is better perceived as a "word" rather than a way to unlock the secrets of the system. For better or for worse, popularity of usage means we are stuck with the names program budgeting and PPBS.

Another RAND economist, Charles J. Hitch, who subsequently

became the Department of Defense Comptroller, deserves recognition as one of the original developers and users of this approach. He indicated a decided preference for the name PPBS as opposed to program budgeting. Hitch, at the direction of Defense Secretary Robert McNamara, instituted the new decision system in the Defense Department in the early 1960s. Its use in the federal government gave the system more fame than its development in the RAND Corporation. It is the judgment of this writer that the acronym is used more extensively in the literature than program budgeting.

Much of the current literature tends to equate program budgeting with PPBS. Some conceive of program budgeting as a subset within PPBS, that is, the programmatic categorization of budgetary accounts. This categorizing can be done without the explicit consideration of systems analysis and the multiyear perspective typically recommended in the PPBS approach. In this limited and special sense, program budgeting may be interpreted as only one phase of the total decision system, the phase that focuses on programmatic classification of budget and expenditure accounts. Thus, there is some justification for attributing separate meanings to the two terms. However, most writers consider program budgeting and PPBS to be synonymous, and, unless detailed discussions clearly indicate otherwise, it is the point of view that prevails in this book.

The semantic problems likely to confront those seeking to understand the decision system are apparent. This is not unusual in new fields. It takes time for terms to acquire specific and standard definitions. A superficial swipe at the literature may not remind the reader that a system by definition is more than any single element within it. Each element can be understood completely only in relation to others rather than as a discrete process. Misinterpretations of the meaning and substance of PPBS can occur when there is a failure to view it as a system of interrelated processes. Errors may be compounded by preoccupation with a single element, such as budgeting, to the neglect of all others. This is not to denigrate the importance of budgeting but rather to suggest that its full potential is most likely to be illuminated when viewed in the perspective of other activities. Overemphasis of one dimension and neglect of others may create an image problem for the system. Thus, schools and universities may conclude that only their "business officials" should be concerned with PPB. As subsequent chapters will demonstrate, program budgeting as an output-oriented management system cannot be implemented unless all top-echelon administrators, including those concerned with program definition (curriculum and instruction), are involved. Although the fiscal dimension is important in the total system, PPBS is more than just another fiscal technique calling for more precise cost-accounting. It is a way of thinking by clarifying objectives, reordering priorities, searching for alternatives, analyzing the cost and benefits for each option, and deciding on the basis of evidence and rationality.

PPBS and Systems Analysis

Although neither of the two most popular titles, PPBS and program budgeting, suggests its use, systems analysis is an important dimension of the decision technology described here. Program budgeting is a subset of the systems approach to educational administration. The author has identified the major elements of this systems approach to include systems analysis, systems design, systems engineering, systems management, and systems evaluation.[6] In general the attitudes and methods of operation of the systems approach can be summarized as follows:

1. *Organization as a system:* viewing the organization as a system with an array of resources focused on a set of objectives to be satisfied according to a predetermined plan
2. *Organization as a delivery system:* considering an organization (or institution) to be a delivery vehicle, that is, a means of converting inputs (resources) into more desirable outputs (results)
3. *Dynamic relationship among elements:* recognizing that elements and subsystems within the total system are interactive and interdependent components
4. *Mission orientation:* emphasizing that identification and clarification of long- and short-range objectives must be the first order of activities in operation of the organization
5. *Inevitability of change:* recognizing change as normal and, therefore, that redefining goals and reordering priorities are continuing functions
6. *Importance of models:* creating models, which identify critical factors and establish patterns of relationships among them, to study any and all dimensions of the organization
7. *Importance of alternatives:* demanding a search to identify alternatives for attainment of each objective and analyzing the cost-benefit index for major alternatives
8. *Importance of long-range planning:* emphasizing long-range planning.

9. *Monitoring operations:* establishing monitoring subsystems to determine deviations from targeted objectives.
10. *Interdisciplinary problem solving:* employing interdisciplinary problem-solving teams.
11. *Scientific decision making:* implementing sophisticated, objective, and scientifically oriented procedures for decision making based on verified data and quantitative analysis.
12. *The evolving system:* recycling operations to revise or improve procedures following experience and the appraisal of experience.

The popularity of systems analysis introduces semantic problems because of different interpretations of what is involved. Operations research and computer-based information systems have something to contribute to the systems approach but should not be confused with the approach itself. Computer systems managers and programmers have unfortunately applied the term *systems analyst* to information-system specialists. There are other systems techniques as well, such as PERT, an acronym for "program evaluation and review technique," which is a technique for evaluating and reviewing progress toward stated goals. A special chapter is devoted to the analysis dimension in program budgeting.

PPBS and Public Expenditure Economics

Economists, first in the RAND Corporation and then in the Department of Defense, did much to develop the basic concepts of PPBS. Haveman argues that, "until the late 1950's and 1960's public expenditure analysis was not generally recognized as a distinct field of economic inquiry."[7] Economists working in the field of public finance were more concerned with taxation than with expenditures of public monies. As Haveman concludes, "with good reason, public finance prior to the late 1950's was widely interpreted as the economics of taxation."[8]

Since that time the very magnitude of governmental budgets and the complexity of decision making about the type and size of public expenditures have stimulated the application of economic analysis to the planning and execution of expenditure decisions. Government purchases of goods and services now constitute about 20 percent of the gross national product (GNP). This spending gave impetus to the development of what Haveman has called "public expenditure economics," which is now recognized as a subset of the broader field of welfare economics. It is wrong to assume that this branch of economics is confined to the study of welfare payments to the indigent. It is concerned broadly with using the tools of economic analysis to help clarify when and how government can intervene in the market economy to accomplish social objectives. Some economists are pessimistic about the ability of economic analysis to relate public decisions to social welfare. But economists no longer hold to the traditional free enterprise assumption that government expenditures are of small consequence. What big government does influences the functioning of the private as well as public economy.

PPBS may be interpreted as a systematic effort to appraise the relative worth of public expenditure options. The development of the field of public expenditure economics gives program budgeting a much needed conceptual and empirical sophistication. Application of the theory and practice of public expenditure economics can contribute to improvement of public decision making on various expenditure alternatives.

In this sense, PPBS applied to education may be defined as a decision technology concerned with the identification, analysis, and appraisal of public school expenditure alternatives by and through the application of the logic of economics.[9] It is apparent that the objectives of education are many and diverse. Its resources, however, are limited. Some system is needed for valuing the inputs as they relate to the outputs achieved.

This approach does exist and is referred to most frequently as benefit-cost or cost-effectiveness analysis. More will be said about these techniques in chapters 10 and 11.

In the late 1950s and early 1960s the focus of economists was expanded to apply the logic of economic analysis to the expenditure side as well as the revenue side of the public budget. It doubtless contributed much to the improvement of governmental budget making as well as decision making with reference to alternative expenditure patterns.

Without question the use of program budgeting contributed much to the growing popularity of economic concepts to education as well as government. Such terms as *input, output, externalities, cost-benefit, cost-effectiveness,* and *cost-utility* have found their way into the education literature from the field of economics. The influence of economic concepts on the author's thinking and writing should be evident.

Program Budgeting in Education Defined

Program budgeting in education is defined as a decision system concerned with improving resource allocation decisions when an educational institution is confronted with competing objectives and limited resources. It is a means to an end. It is a valuable adjunct to the administration of educational institutions to the extent that it actually does improve expenditure decisions. The fact that it does so through "the application of the logic of economics" or that it may be perceived as a subset of public expenditure economics is not important. Planning, programming, and budgeting mean little if they cannot be translated into useful results. The value of PPBS is derived from the fact that it gives an administrator a capability he did not possess when other techniques were applied. The "go or no-go" decision to implement program budgeting should be made on this basis.

Why Worry about Program Budgeting in Education?

The literature on program budgeting in general is rapidly expanding. The literature on the application of these concepts to the field of education has grown by leaps and bounds since 1967. The writers appear to be a diverse group: a mix of professors, educational administrators, and public figures. Some are concerned with defining the terms, others with describing the processes in a general way, and many simply with exhorting schools to institute program budgeting. An increasing number of education periodicals feature success stories of how a particular agency or school established PPBS. Separating truth from fiction in such tales is not easy. There remains a dearth of research-based writing. A journalistic style prevails, with comparatively little documentation to support conclusions. In general, more rhetoric than substantive writing characterizes the literature on PPBS in education, although there are some noteworthy exceptions.

The PPBS literature has become so extensive that bibliographies on program budgeting are no longer uncommon. They have been produced by an ERIC center, the RC–ASBO project, and even an R & D center focusing on the application of program budgeting to vocational education. The author has identified over 300 separate pieces on or related to program budgeting in general and as applied to education, and this was by no means an exhaustive listing. Sifting through this mass of material and sorting the good from the bad is a major task that can consume much time.

As of 1972, there have been legislative recommendations or mandates in about twenty states calling for the establishment of program budgeting in education. PPBS is far more complex than most people anticipated five years ago. It is not a cure-all or a way to reduce expenditures during an inflationary period or when people are demanding more rather than less from educational institutions. It may contribute to optimizing resource use. To paraphrase the military men who are forever seeking ways to produce "more bang for the buck," PPBS may help to get "more pedagogy for the penny."

The popular educational term in the early 1970s is *accountability*. It is a goal-referenced term. It is meaningless unless one specifies accountability for what, to whom, and under what conditions. PPBS may be perceived as a method or part of an accountability system. Program budgeting does specify objectives and emphasize outcomes. These are important in establishing an accountability system.

This book develops a conceptual base for PPBS by defining key concepts within the system and then illustrating what they mean in operational terms. It does not stop at this level, but moves to the practical concerns of identifying what a school or university operating in the PPBS mode would look like. This includes the most frequently discussed dimension, namely, what do program budgets look like? In addition strategy is suggested for moving toward or implementing the PPBS approach, specifically in educational institutions. The illustrations are extracted from public and private elementary, secondary, and higher educational institutions.

In short, the objective is to give the reader a comprehensive review of the nature and substance of program budgeting, but the concepts are presented with a definite practical flavor that may be helpful in making it work in a given educational institution. The history and development of PPBS are described next, in chapter 2.

Summary

Program budgeting and PPBS may be the most popular but they are not the only ways of identifying a revolutionary development in the science of management. There are PPBES (planning, programming, budgeting, and evaluating system), EPPBS (this time E stands for education), and ERMS (educational resource management system). Use of PPBS as a way of identifying the system has been criticized because it emphasizes the wrong thing (processes rather than outcomes) and is incomplete (many important processes are not evident from the four-letter acronym). The author suggested PPBADERS to correct the latter objection by giving recognition to analyzing, deciding, evaluating, and recycling. This made it more accurate but more cumbersome, and failed to emphasize the purpose behind the system. The author's second acronym was RADS, which viewed it as a resource allocation decision system. The reason for getting excited about the system at all is that it may improve decisions made about how scarce resources can be allocated to competing objectives. In the end PPBS was accepted as a four-letter word representing a broader concept, rather than an abbreviation for what the system is all about.

Novick preferred the term program budgeting, but Hitch liked PPBS better. Since the system gained its fame when Hitch, as comptroller, installed it in the Department of Defense, PPBS became the most popular appellation. The two terms are used interchangeably here unless stipulated to the contrary.

PPBS is related to other techniques that make up what is known as the systems approach to school administration. Its concepts were developed first by economists (in the RAND Corporation and later in the federal government) with experts from other disciplines chipping in ideas during the 1960s.

Public expenditure economics, a branch of welfare economics, came into being fairly recently. The growth of government expenditures made analysis of spending as well as taxation an important part of public finance. PPBS may be perceived as a subset of public expenditure economics. Thus, program budgeting in education may be defined as decision technology concerned with the identification, analysis, and appraisal of public school expenditure alternatives by and through the application of the logic of economics.

PPBS is a means, not an end. The "go or no-go" decision to implement it should be based on the probability that it will help administrators get "more pedagogy for the penny." It is not a cure-all or a way to reduce costs during an inflationary period or when people demand more from educational institutions; rather it is a method of optimizing use of resources.

The literature on PPBS has grown so rapidly that it is a time-consuming chore to sift it all. More rhetoric than substance characterizes the writing in education, although there are some noteworthy exceptions. Bibliographies on the topic are no longer a rarity and have difficulty maintaining currency.

Program budgeting can contribute much to the operation of an accountability system for education. Accountability is a goal-referenced term; it demands definition of accountability for what, to whom, and under what conditions.

Notes

1. L. Merewitz and S. H. Sosnick, *The Budget's New Clothes* (Chicago: Markham Publishing Co., 1971), p. 273.

2. Ibid., p. vii.

3. W. H. Curtis, *Educational Resources Management System*, special report, Association of School Business Officials Research Staff on a Planning-Programming-Budgeting-Evaluating System (Chicago: Research Corporation of the Association of School Business Officials, 1972), pp. 9-16.

4. S. J. Knezevich, ed., *Administrative Technology and the School Executive* (Washington, D.C.: American Association of School Administrators, 1969), pp. 70-71.

5. F. S. Hoffman, "Public Expenditure Analysis and the Institutions of the Executive Branch," in *Public Expenditures and Policy Analysis*, ed. R. H. Haveman and J. Margolis (Chicago: Markham Publishing Co., 1970), p. 424.

6. S. J. Knezevich, *Administration of Public Education*, 2d ed. (New York: Harper & Row, 1969), chap. 29.

7. R. H. Haveman, "Public Expenditures and Policy Analysis: An Overview," in *Public Expenditures and Policy Analysis*, ed. R. H. Haveman and J. Margolis (Chicago: Markham Publishing Co., 1970), p. 1.

8. Ibid., p. 2.

9. Ibid., p. 3; this definition is from Haveman's phrase about applying "the logic of economics to public expenditure decisions."

Selected References

Haveman, R. H. "Public Expenditures and Policy Analysis: An Overview." In *Public Expenditures and Policy Analysis*, edited by R. H. Haveman and J. Margolis. Chicago: Markham Publishing Co., 1970.

2. History and development of program budgeting

Complex ideas are not born fully developed on any given day in history. They evolve over time; ideas that may appear initially to be divergent but related are synthesized to generate new concepts of greater significance and potential than the individual precursors. How program budgeting took its rise can be traced only after the term is defined with specificity. As David Novick, the RAND Corporation economist, put it, "certain elements of program budgeting are as old as civilization."[1] On the other hand, modern roots of its *popular* usage can be traced to President Lyndon Johnson's news conference of August 25, 1965, at which he announced: "This morning I have just concluded a breakfast meeting with the Cabinet and with the heads of federal agencies, and I am asking each of them to immediately begin to introduce a very new and very revolutionary system of planning and programming and budgeting throughout the vast federal government, so that through the tools of modern management the full promise of the finer life can be brought to every American at the lowest possible cost." He directed each cabinet member and agency head to develop a special staff of experts to define goals and to engage in "modern methods of program analysis."

Shortly thereafter, the famous Bulletin 66-3 of October 12, 1965 (reproduced in Appendix A of this book), was sent to the heads of federal executive departments and establishments from the Executive Office of the President, Bureau of the Budget. This historic memo announced the introduction of an integrated planning-programming-budgeting system (PPBS) in the executive branch, and gave some instructions for its establishment. It gave rise to other Bureau of the Budget bulletins on the application of PPBS to the federal government, such as the Supplement to Bulletin 66-3 of February 21, 1966 (reproduced in Appendix B), Bulletin 68-2 of July 18, 1967 (reproduced in Appendix C), and Bulletin 68-9 of April 12, 1968.

Perhaps as famous as the original Bulletin 66-3 of 1965 was a message released by the Office of Management and Budget in September 1971. Addressing the heads of federal departments, OMB Director George B. Shultz called for a significant revision in many of the components of PPB. More will be said about this in later chapters.

There can be no question that the modern synthesis of ideas brought together under the label of PPBS, and the detailed procedures for implementing what is considered by many as potentially the most significant management improvement in the history of American government, can be traced to events and practices in the federal government as early as 1961. The contributions of the RAND Corporation, in particular, during the 1940s and 1950s deserve to be recognized. In this unique "think tank," many of the ideas that were applied on a grand scale in the Department of Defense in 1961, in the Department of Agriculture in 1962, and then in many other federal agencies after 1965, were first generated. The promising experiences in the early 1960s doubtless stimulated President Johnson's directives in the last half of 1965 to apply the concepts and procedures to all aspects of government.

The Antecedents of Program Budgeting

Those who argue that PPBS does not constitute anything radically new in the management of complex institutions refer to the history of particular elements within the technique and not to the complete set of ideas. To illustrate, benefit cost-analysis has a history of its own that can be traced back over 100 years before its use in PPBS. Merewitz and Sosnick, in a brief history of benefit cost-analysis, referred to its use in 1844 by a French engineer, Jules Dupuit, who discussed measurements of the benefits of public works.[2] The relationships between benefits likely to accrue and costs likely to be incurred were computed by planners in the Tennessee Valley Authority in developing water resource use plans during the 1930s. In 1937 benefit cost-analysis was used by the state of Oregon in

evaluating highway projects. Before World War II, a number of
federal agencies concerned with such national problems as flood
control, rivers and harbors, navigation, and hydroelectric projects
employed such quantitative analysis techniques. The evidence is clear
that benefit cost-analysis was generated, considered, and used in
public works projects long before it was incorporated as an important element of PPBS.

Systems analysis, also identified closely with program budgeting, is
as old in spirit as logical thinking, although many of the techniques
used to sharpen such thought are relatively new. Novick stated that
"probably the greatest innovations in systems analysis were initiated
in the 1920's in the Bell Laboratories."[3] Others contend that the
work of the great inventor Thomas Alva Edison was based on
principles related to systems analysis and operations research. Some
references can be found to efforts of the United States Navy Department during World War I to use operations research, which is closely
related to systems analysis. Operations research, however, traces its
modern origins to scientific efforts in some British universities during
the 1930s, and to the early years of World War II. The weapon
systems analysis done for the United States Department of Defense
by the RAND Corporation in 1949 was based on the Bell Lab
method of analysis of the 1920s and sophisticated improvements of
it made during World War II. The RAND publications on weapon
systems analysis appeared in 1949. It is apparent that quantitative
analysis approaches were used in selecting alternatives four or five
decades before their inclusion within the PPB system.

Federal Budget Origins and Reform Efforts

Budgeting in the federal government traces its formal beginning to
the Budget and Accounting Act of 1921. Other governments instituted the practice much earlier. A full-fledged budgeting system
began in the British government in 1822.[4] There were study commissions and debates about the need for establishing a federal budget in
this country during the first two decades of this century. Budgeting
was inaugurated in some of the major American cities before its start
in the federal government. "The establishment of the New York
Bureau of Municipal Research in 1906 gave even greater impetus to
the development of city budgeting."[5]

Federal budgeting immediately following the 1921 act emphasized
the development of an adequate system of expenditure control
rather than the use of budgeting as an instrument in strategic plan-

ning, as specified by operations in the PPB mode. Even the concept of generating program memorandums has a history that antedates PPBS. Thus, Schick points out that "in 1907 for example the New York City Bureau of Municipal Research published a 'program memorandum,' that contained some 125 pages of functional accounts and data for the New York City Health Department."[6]

Novick pointed out that the General Motors budget of 1924 "included a basic feature of the PPBS method, which is to identify major objectives, to define programs essential to these goals, to identify resources with specific types of objectives, and to systematically analyze the alternatives available."[7] The scheme called the Production Requirements Plan that Novick developed early in 1941 to break the logjam in production of scarce war materials in the early years of World War II attempted to deal with priority and allocation problems. It generated the Controlled Materials Plan of late 1942 used by the War Production Board for budgeting critical materials such as copper and aluminum rather than dollars. Novick argues that the system of production for the balance of World War II from 1943-45, and the distribution of the output from that system, "were effectively regulated through the Controlled Materials Plan, which was the first federal program budget."[8] It lacked the sophisticated cost-effectiveness analysis that characterizes program budgeting today, but this does not deter Novick from identifying the Controlled Materials Plan accomplishments with those of program budgeting.

What RAND did in its weapon systems analysis studies, completed in 1949, led in 1953 to a publication that "proposed the first program budget to be applied to the Air Force."[9] Publications in 1954 and 1955 by RAND extended these ideas and applied them to all military components.

The Hoover Commissions

Another stream of somewhat independent activities influenced development toward program budgeting. It took the form of a series of studies by specially appointed federal commissions seeking to improve total governmental operations, particularly budgeting, during the late 1930s and the 1940s. Schick notes that "the President's Committee on Administrative Management (1937), castigated the routinized control minded approach of the Bureau of Budget and urged that budgeting be used to coordinate federal activities under presidential leadership."[10] It was during the 1930s that the TVA and the Department of Agriculture experimented with a then new approach called *performance budgeting*. The so-called Hoover Commission, known formally as the United States Commission on the Organization of the Executive Branch of the Government, came into being in 1947. In 1949 it recommended that federal budget classification move away from simply specifying objects and toward identifying functions, activities, and projects. Its task force suggested the term "program budgeting." Other of their writers describing the same thing called it performance budgeting. Thus, the Hoover Commission used two new terms to denote budget innovations for that period, and its "program budgeting" was not what David Novick meant by that term. In the 1940s the Hoover Commission and other writers equated performance budgeting with "program budgeting"; in the 1960s program budgeting became synonymous with PPBS, and there are significant differences between performance budgeting and PPBS. The Committee for Economic Development in 1955 recommended restructuring the total federal budget to reflect "program" concerns. The committee was influenced by Hoover Commission writers rather than RAND economists at that time. The point here is that efforts at reforming the federal budget were being made during the 1930s and 1940s independently of RAND Corporation activities. The writings of the 1950s, which were stimulated by the first Hoover Commission report, extolled the virtues of performance budgeting, but did not evolve into PPBS. It was in a 1954 RAND report that Novick, working independently of the Hoover Commission, defined program and program budgeting.

Later Federal Government PPBS Activities

As indicated previously, although parts of program budgeting are as old as civilization, these elements were not unified into a powerful management tool until recently. Federal government practices during the 1960s put it all together into a new concept. Admittedly, the antecedents of PPBS are many and diverse, but the basic thinking and development of the RAND economists of the 1950s brought PPBS into being. It was tested initially for feasibility as a management system in the Air Force in the 1950s. Program budgeting entered the federal government in a more formal and comprehensive manner under the direction of then Secretary of Defense Robert McNamara in 1961. Charles J. Hitch, who had been chief economist at RAND, became Assistant Secretary of Defense (Comptroller). With Secretary McNamara's encouragement he prepared the fiscal

1963 Defense Department budget in program terms.[11] It was under Hitch's leadership that the system was implemented successfully in the Department of Defense. Hitch and McKean wrote the famous *Economics of Defense in the Nuclear Age,* published first by RAND and then others, which expanded on the use of cost-benefit analysis.[12]

In 1962 the Department of Agriculture developed a dimension of program budgeting to be applied to the 1964 agency budget. It was called zero-base budgeting. Programs were analyzed in terms of present, not past, contributions and whether their continuance could be justified with or without changes in fiscal support for a given fiscal year.

The extension of PPBS to all levels of the federal government, by President Johnson's directive in 1965, called for a significant increase in the number of federal staff members with special expertise to implement the concepts. Merewitz and Sosnick note: "The U.S. government quietly abandoned its compulsive version of PPB" in June 1971.[13] By this they mean that the Office of Management and Budget discarded demands for "program accounting, detailed description of activities, and zero-base budgeting, and it has restricted multi-year costing and benefit-cost analysis to expenditures that would represent new policy decisions."[14]

PPBS in Business

The General Motors budget of 1924 was based on procedures strikingly similar to what is now called program budgeting. During the early 1920s General Motors faced several financial crises. The DuPont Corporation contributed to GM both capital and a young assistant treasurer who introduced the concept of rational return on investment analysis to facilitate planning and decision making.

"Some authorities claim that PPB was a contribution of *business* to government management."[15] This is clearly a minority point of view. There can be no debate on the point that popularization of the technique can be traced to its application to federal government operations, not to business and industry.

Ford Motor Company in the years following World War II employed a group of young men as a management team who had previously served in the federal government and introduced systems management concepts to the war effort. Among them were Robert McNamara, later of the Department of Defense, and Charles Thornton, later of the Litton Corporation. They introduced at least quantitative analysis concepts to business management in the late 1940s. Smalter argues that the International Minerals and Chemicals Corporation implemented a planning and budgeting approach that was similar to, but developed without benefit of observing, practices in the Department of Defense.[16] Merewitz and Sosnick conclude, "the question of where PPB originated is moot," but they suggest clearly that there was a "symbiosis" between private and public sector pioneers.[17]

There is relatively less in the literature dealing with the application of PPBS to business and industry than to the various levels of government. Organizations such as the Committee for Economic Development and the United States Chamber of Commerce approved the use of PPB concepts at all levels of government.

PPBS in State and Local Governments

It can be argued that what works well at the federal level could be applied to public expenditure decision making at the state and local levels as well. PPBS can be seen as a means of overcoming organizational and managerial shortcomings at these levels. In his 1967 state of the Union message, President Johnson declared:

> Each state and county and city needs to examine its capacity for government in today's world as we are examining ours, and as I see you are examining yours. Some will need to reorganize and reshape their methods of administration as we are doing. Others will need to revise their constitutions and laws to bring them up-to-date as we are doing. Above all, I think we must work together and find ways in which multitudes of small jurisdictions can be brought together more efficiently.

The chairman of the Subcommittee on Intergovernmental Relations, Senator Edmund Muskie, stated in 1967, "as a tool for improving the efficiency and effectiveness of state and local governments, PPB systems seem to hold a promise well worth pursuing."[18] He went on to cite the many organizations that were urging the demonstration and testing of PPB in state and local governments: the Council of State Governments, the International City Managers Association, the National Association of Counties, the National Governors Conference, the National League of Cities, and the United States Conference of Mayors.

To stimulate the use of PPB in states and local agencies the Ford Foundation in 1966, and for some years thereafter, financed the State-Local Finances Project at George Washington University, directed by Dr. Selma J. Mushkin. This project is sometimes referred to as the "five by five by five" project, because five states, five counties, and five cities were selected as PPBS demonstration centers. These were California, Michigan, New York, Vermont, and Wisconsin; Dade County, Florida, Davidson County, Tennessee, Los Angeles County, California, Nassau County, New York, and Wayne County, Michigan; and Dayton, Ohio, Denver, Colorado, Detroit, Michigan, New Haven, Connecticut, and San Diego, California. Hatry and Cotton[19] prepared a monograph for state and local government officials considering the adoption of PPBS.

PPBS was applied to state and local government levels about five years after its introduction in the Department of Defense. Some sources trace New York state and city efforts to implement PPB as far back as 1964.[20] California embarked on its "programming and budgeting system" (PABS) in 1966. Pennsylvania was not a part of the five by five by five project and considered PPBS in 1967.

Several state legislatures in the late 1960s began to mandate or recommend implementation of program budgeting. It is estimated that by 1972 approximately twenty states had either mandated or recommended the application of PPBS to state and local governments as well as school districts. At first the legislatures were prone to pass laws in one year and demand implementation of program budgeting the next. This proved to be precipitous and unrealistic. More recently the Indiana law of 1971 mandated that all public school districts without exception are to implement "a system of programmed budgeting" by no later than July 1, 1977.

A great deal of rhetoric continues to surround the application of PPBS to local governments. Comparatively few, other than very large urban centers, had the staff capability to fulfill the demands of a sophisticated PPB system as late as 1972. More was being accomplished in state governments, but the political process makes it difficult to establish PPBS at these levels as well.

Program Budgeting in Education

In 1964 Novick edited a series of RAND publications and produced the first definitive volume on program budgeting.[21] Prior to that time most articles on the subject appeared in separate monographs and periodicals. Within Novick's collection was an article by Hirsch entitled "Education in the Program Budget."[22] It was rather general in its treatment of PPB and hence its impact was not felt immediately.

As in state and local governments, program budgeting in education generally followed and was influenced by practices in the federal government. Federal grants as early as the mid-1960s were awarded often on condition that program budgeting be implemented at least for federally supported activities.

Perhaps the most comprehensive, carefully planned, and widely publicized project adapting program budgeting concepts and techniques to the purposes of education was a rather sizable federal government grant, awarded jointly to the Research Corporation of the Association of School Business Officials and Dade County, Florida, public schools . This "PPBES" project sought to develop and field test program budgeting concepts and practices in several public elementary and secondary school districts in the nation. Many of its accomplishments can be traced to the outstanding leadership and tireless efforts of the project director, Dr. William H. Curtis. To help develop, test, and disseminate the concepts, a number of pilot school districts were added from across the nation: Clark County (Las Vegas), Nevada; Douglas County, Colorado; Herricks, New Hyde Park, Long Island, New York; Memphis, Tennessee; Milwaukee, Wisconsin; Montgomery County, Maryland; Peoria, Illinois; and Westport, Connecticut. The project was completed in 1971, and a special report was published by RC–ASBO early in 1972.[23] During the late 1960s other school districts, such as Baltimore, Chicago, Los Angeles, Memphis, New York, Philadelphia, Sacramento, California, Skokie, Illinois, and Pearl River, New York, either revised their budgetary formats or implemented what each defined as PPBS in education. State departments of education, the Government Studies Center at the University of Pennsylvania, and various regional educational development agencies advocated the PPBS concepts and techniques in education. The Center for Vocational and Technical Education at Ohio State University focused on the special problems of vocational-technical schools seeking to implement program budgeting. By 1970 much had been written about PPBS in education; many schools were involved to various degrees with the system; and a number of educational organizations were studying and disseminating its concepts.

The U.S. Office of Education, at the time of this writing (1972), is revising its handbook *Financial Accounting* (Handbook II, revised) to further stimulate interest in PPBS by emphasizing program accounting.

In the field of higher education efforts to establish PPBS were evident as well. In the late 1960s, the Western Interstate Compact for

Higher Education (WICHE) funded a series of studies on the use of PPBS in institutions of higher learning. One's evaluation of the success of this use depends upon one's perception of what PPBS is. Some argue that the difficulty of developing a program structure for higher education makes adaption of PPBS impractical. Others engage in sophisticated cost accounting and unit cost analyses and label this PPBS.

Hartley in 1968 produced the first book applying PPBS concepts to education.[24] A sizable number of articles on program budgeting in education appeared in educational periodicals or as separate monographs during the last few years of the 1960s and the early 1970s. Books of readings (collections of PPBS articles combined in book form) were aimed at the political science or economics market rather than at education students.

Although there was a considerable amount of interest in PPBS as applied to education in the 1960s, by the early 1970s there was still a great deal more conversation than actual practice in implementing the system in public elementary, secondary, vocational-technical, and higher education schools. In 1973 many school districts assumed a more modest posture and claimed only to be moving toward implementing one or more phases of PPB, hoping to complete installation by the end of this decade. The American Association of School Administrators, acting through its National Academy for School Executives, began to disseminate information about program budgeting and its application to education, in Canada as well as in the United States, as early as 1969. A number of other agencies—private, quasi-public, and public—followed suit with conferences on the subject.

By the early 1970s PPBS in education had gained sufficient popularity to provoke attacks by some teacher groups as being too costly. Even some of the far-right extremists began to attack PPBS as a "sinister program" guilty of destroying human privacy. Perhaps this is the inevitable fate of a promising idea that has the misfortune of being misinterpreted because of its popularity. Such reckless and unwarranted attacks will not delay the implementation of a management system of promise and significance. Many feel that PPBS is an idea whose time has come.

Summary

Specific dimensions of program budgeting are said to be as old as civilization. They began as soon as man had to grapple with the problem of accomplishing more than he has resources to accomplish. The roots of the modern PPB system are of more recent origin, going back to pregnant ideas developed in the 1950s and applied to federal government operations in the 1960s. President Johnson's actions in 1965 gave the thrust that disseminated PPBS more widely in the federal government and thus extended the popularity of this management system.

The antecedents of PPBS are many and varied. Some elements, such as benefit-cost analysis, had their origins in 1844 when a French engineer demonstrated concern for the worth of public works. Considerable use was made of benefit-cost analysis in United States public works projects in the 1930s. Systems analysis used in PPBS can be traced to efforts in the 1920s in the Bell Laboratories and to British developments during World War II.

Budgeting did not begin with "program budgeting" either. The British government established it in 1822, some U.S. cities in the early 1900s, and the U.S. government in 1921. Budgetary reforms have been debated ever since General Motors in 1924 used an approach very similar to what Novick called program budgeting. Activities during World War II in the United States showed seeds of the idea developing. Hoover Commission efforts represented another stream of thought aimed at budgetary reform; the commission recommended "performance budgeting," which is different from program budgeting.

The RAND studies for the defense establishment during the late 1940s and the 1950s generated the present concept and techniques of PPBS. RAND economists such as Novick, Hitch, McKean, and Quade can be said to have systematized all the elements to produce the PPB system. It was formally instituted in the Department of Defense in 1961, under the leadership of Defense Secretary Robert McNamara and DOD Comptroller Charles Hitch. For a summary of the significant dates and events in the development of PPBS, see table 2-1 on pages 25-26.

Although parts of PPBS were used in private industry, most sources agree that popularization of the concepts and techniques came from their use in the federal government.

By the mid-1960s PPBS concepts were being extended to apply to state and local governments as well. The famous "five by five by five" project, started in 1966, used five states, five counties, and five cities as pilot centers for the adaptation of program budgeting to these levels of government. Federal government officials used their influence to improve the efficiency and effectiveness of state and local governments through PPBS. Larger units of local government were more likely to implement the system than smaller entities.

Schools followed the PPBS practices in other governmental levels. In 1968, the joint "PPBES" project undertaken by the Research Corporation of the Association of School Business Officials and Dade County, Florida, provided a major stimulus to disseminating PPBS in education. Federal grants helped to establish the system elsewhere. A number of school districts reported operations in the PPBS mode by the late 1960s and early 1970s. Each district seemed to have its own definition of PPBS. The literature on applying PPBS to education has grown rapidly in the last five years. The U.S. Office of Education is seeking to stimulate further interest in PPBS in education by designing its forthcoming revision of *Financial Accounting* (Handbook II) to reflect program accounting and other PPBS concepts. Efforts to apply PPBS to vocational-technical education and institutions of higher learning were evident in the late 1960s.

In short, interest in applying PPBS to education started in the mid-1960s and grew substantially in the late 1960s. By 1972, however, there was still a great deal more talk than action to implement sophisticated PPB systems in education. One indication of the popularity of PPBS is that it is being attacked by some far right extremists.

Table 2-1. Brief chronological history of developments
related to program budgeting

Dates	Events or activities
Probably at the beginning of civilization	Attempts to use rational thinking to decide how to allocate scarce resources among multiple competing objectives
1844	Jules Dupuit, French engineer, considers benefit-cost analysis for some public works projects
1907	New York City Bureau of Municipal Research publishes program memorandums to accompany budget document
1920s	Bell Laboratories use systems analysis
1921	Federal Budgeting and Accounting Act enacted
1924	General Motors Corporation budget incorporated basic features of PPBS

Dates	Events or activities
1930s	Benefit-cost analysis used for Tennessee Valley Authority (TVA) projects, state highway projects, etc.
	Performance budgeting experiments in TVA and Department of Agriculture
1941	Production Requirements Plan adopted during World War II to relate resource analysis to priority war needs
1942-45	War Production Board's Controlled Materials Plan used to budget critical materials rather than dollars (an unusual first federal program budget)
1946	Project RAND (precursor to the RAND Corporation) created by the United States Air Force
1949	RAND Corporation weapon systems analysis studies
	Hoover Commission report recommending performance budgeting
1953-55	RAND proposals for first Air Force program budget
1960	RAND publications of *The Economics of Defense in the Nuclear Age* and *New Tools for Planners and Programmers*
1961	**Launching of PPBS in the Department of Defense**
1964	Publication of Novick's book, *Program Budgeting*
1965	President Johnson's release of the famous Bulletin no. 66-3, directing use of PPBS in all federal departments and agencies
1966	Inauguration of State-Local Finances Project (five by five by five project)
1966-69	Various state and local government agencies experiment with PPBS
1968	RC—ASBO/Dade County, Florida, PPBES project launched
1968	Local school districts start to develop and implement PPBS
1971-72	RC—ASBO/Dade County, Florida, PPBES project completed and reported as *Educational Resources Management System*

Notes

1. D. Novick, "The Origins and History of Program Budgeting," *California Management Review* (fall 1968): 7-12.

2. L. Merewitz and S. H. Sosnick, *The Budget's New Clothes* (Chicago: Markham Publishing Co., 1971), pp. 9-12.

3. Novick, *op. cit.*

4. J. Burkhead, *Government Budgeting* (New York: John Wiley & Sons, 1956), p. 2.

5. S. H. Knezevich and J. G. Fowlkes, *Business Management of Local School Systems* (New York: Harper & Row, 1960), p. 18.

6. A. Schick, "The Road to PPB: The Stages of Budget Reform," *Public Administration Review* 26, no. 4 (December 1966): 243-58.

7. Novick, *op. cit.*

8. Ibid.

9. Ibid.

10. Shick, *op. cit.*

11. Merewitz and Sosnick, *op. cit.*, pp. 2-3.

12. C. J. Hitch and R. McKean, *Economics of Defense in the Nuclear Age* (Cambridge: Harvard University Press, 1960).

13. Merewitz and Sosnick, *op. cit.*, p. 301.

14. Ibid., p. 302.

15. Ibid., p. 7.

16. D. J. Smalter, "The Influence of DOD Practices of Corporate Planning," *Management Technology* 4, no. 2 (December 1964): 37-61.

17. Merewitz and Sosnick, *op. cit.*, p. 8.

18. U.S. Senate, Committee on Government Operations, Subcommittee on Intergovernmental Relations, *Criteria for Evaluation in Planning State and Local Programs* (Washington, D.C.: Government Printing Office, 1967), p. iv.

19. H. P. Hatry and J. F. Cotton, *Program Planning for State, County, and City* (Washington, D.C.: State-Local Finances Project, George Washington University, 1967).

20. H. J. Hartley, *Educational Planning-Programming-Budgeting* (Englewood Cliffs, N.J.: Prentice-Hall, 1968), p. 103.

21. D. Novick, ed., *Program Budgeting* (Washington, D.C.: Government Printing Office, 1964), a 236-page volume.

22. Ibid., chap. 6.

23. W. H. Curtis, *Educational Resources Management System*, special report, Association of School Business Officials Research Staff on a Planning-Programming-Budgeting-Evaluating System (Chicago: Research Corporation of the Association of School Business Officials, 1972).

24. Hartley, *op. cit.*

Selected References

Curtis, W. H. *Educational Resources Management System*. Chicago: Research Corporation of the Association of School Business Officials, 1972.

Hatry, H. P., and Cotton, J. F. *Program Planning for State, County, and City*. Washington, D.C.: State-Local Finances Project, George Washington University, 1967.

Merewitz, L., and Sosnick, S. H. *The Budget's New Clothes,* chap. 1. Chicago: Markham Publishing Co., 1971.

Novick, D. "The Origins and History of Program Budgeting." *California Management Review* (fall 1968).

_____, ed. *Program Budgeting.* Washington, D.C.: Government Printing Office, 1964.

Schick, A. "The Road to PPB: The Stages of Budget Reform." *Public Administration Review* 26, no. 4 (December 1966): 243-58.

3. The planning dimension of program budgeting

Although not evident in the abbreviated title program budgeting, the first P in PPBS represents planning and the second, programming. The first parts of the popular acronym, planning and programming, may well be the least discussed and most neglected dimensions of PPBS in education. Both processes are important points of departure for operation in a systems mode. Programming is a relatively unfamiliar term in education and a source of considerable confusion, if reports from schools alleged to have adopted program budgeting are any indication of the status quo.

Novick makes it clear that, "planning and programming are really aspects of the same process; they differ only in emphasis."[1] To him planning is "a more informal process than programming, more a matter of attitude than procedures."[2] He visualizes programming as being the more specific determination of courses of action generated through planning. Plans are translated into programs. In all cases planning precedes programming, and for that reason it is reviewed at this point while discussion of programming is delayed until chapter 6.

From the systems point of view planning is a mechanism by which a system adapts its goals, priorities, and resources to changing environmental and internal forces. It can be conceptualized as a vehicle for systems change. It rightfully occupies a position of importance within an organizational hierarchy, and relatively more of the

administrator's time is devoted to planning than to other administrative functions as he moves up the executive hierarchy.

A dynamic environment generates uncertainty, which in turn
alters missions, modifies priorities, and changes procedures. During
such times planning becomes a critical function; it is the means by
which the organization copes with uncertainty. The more complex
the organization and the more turbulent the society, the more
necessary it becomes for administrators to dedicate more time and
resources to the planning functions. Therefore, at this point in time
anticipation of the future through planning has assumed great importance and high priority in the administration of educational
institutions.

Planning Defined

Planning is a word that rolls easily from the pens of writers and
tongues of speakers. Unfortunately, popular use makes it a relatively
vague concept, and the developers of program budgeting did not help
matters much by assigning by implication two somewhat different
dimensions to planning. In one sense planning "seeks a continual
review of objectives."[3] In another it implies generation of sets of
alternatives for use in reaching or satisfying an objective. In still
another it becomes the initial thrust toward systems analysis by
"selection of courses of action through a systematic consideration of
alternatives."[4] In the first case the output of the planning process is
a well-defined or more realistic set of objectives. In the second the
end product is a set of feasible alternatives. In the third the outcome
is selection or specification of a preferred alternative for attainment
of the objectives.

The emphasis of this and the next few chapters will be on planning
as a process resulting in the determination and clarification of objectives. Planning as the generation and analysis of alternatives will be
reviewed in later chapters. Perhaps it would be more precise to use
the acronym GOPBS, where GO stands for "goal orienting." This
implies that the first stage in program budgeting is to orient the
organization toward its goals. Stated another way, PPBS is a mission-
oriented management system. This should be implied by the first "P"
representing the planning process. Without planning in this sense,
programming, or the clustering of activities around objectives, would
be difficult if not impossible to execute in a meaningful way. In this
sense, planning starts by defining the objectives or outcomes to be
accomplished and concludes by suggesting procedures for attaining
the objectives in an optimal fashion.

It has been suggested that although planning has been a popular word throughout history, it is nonetheless an elusive concept. Only recently have there been efforts to develop a systematic approach to the study of planning. Much of the early planning literature consisted of exhortations on the importance or desirability of planning rather than analyses of the substance of issues, significant techniques, or operational demands. As a result the word *planning* is as much abused in administration as it is in other walks of life. The considerable rhetoric surrounding the term gives it a status similar to motherhood; no one dares to oppose planning.

Dror argues that there is "a large and growing literature dealing with different kinds of planning" and considering it "as a methodology of rational thought and action," rather than simply an ideological discourse on its desirability.[5] He compiled an impressive list of definitions of planning from various sources. The substance of these definitions is submitted below:

1. Deciding in advance what is to be done, that is, a plan is a projected course of action.

2. The working out in broad outline of the things that need to be done and the methods for doing them to accomplish the purpose set for the enterprise.

3. An organized effort to utilize social intelligence in the determination of national policies.

4. Consists in the systematic, continuous, forward-looking application of the best intelligence available to programmes of common affairs in the public field.

5. A continuous process, and necessitates the constant reexamination of the trends, tendencies, policies in order to adapt and adjust governmental policies with the least possible friction and loss.

6. Not an end, but a means, a means for a better use for what we have.

7. One of the functions of the manager and, as such, involves the selection, from among alternatives, of the enterprise objectives, policies, procedures and programmes. It is thus decision-making affecting the future course of an enterprise.

8. An intellectual process, the conscious determination of courses of action, the basing of decisions on purpose, facts and considered estimates.

9. Equivalent to rational social action, that is, as a social process for reaching a rational decision.

10. The fullest and most rational utilization of all work and of all the material resources of the community, in the light of a scientific forecast of the trends of economic development and with strict observance of the laws of social development.

11. An activity by which man in society endeavors to gain mastery over himself and to shape his collective future by power of his reason.

12. Essentially a means of improving decisions and is therefore a

prerequisite to actions. It seeks to answer two vital questions: What is the purpose of an agency or program, and what are the best means of achieving that purpose?

From this review of other thoughts, Dror derived his own definition of planning in the context and purposes of administrative sciences. This excellent definition is used in this volume. According to Dror, "planning is a process of preparing a set of decisions for action in the future, directed at achieving goals by optimal means."[6] All definitions emphasize the future orientation of planning, its focus on goals, and its emphasis not only on decisions but also on actions based on those decisions. Planning is a general process for accomplishing many different outcomes. It may be defined by the rational approaches used during the process or by the substantive problems attacked. More often than not the latter prevails, and one hears of urban planning, school plant planning, financial planning, etc. The context of planning may determine the techniques to be used in meeting future demands.

Planning in PPBS

It is obvious that planning is important to many, if not all, management systems. The PPB system is neither the first nor the last to stress the process. Writers in administration refer to a hierarchy of plans, ranging from broad plans that serve as guidelines for top-level executives to highly detailed plans for operating units within an organization. Another categorization, based on time, distinguishes long- and short-range plans. Plans may also be classified by whether they apply to repetitive activities, such as standard operating procedures, or nonrepetitive activities, such as single use plans for unique situations.

Program budgeting was stimulated in the federal government partly by the desire to improve high-level planning in the Department of Defense. According to Charles Hitch, PPBS was introduced in 1961 to improve the department's planning function, which was believed to be in disarray because it was not as realistic as necessary, lacked criteria on which to render judgment when confronted with difficult choices, and failed to consider the fiscal implications of its decisions. In other words, criticisms were based, not on the absence of planning, but on the kind of planning that existed. It failed to generate the information and interpretations necessary to improve decision making, particularly on a long-range basis. To illustrate, substantive planning (called military planning in the department), which was concerned with both ultimate and intermediate objectives, was divorced from fiscal planning, and more often than not failed to consider ultimate objectives. PPBS was inaugurated to supply management techniques for relating resource requirements to objectives.

Planning is an important process in PPBS, providing a disciplined approach to (1) force specification of objectives, (2) anticipate a set of long- and short-range futures, (3) identify alternative courses of action, (4) stimulate the use of sophisticated analysis tools or techniques, and (5) improve rational decision making on resource allocations. Missions are specified and clarified through the planning process. Since many important problems cannot be solved within short periods, PPBS also includes a time dimension. It calls for multiyear planning, with the stipulation of how much can be hoped to be accomplished in the traditional one-year period. In a sense, this can be interpreted as a call for strategic planning to supplement tactical planning.

Through the planning process it is possible to define a predetermined course of action for an organization, based on certain assumptions and constraints, to optimize a desired future condition. Program budgeting is often depicted as a vehicle for strengthening, as Novick puts it, "an organization's capability to do long range planning and to provide a systematic method for resolving major resource allocation issues."[7] This puts a time dimension on planning in the program budgeting system. The single fiscal year is deemed to be too short a period for arriving at prudent resource allocation decisions.

To some, estimating what will be happening in the distant future is frustrating. Even five years in the future is a long time. Long-range planning implies that attention must be focused on the plan of action developed five years previously. The likely inaccuracies in this approach are not the point. The significance of long-range projection is that it focuses attention on long-term commitments. These may or may not reinforce commitments that appeared reasonable in the short run.

As Hatry and Cotton put it, "many, if not all, decisions on allocation of resources have future implications and therefore imply future commitments."[8] In PPBS, more than in other management systems, the future implications of actions taken must be explicitly defined. Therefore, multiyear program and financial documents (plans) are important outcomes of the planning process, and it can be said that an organization cannot claim to operate in the PPBS mode unless its planning horizons display program and financial plans that cover more than one, and preferably five fiscal years. More prudent *current* resource allocation decisions are possible only to the extent that estimates of future expenditures and outcomes are made explicit as possible. To use the words of Hatry and Cotton again, "an integral part of the PPBS concept is the estimation of the time phased expenditure requirements and outputs of each program for each alternative mix of programs being considered."[9] One of the major defects of the traditional annual budgets is that they are limited to a short time span. PPBS seeks to remedy this defect by emphasizing long-range planning through multiyear expenditure and outcomes budgeting.

The continuity of planning deserves to be stressed as well. Projecting plans into a five-year future period does not imply that the task is accomplished once and for all. Rather it suggests that new data will become available and future plans will be updated, modified, or replaced. Planning then becomes a continuous activity of relating organizational activities to goals. Again, PPBS plans for a single year are simply one slice of a multiyear planning approach.

Another aspect of planning that deserves consideration is its tendency to encourage serendipity: the art of discovering the unexpected. For example, Elton Mayo sought to determine the effect of lighting and fatigue on worker productivity, and he discovered the small social groupings and the "Hawthorne effect" along the way. Roentgen inadvertently left a key on a well-wrapped but undeveloped photographic plate and discovered X-rays. Thus, one by-product of planning may well be the unexpected bonanza as well.

According to one source, "the purpose of planning is to provide a mechanism by which alternative goals, programs, and their costs and benefits can be organized, analyzed and summarized."[10] This statement views the basic output of the process as analysis of alternatives. In stipulating the steps in planning, the following are included by the same source:

1. Development of long range goals by major functional areas
2. Projection of basic population, economic, social, and physical data
3. Development and maintenance of a process whereby program alternatives can emerge
4. Development and improvement of methods for quantifying data on goals, programs and resources associated therewith[11]

This perception gives planning a more comprehensive scope than is implied in the statement of its purposes.

Why Planning Does Not Always Work

Planning has a pleasant sound to it, and we instinctively believe that only good can come of it. It is a demanding process, however, and without complete understanding and a disciplined approach, planning may fall far short of our expectations. The point is that planning is not an automatic thing. It may result only in wasted time, for difficulties abound in its implementation.

One European writer, viewing planning from a business perspective, identified the five simple elements of planning and put together the acronym PIPOS for philosophy, inputs, process, outputs system.[12] He summarized the elements in table 3-1.

After surveying planning in over 350 companies in Europe and America, Ringbakk came up with ten major reasons for planning failures:[14]

> 1. Corporate planning is not integrated into the total management system.
> 2. The different dimensions of planning have not been understood.
> 3. Management at all levels is not engaged in planning activities.
> 4. Responsibility for planning rests solely in a planning department. (Ringbakk argues that the "planning department should not plan" for this may bring line management departments to abdicate the planning function to such departments.)
> 5. Management expects the plans to come true as planned.
> 6. Too much is attempted at once.
> 7. Management fails to operate by plan.
> 8. Extrapolation and financial projections are confused with planning.
> 9. Inadequate information inputs are used.
> 10. Too much emphasis is placed on only one aspect of planning. (It is too easy to get hung up on little details when the overall picture is missing.)

PPBS may be perceived as a disciplined planning approach. It calls for both long- and short-range planning. It seeks to anticipate the future and forces those within the organization to specify objectives. The latter concern will be pursued further in the next chapter. Planning is also based on sophisticated tools. This dimension of the complex planning process is very similar to the analyzing in the PPBADERS acronym. More will be said about planning as it relates to systems analysis in yet another chapter. For the purposes of this chapter the concept was clarified, defined and then related to PPBS.

Table 3-1. The five simple elements of planning[13]

Philosophy	Inputs	Process	Outputs	System
Corporate management engaged in and fostering planning	*Studies of the future* *Environmental surveillance* ⎫ *Opportunities and threats*	*Strategic administrative operating* ⎬ *Decision areas (kinds of planning)*	*Specific objectives and policies* *Strategies to attain them* *Contingency provisions*	*Organizing and leading* → *Implementation* → *Monitoring and control*
Operating management engaged in and doing planning	*Corporate audits* *Evaluation and control of past performance* ⎫ *Strengths and weaknesses*	*Formulate objectives and sub-objectives* ↓ *Develop alternative strategies and action programs* ↓ *Evaluate these in terms of resources, profitability, and risk* ↓ *Decide by choosing alternatives and commit or decommit the corporate resources* ↓ *Programming and derivative planning*	*Considerations of environmental factors* *A practical timetable* *Clear delineations of operating and staff executives' responsibilities* *Specifying purposes in terms of financial and quantitative schedules*	

Its relationship to mission statements and management by objectives will be reviewed in subsequent chapters. Planning is not a vague or idle process, but action oriented.

Summary

Planning is the first process suggested in the acronym PPBS, and programming the second. The two processes are related but differ in emphasis. From the systems point of view, planning is a mechanism through which a system adapts its goals, priorities, and resources to changing forces. Therefore, planning becomes a critical function during times of great ferment. The higher up he goes in the hierarchy, the more important planning becomes to the administrator.

Although popular and widely used, planning is often described in relatively vague terms. There are many definitions in the literature. Most suggest a concern for the future, focus on goals, and relate planning to decision making and actions. It is a general process for accomplishing different outcomes. The context or expected outcomes of planning influence the approaches used in the planning process. For the purposes of this volume, planning is defined as "a process of preparing a set of decisions for action in the future, directed at achieving goals by optimal means."

The idea and importance of the planning function were not original to PPBS. Other management systems stress the significance of planning and the development of a hierarchy of plans, time-phased plans, and repetitive versus nonrepetitive plans. Program budgeting sought to improve the quality of planning in the Department of Defense, not to begin planning, which had existed for some time before the introduction of PPBS. PPBS did supply a management technique that better related resource requirements to objectives.

Planning is an important process in PPBS, providing a disciplined approach to (1) force specification of objectives, (2) anticipate a set of long- and short-range futures, (3) stimulate the use of sophisticated analysis techniques, and (4) improve resource allocation decisions. Strategic planning, that is, specifying the future implications of current resource allocation decisions, receives special emphasis. Therefore, multiyear rather than single-year expenditure requirements are important in program budgets.

Planning continuity implies reviewing long range estimates through modifications based on more recent data. Identification and subsequent clarification of objectives is one outcome of the planning process in PPBS. It is described more fully in the chapters that

follow, while discussion of the analysis concerns of planning are
reserved for later chapters.

Notes

1. D. Novick, ed., "The Department of Defense," in *Program Budgeting*
(Washington, D.C.: Government Printing Office, 1964), p. 58.

2. Ibid., p. 69.

3. Ibid.

4. Ibid., p. 58.

5. Y. Dror, "The Planning Process: A Facet Design," *International Review of
Administrative Sciences* 29, no. 1 (1963): 44-58.

6. Ibid.

7. D. Novick, "Long Range Planning Through Program Budgeting," *Business
Horizons*, February 1969, pp. 59-65.

8. H. P. Hatry and J. F. Cotton, *Program Planning for State, County, and
City* (Washington, D.C.: State-Local Finances Project, George Washington University, 1967), p. 19.

9. Ibid.

10. J. H. McGivney and W. C. Nelson, *Program Planning Budgeting Systems
for Educators*, vol. 1, *An Instructional Outline*, Leadership Series no. 18 (Columbus, Ohio: Center for Vocational and Technical Education, 1969), p. 58.

11. Ibid.

12. K. A. Ringbakk, "Why Planning Fails," *European Business*, reprinted in
Notes and Quotes (Hartford, Conn.: Connecticut General Life Insurance Co.,
1972).

13. Ibid.

14. Ibid.

Selected References

Dror, Y. "The Planning Process: A Facet Design." *International Review of
     Administrative Sciences* 29, no. 1 (1963): 44-58.
Novick, D. "Long Range Planning Through Program Budgeting." *Business Hori-
     zons*, February 1969.
_____, ed. "The Department of Defense." In *Program Budgeting*. Washington,
     D.C.: Government Printing Office, 1964. Chapter 3.
Ringbakk, K. A. "Why Planning Fails." *European Business*. Reprinted in *Notes
     and Quotes*. Hartford, Conn.: Connecticut General Life Insurance Co., 1972.

4. Generating the quality and types of objectives needed to operate in the PPBS mode

PPBS is a mission-oriented, or outcomes-oriented, management system. As we saw in chapter 3, the two basic dimensions of planning include orienting the organization toward its goals, identifying alternative courses of action, and rational analysis of alternatives to ascertain the optimal means of reaching objectives. There can be no program budgeting without identification and clarification of objectives. The quality and type of objectives needed to operate in the PPBS mode is the subject of this chapter. An important administrative skill for those seeking to implement program budgeting is the ability to identify and prepare performance objectives.

Therefore, it is difficult to overemphasize the importance of objectives in the PPB system. This decision technology demands clarification of the directions for the organization. Again, this is not the first management system calling for establishment of objectives. Many an administrator has been admonished to "Know your objectives." Unfortunately, one of the most difficult problems encountered in implementing PPBS in education is the translation of often vague, general statements of educational objectives into specific guides for action. More often than not system-wide goals degenerate into slogans rather than specific directives for positive action. Statements of educational objectives were developed long before PPBS was ever thought of. Most school systems have such statements gathering dust in a drawer. Recommending that administrators as well as teachers define objectives is another ancient and honorable rite. It is probably the most widely accepted and least questioned principle of operation. Despite the seeming popularity of spelling out where you want to go, before you worry about how you get there, the process of goals determination or objective specification has proved worrisome, bothersome, time-consuming, and of little practical value.

Reform in Specifying Objectives

In the past, educational objectives have been stated as the Seven Cardinal Principles, the four groups of the Objectives of Education in an American Democracy, the ten Imperative Needs, the four dimensions of the Task of the School, and the Imperatives in Education. Practically all general treatises in education, as well as those that focus on its administration, contain one or more of these educational concerns. Doubtless there will be others as increasing numbers of new burdens are assigned to schools. Schools are being pressured to assume a more dynamic role in the solution of many social ills.

Therefore, PPBS cannot lay claim to being the first management system calling for the establishment of goals or objectives as guideposts to future operations and criteria for subsequent evaluation. What makes the program budgeting emphasis on objectives unique is the manner in which objectives are phrased and the degree to which they influence actions and specify value judgements to be applied to the organization. This is not to imply that performance objectives trace their origins to program budgeting: other forces have helped to stimulate reform in the way educational outcomes are defined and applied to its related processes such as instruction and administration. For example, the use of programmed instruction—as well as other new instructional systems, such as computer-assisted instruction, individually prescribed instruction (IPI), or individually guided education (IGE)—called for the restructuring of the manner in which educational objectives were written and applied to various endeavors. The revolution in objectives writing in education has been going on for more than a decade and doubtless will continue. It is a timely one, for precepts in the instructional field can also be adapted to the administration and supervision of educational institutions.

Special taxonomies of educational objectives were stimulated in large part by Bloom and Kratwohl writing for the American Education Research Association.[1] There is a growing literature that speaks of educational objectives in the cognitive, affective, and psychomotor domains. Bloom, Krathwohl, and others generated a taxonomy or logical scheme to bring order into the confusion and chaos that typified the field of educational objectives for so long. The emphasis was on actual behaviors desired after completion of a unit of instruction by the learner. The system of classifying objectives did not attempt to suggest or in any way constrain the teaching strategies used for achieving them. The new emphasis grew to a point where a unique instructional objectives exchange (IOX) was created, which now includes taxonomies of objectives that encompass more than thirty-five different subject fields.[2] Another source of curriculum and instructional reform has been the specification of new types of objectives referred to as behavioral objectives. Although a considerable effort was evident in the 1950s and 1960s to make educational objectives more functional in curriculum and instruction, and therefore more useful to the teachers, the beginnings can be traced to Tyler's work in the 1930s and thereafter.[3]

As the name implies, a behavioral objective states the desired learning outcome in terms of behavior exhibited by the learner or evidence of attainment of a measured level of performance. Some prefer the term performance objective. Others argue that a performance objective is a special kind of behavioral objective, that is, one that includes a criterion for measuring whether the specified level of competence has been satisfied by the learner. For the purposes of this volume, however, the two terms will be considered synonymous.

Peter Pipe defines a behavioral objective in further detail by specifying the following characteristics:[4]

> 1. It describes the observable *action* which is to be evidence of competence.
> 2. When necessary, it describes the *conditions* under which the action is to be performed.
> 3. When necessary, it describes the *criteria* by which to judge acceptable performance.

What the emphasis on behavioral objectives did was to sharpen the terminology used. To illustrate, objectives often were stated in such vague terms as helping the student "to understand" something. "To understand" is subject to many interpretations, implying among other things the ability to recall something, to use it in a particular way, and to interpret its significance.

Leles and Bernabei viewed a behavioral objective as an indication of a "teacher's intention by denoting behavior which a student must demonstrate" after successful completion of the learning activity.[5] They added that such an objective "includes descriptive phrases about expected terminal behavior, conditions, and criterion."[6] They recommended abandonment of words open to many interpretations, such as *know, want, appreciate, learn,* and *like,* in favor of other more specific terms, such as *identify, construct, demonstrate,* and *order.* In all cases the performance objective must specify what the learner must be able to do or perform. Being able to discriminate between ambiguous or vaguely defined objectives and those stated in performance terms is a prerequisite to preparing behavioral objectives.

Leles and Bernabei[7] identified the following questions to be answered to ascertain the essential elements as standards for preparing a behavioral objective: (1) "Who?"; (2) "What will he do?" (behavior); (3) "What material is to be used?" (conditions); (4) "Who initiates the action?" (conditions); (5) "What are acceptable responses?" (performance level); and (6) "Are there special restrictions or requirements?" (conditions). This can be applied to a phase of administration as:

> The Director of Transportation shall submit to the superintendent a written report on all school bus accidents within twenty-four hours of the incident, stipulating the name and parents of the injured pupils or others; extent of injuries; circumstances surrounding the accident such as time, place, and factors relating to the event; name, age, and experience of bus driver; subsequent treatment of the injured; information related to police and insurance officials; and other matters of importance.

The who in this case is the transportation director and the behavior is the filing of an accident report. The various "conditions" are specified. The performance level is indicated as a written report, filed within twenty-four hours of the incident, submitted to the superintendent, and in the detail noted. A performance objective for an administrative situation becomes a performance policy, which states in behavioral terms what shall be done by an administrator or supervisor and under what conditions. The performance policy statement could be rephrased in objectives language as "it shall be the objective of the Director of Transportation to file a written report with the superintendent. . . ."

Taba called for a sharpening of educational objectives by having objective statements describe the behavior expected, indicate the context to which the behavior applies, clearly distinguish the learning experiences required to satisfy various behaviors, specify its developmental tasks, be realistic, and be broad enough to encompass all types of outcomes.[8]

Hierarchies of Outcome Statements

There have been efforts to categorize and establish hierarchies of objectives. References are made to "product-oriented" or "output" objectives in contrast to "process-oriented" objectives. The classical separation has been between general and specific objectives. Objectives may be further classified by function at the teaching-learning level, at the administrative level, and at the system level. The same objective may be rephrased with varying degrees of explicitness for each level of operation. Some may be classified by time frame according to immediate, intermediate, and long-term objectives. The school administrator must work with teachers who communicate their efforts in terms of instructional performance objectives. In addition, top-echelon administrators work with other executives. The objectives at this level may be stated as "performance policies" rather than "behavioral objectives." There are a number of semantic pitfalls in clarifying statements of objectives to satisfy the demands of those who seek to operate in the program budgeting mode.

In this book the general term *outcome* is used to embrace all other terms such as *mission, goal,* or *objective.* The description of various types of outcomes carry titles such as "mission," "goal," "objective," "performance objective," and "targeted performance objective." In other words, the latter descriptors are subsets of the universal outcomes. The relationship between and discrimination among outcomes descriptors useful in administration are summarized in table 4-1. It represents one effort at distinguishing among terms that are used either interchangeably or inconsistently by writers in education, or for that matter, in other disciplines.

To illustrate, a mission statement reflects the hopes and aspirations of the organization as it relates to its culture or society. It represents a general intention, which either stimulated the formation of the organization or justifies its continued existence. Mission statements are found at the policy or system-wide level. They are useful to boards of control and top-level administrators who operate on an organization-wide basis. They are akin to broad aims and general purposes. It is here where "educational objectives," the broad generalizations or global concerns, may be useful as guidelines.

Table 4-1. Differentiation of various descriptions of administrative outcomes by levels and activities

Levels	Outcomes descriptor	Time reference	Organization levels at which appropriate	Processes emphasized	Actions indicator	General definition
A or 1	Mission	Very long-range	System-wide; top echelon; organization-wide	Formulating policy	Intentions	Hopes and aspirations; societal desires; general intentions that justify the organization's reason for being; resolutions to guide future actions, abstract descriptions of broad generalizations about the global concerns of the organization. Synonyms: "Broad Aims," "General Purposes," "Educational Objectives."
B or 2	Goal	Long-range	Subsystem levels; executive cabinet level; supt. to assoc. supt. portions	Planning and appraising	Functions	The general pointing of directions to be pursued to reach missions; the general and/or fundamental processes pursued as terminal points. Synonym: "Broad Objectives."
C or 3	Objective	Medium-to-short-range	Major component; division	Programming	Programs	Strategic positions or significant and measurable outcomes to be achieved by each of the major components of the organization; outcomes that give very specific directions and suggest challenges to be met; terminal behaviors to be attained.
D or 4	Performance objective	Short-range	Category; department	Implementing and monitoring	Activities	Short term outcomes that are specific and measurable; a well-defined set of specific products, processes, or other achievements.
E or 5	Targeted performance objective	Immediate-to-short-range	Element; basic operational unit	Operating, interacting, and producing	Specific operations	Realistic and specific outcomes that are challenging, measurable, and criterion-referenced and focus on a single product, specific process, or other detailed achievement. In addition the outcomes are focused on a well-defined cluster of actors or recipients.

A goal is an expression of outcome that is one step removed from a mission statement. It, too, has a long time reference. It indicates the general direction to be pursued in reaching a mission. A goal statement describes a general end or fundamental process, that is, a terminal point. It, too, is much too broad to be useful in defining a specific administrative or supervisory activity. It is useful at an executive cabinet level or subsystem level concerned with overall plan for the organization and appraising its direction and outputs.

An objective as a statement of an outcome is placed at level 3 and by and large applies to a major component or division of an organization. It is important to programming within an organization, that is, to the clustering of activities related to achievement of a goal. Without statements of objectives, there can be no organizational programs. In a sense, an objective is a strategic position or significant outcome to be achieved by each of the major components of the organization. Outcomes at this level of operation give very specific directions and suggest challenges to be met or terminal behaviors to be obtained.

Performance objectives are more sharply focused objectives specifying measurable outcomes against a standard or criterion. They have significance in the short time range, apply primarily to categories or departments within an organization, give well-defined meaning to activities. In summary, performance objectives can be viewed as short-term outcomes that are specific in nature and measurable by degrees of achievement when conditions are known and given products, processes, or other achievements can be defined.

Targeted performance objectives represent a further refinement toward even greater specificity for basic operational units or elements within an organization. They are outcomes statements that influence specific and detailed operations where teachers interact with learners, in the case of schools, or where the lowest level administrators interact with clientele to be served or an operations unit. As such they are realistic and specific outcomes and are challenging, measurable, criterion-referenced and focused on a single product, specific process, or other detailed achievement. In addition, these outcomes are focused on a well-defined cluster of actors or recipients of services.

Jenkins and Deno have developed a classification system for curriculum and instruction objectives based on their "degree of abstractness or distance from observable data."[9] This taxonomy is similar in spirit in some respects to what is presented in table 4-1. Their level A is defined as "abstract educational goals" that "are usually established by some reputable group." Producing "good citizens" is an illustration of the "general global educational objective." "If a student knows X, appreciates Y, and values Z (curriculum objectives), he will likely be a good citizen (educational objective)."[10]

Their level 2 objectives are the "locus of continuing struggle between behavioral and non-behavioral curriculum writers." This level bridges the gap between global and specific outcomes. Jenkins and Deno suggested that "events such as 'knows,' 'understands,' 'appreciates,' and 'values' are hypothetical dispositional states."[11]

Level 3 objectives, in turn, identified student capabilities. Level 4 objectives were the most specific and, therefore, the least abstract.

Identifying Performance Objectives

A sizable volume of literature is devoted to the use of behavioral objectives for instructional purposes, but very little can be found on the application of the concept to administration and supervision outcomes statements as a means to an end. These statements should be written at the level of specificity appropriate to the administrative echelon; an encyclopedic list of targeted performance objectives could drown a top-echelon executive in data rather than help him.

The reader is cautioned that not all writers concur with the hierarchy of outcomes shown in table 4-1 or with the definition or sequencing of outcomes descriptors. Some writers view a goal as being more specific than an objective. All concur that performance objectives are a subset of the general class of objectives. The term *performance objectives* is synonymous with what others call *behavioral objectives*. Very often the key in identifying a performance objective is the action verb.

The following are outcomes statements that may or may not be written in behavioral terms. Some are instructional behavioral objectives; others are administrative performance objectives or performance policies. The reader can test his ability to distinguish which outcomes are stated in behavioral terms (B) and which are not (NB). The correct answers to the classification of outcomes statements appear at the end of the chapter summary. If you score less than 90 percent, it might be well to reread the chapter or spend more time with the references on behavioral objectives.

 1. To provide educational experiences of the highest quality to all learners at the least possible expenditure of tax dollars.
 2. To ensure positive educational leadership for all professional and other employees in the school district.

3. To promote safe, adequate, and efficient pupil transportation.

4. At least 85 percent of students without serious educational, physical, or emotional handicaps will be graduated from high school with a diploma that recognizes that current state requirements have been satisfied.

5. To have the school business office to disburse payment for at least 90 percent of all approved bills for goods or services received and for which unencumbered funds are available within thirty days of such approval.

6. To ensure that all expenditures have been kept within amounts budgeted for the fiscal period.

7. To help students through writing exercises develop a sense of structure for the English language.

8. The child will add two new words to his reading vocabulary for each day in attendance at school.

9. The student will understand how to prepare chemical equations involving oxidation and reduction interactions by the end of the first semester of chemistry study.

10. Given the names of the fifty states, the pupil will be able to match the name of the capital with the correct state with 95 percent accuracy.

11. The child will be able to write a creative story ending after listening to the beginning of the story.

12. After viewing and interacting with a set of solid objects of differing geometric shapes, the child will be able to sense that each unique shape feels different.

13. By the end of one year of reading instruction, 80 percent of the children will be able to select the word in a series that is phonetically similar to a key word 80 percent of the time.

14. At the end of one year of instruction, 75 percent of the children will demonstrate the capability of naming and describing up to four main characters in a story told by the teacher at the 80 percent competency level.

15. From a selected list of current social problems the student at the end of the course shall be able to sense the importance of each one quickly and accurately.

16. To help the learner gain the knowledge necessary to use musical opportunities as a means for exploration and development of musical appreciation, interest, and talents.

17. Given a set of numbers, 80 percent of the students will be able to discriminate between rational and irrational numbers with 90 percent accuracy.

18. To help the adolescent gain an appreciation and knowledge of significant body changes during puberty.

19. At least 90 percent of the guidance counselors in the school system will submit five-year plans for operation of a comprehensive achievement-testing program in grades 1-12, which will include estimated costs, numbers, and types of tests; schedules for test administration; and test data-processing procedures and target dates.

20. To operate a school bus transportation system for the year in

such a way as to reduce accident rates by 33 1/3 percent from the previous year without a decrease in the number of pupils transported or the number of miles covered or an increase in operating costs.

Keep in mind that a behavioral objective can be distinguished by the use of action verbs to describe behavior to be exhibited, the specification of conditions, and indication of criteria for measurement of the desired outcome. Performance objectives enable an instructor (in the case of instructional activities) or an administrator to clarify for himself the intent of the instructional or administrative efforts.

It is important for those who seek to operate in the PPBS mode to be able, not only to identify performance objectives, but also to write them. A rather sizable volume of literature exists on the application of performance objectives to instruction, but there is very little, if anything, on the application of objectives to administrative and supervisory responsibilities. More will be said about this in chapter 5, which relates operation in a management-by-objective mode to PPBS.

Criticisms of Objectives

More than one administrator has been frustrated by the discrepancy between time devoted to writing objectives and the relatively minor benefits achieved. Bitter philosophical disputes, as well as aimless wheel spinning for two or three years, are not unusual among educational personnel involved in preparing sets of objectives. Some question whether statements of objectives are as helpful as others claim them to be. For example, in writing about some of the difficulties encountered in writing objectives, Merewitz and Sosnick declare that, "being candid about objectives may be embarrassing or offensive, and it may also alert opponents and give them something specific to attack."[12] They argue further that, "neither would having a precise statement of objectives settle how any given amount of money that might be allocated to a program should be spent."[13] They conclude that (1) "describing objectives has no effects that we regard as beneficial"; (2) "a statement of objectives, even though it has no factual input and need not be prepared annually does have periodic preparation and revision costs"; (3) "a statement of objectives may impair flexibility"; and (4) "describing objectives is not worth the cost."[14]

This is a rather sweeping condemnation of what many consider to be an essential aspect of operation in the PPBS mode. There is no question that time and resources are required to generate objectives. In the author's opinion, however, they cannot and should not be avoided. The viewpoint of Merewitz and Sosnick "that having a statement of objectives yields no benefits"[15] is subject to question. Well-developed and meaningful objectives are vital, and one cannot move very far in PPBS without them. Detailed descriptions of what it is hoped will be accomplished, followed by programs to reach the goals, represent one of the distinguishing features of program budgeting. In a sense, outcomes may be construed as benefits being sought. Nevertheless the attacks by Merewitz and Sosnick have a useful purpose: that of alerting administrators to the dangers of poorly written and meaningless statements of outcomes.

Objectives preparation can be considered a never-ending task; no one set will suffice forever. It is unrealistic to believe that missions, goals, objectives, performance objectives, and targeted performance objectives emerge in perfect form at the first effort, no matter how long the effort takes. A statement of objectives or performance objectives or targeted performance objectives should be prepared within a stipulated time and then put to the test to see if they can serve as effective guides to action. The statements are continually recycled and revised to serve useful purposes.

The problem of preparing objectives is particularly acute in educational institutions in which there are many objectives and most of them are difficult, if not impossible, to measure over relatively short periods of time.

This has been a general introduction to the issue of mission statements and objectives in program budgeting. The next chapter focuses on the operational implications of such statements in a PPB system.

Summary

There can be no operational program budgeting system without first identifying and clarifying objectives. PPBS is neither the first, nor is it likely to be the last, management system exhorting an administrator to "know your objectives."

One of the most difficult problems encountered in implementing PPBS in education is the translation of vague, general statements of educational objectives into more specific guides to action. Most school systems have such outcome statements gathering dust in a drawer. Despite the popularity of the idea, the actual process of goals determination has proved to be a bothersome and time-consuming chore.

The factors that make the program budgeting emphasis on objectives unique are the manner in which outcomes are phrased and the degree to which they influence actions and specify value judgements. Other forces in education stimulated the development of performance objectives. The revolution in objectives preparation has been going on for more than a decade. Significant strides have been made in developing taxonomies of education objectives in the cognitive, affective, and psychomotor domain. In addition hierarchies have been established to distinguish between product- and process-oriented, general and specific, and short- and long-range objectives.

The most significant development is the behavioral or performance objective, which couches the desired outcome in measurable and behavioral terms. It is characterized by some observable action on the part of the learner, specific conditions, and definite criteria for acceptable performance. The use of behavioral objectives sharpens the terminology and clarifies the intent of a given activity.

The general term *outcomes* embraces other terms, such as *mission, goal, objective, performance objective,* and *targeted performance objective.* The most abstract or broadest generalization and description of an outcome is the mission statement. At the other extreme is the specific, sharply focused, measurable, and criterion-referenced targeted performance objective. Not all writers agree on the sequence of abstractions for outcomes. For this volume the sequence flows from mission to goal to objective to performance objective to targeted performance objective. Highly detailed targeted performance objectives, imperative to direct activities at the operational level, could drown the top-echelon administrator. The degree of specificity necessary for outcomes statements is related to the operational level in the organization.

Generating objectives takes time and other resources. One unusual view holds that describing objectives impairs flexibility, can alert opponents where best to direct specific attacks, and in general leads to no discernible benefits. Detailed descriptions of outcomes is one of the distinguishing features of PPBS. In the author's opinion a detailed and meaningful outcomes statement is essential to operation in the PPBS mode.

Identifying the action verbs, conditions, and criteria help in discriminating behavioral and nonbehavioral objectives. In the list of outcomes on pp. 46-48, the following meet the test of behavioral objectives: 4, 5, 8, 10, 13, 14, 17, 19, 20. A rather sizable volume of literature exists on the application of performance objectives to instruction, but little can be found on the relation of outcome descriptions to the tasks of administration and supervision. Chapter 5 will deal with the operational implications of these descriptions.

Notes

1. B. Bloom, ed., *Taxonomy of Educational Objectives, Book I: Cognitive Domain* (New York: David McKay, 1956); D. R. Krathwohl et al., *Taxonomy of Educational Objectives: The Classification of Educational Goals, Handbook II: Affective Domain* (New York: David McKay, 1964).

2. These taxonomies can be obtained from IOX—The Instructional Objectives Exchange, P.O. Box 24095, Los Angeles, California 90024.

3. R. W. Tyler, *Constructing Achievement Tests* (Columbus, Ohio: Ohio State University, 1934).

4. Peter Pipe, "Putting Behavioral Objectives to Work: Some Definitions," mimeographed (AASA National Academy for School Executives Clinic, 1970).

5. S. Leles and R. Bernabei, *Writing and Using Behavioral Objectives* (Tuscaloosa, Ala.: University Supply Store, University of Alabama, 1969), p. 30.

6. Ibid.

7. Ibid., p. 48.

8. H. Taba, *Curriculum Development: Theory and Practice* (New York: Harcourt, Brace & World, 1962), pp. 194-210.

9. J. R. Jenkins and S. L. Deno, "A Model for Instructional Objectives," *Educational Technology,* December 1970, pp. 11-16.

10. Ibid.

11. Ibid.

12. L. Merewitz and S. H. Sosnick, *The Budget's New Clothes* (Chicago: Markham Publishing Co., 1971), p. 56.

13. Ibid., p. 57.

14. Ibid., pp. 57-58.

15. Ibid., p. 57.

Selected References

Bloom, B., ed. *Taxonomy of Educational Objectives, Book I: Cognitive Domain.* New York: David McKay, 1956.

Jenkins, J. R., and Deno, S. L. "A Model for Instructional Objectives." *Educational Technology,* December 1970, pp. 11-16.

Krathwohl, D. R. et al. *Taxonomy of Educational Objectives: The Classification of Educational Goals, Handbook II: Affective Domain.* New York: David McKay, 1964.

Leles, S., and Bernabei, R. *Writing and Using Behavioral Objectives.* Tuscaloosa, Ala.: University Supply Store, University of Alabama, 1969.

Merewitz, L., and Sosnick, S. H. *The Budget's New Clothes.* Chicago: Markham Publishing Co., 1971.

Taba, H. *Curriculum Development: Theory and Practice.* New York: Harcourt, Brace & World, 1962.

5. PPBS and its relationship to management by objectives (MBO) and accountability

PPBS is a means, not an end. Implementation of this system enhances an administrator's capability to make more prudent resource allocation decisions. As Miller and Starr put it, "the reason for making the decision is a desire of the decision maker to achieve some future state of affairs—his objectives." They add: "the precise formulation of the objective is the first major problem facing the decision maker."[1] In short, a decision technology is based on objectives.

The basic theme of the previous chapter was that there can be no operational program budgeting system without clearly specified organizational outcomes. Program budgeting may be perceived as "budgeting by objectives," that is, a system of classifying anticipated expenditures around a set of objectives (or related programs for the achievement of objectives). Some increase the importance attached to objectives and declare that *all* managerial activities in organizations operating in the PPBS mode are governed by objectives. To fulfill these demands means implementing what is called the "management by objectives" approach, frequently identified by the acronym MBO.

In short, both PPB and MBO place stress on the importance of objectives. Are they the same? This issue is explored in this, the last of three chapters on the first dimension of PPBS: the planning process as it is related to orienting the organization toward its objectives.

Various Conceptualizations of MBO

The relationship between MBO and PPBS will be determined in large part by how MBO is conceptualized. All writers agree that MBO means management by objectives, but after that is said agreements are few and far between. Many different interpretations are attached to this seemingly simple concept.

The term MBO began its climb to popularity in the literature on business and industrial management through the writings of Peter Drucker and Douglas McGregor during the 1950s.[2] It was believed that progress can best be measured in terms of what one is trying to make progress toward, that is, through the clarification of objectives. The emphasis is on results of work rather than its related activity; it may be called "management by results." Drucker and McGregor sought ways to measure managerial performance rather than objectives per se.

There are two basically different interpretations of the substance of MBO. One may be identified as being "human relations oriented" and the other "systems management oriented." Each deserves further identification and description.

Within the broad human relations classification there are at least four subsets. The first presents MBO as being in reality a "results-oriented management personnel appraisal." In other words, what some call MBO is identified more accurately as "management-personnel-evaluation by objectives" or MPE—BO. According to Odiorne, it is staff evaluation "where stated goals replaced personality traits as appraisal criteria."[3] The transfer of focus is from what a manager does, that is, what activities consume his time schedule, to the products generated as the result of his efforts. To Odiorne, MBO in this light becomes "a narrowly applied kind of criteria development for performance review" and sometimes is interpreted as "another personnel department gimmick."[4]

Managerial appraisal based on end products can be executed in a number of ways. For example, the top level executive can sit down with a subordinate and establish measurable, meaningful, and challenging objectives. Another method is the works standards approach in which directives are issued unilaterally from the top level.

In education these types of evaluation are identified as "cooperative appraisal" and the "job target" approach rather than MBO. Some school systems, however, have adopted the MBO acronym and talk of "management contracts" between a superior and subordinate as the document defining objectives to be accomplished.

It is apparent that MBO as a results-oriented managerial appraisal system borders on a new way for arriving at a job or position description. Rather than using vague generalizations to describe what is expected from a person in a given position, the system focuses on specific products or outcomes to be achieved by a stated time and within the resources allocated. This narrow conceptualization of MBO may end up as a refined outcomes-oriented job description called a "management contract."

A step away from appraisal is MBO as a basic way to motivate managers and other personnel. The concerns for the human element in an organization remain. McGregor argues that it is a mistake to assume that personnel are lazy, uncreative, selfish, untrustworthy, undependable, and hard-to-stimulate people who must be carefully monitored or supervised if anything is to be accomplished in an organization.[5] This interpretation of human behavior he labeled "Theory X." In his "Theory Y" he suggests that personnel can become self-directed and increase productive capabilities if properly approached, motivated, and supervised. In short, MBO is a leadership style, that is, a way for top executives or leaders to relate to subordinates.

MBO then becomes a way to motivate greater productivity not by appraisal but by helping an employee find greater job satisfaction through advance knowledge of what is expected of him. The emphasis is on human relations techniques that stimulate greater job satisfaction and thereby increase productivity. The aim of this conceptualization of MBO is to develop the employee's feeling of direction by defining his job targets and generating understanding of what is expected of him. The assumption is that an administrator fails when subordinates or co-workers fail. People generally work below par, and it is the leader's responsibility to motivate his people to perform closer to their full potential. The prime mechanism for helping subordinates to perform to potential is the work objective. The employee in this approach is encouraged to set his own performance goals, a process that helps develop self-directed individuals. MBO becomes a leadership style for stimulating greater productivity. It can be called "leadership by objectives."

A third subset of the human relations interpretation of MBO is related to but much broader in scope than the previous two. Here the primary end product is a management development system rather than simply a management appraisal approach or worker motivation strategy. Appraisal and motivation are parts of the management development system, but the emphases are on giving the manager an opportunity to know his job better than anyone else, integrating company objectives with managerial efforts, and helping the manager become a self-starter in the organization. A work climate is created to encourage individuals to develop to their fullest while executing their responsibilities for fulfilling the objectives of the organization.

Again, the chief strategem is to obtain agreement on objectives so that the manager has a clearer idea of what is expected of him, what demands and opportunities are available to him, and how well he is doing. You accomplish this by setting up a series of training programs to help him continue to grow professionally. In this sense MBO is operationalized through a set of training programs that is part of the human development system focusing primarily on managerial personnel as key individuals in the organization. This subset may be called "development by objectives."

The fourth subset within the realm of MBO as a way to improve human relations or productivity is similar to what others call "sensitivity training." The purpose is to understand what makes people tick. Such insights may be gleaned through a fuller comprehension of a person's value systems. The value systems are operationalized through the goals to which people subscribe. Few writers subscribe to this interpretation of MBO.

Levinson summarizes a rather comprehensive human relations conceptualization of MBO as a practice intended to

> measure and judge performance, integrate individual performance with organizational goals, define the job to be done and the expectations of accomplishment, stimulate increasing competence through the continuing growth programs for subordinates, sharpen communications between a superior and his subordinates, serve as a basis for judgment about salary and promotion, motivate the subordinate, and serve as a device for organizational control and integration.[6]

This is the behavioral scientists' interpretation of MBO as a sounder basis for evaluating individual job performance, improving worker motivation, enhancing productivity and better understanding human hopes and aspirations. This interpretation is not related closely to PPB as a way to improve resource allocation decisions. Thus, even though in this particular conceptualization of MBO the individual in an organization is planning his work in terms of objectives he has set by himself or with his superior's help, it cannot be equated with a significant aspect of PPB.

Howell argues that the full potential of MBO will never be realized if it is conceived only as a way to improve performance evaluation.[7] He stresses instead that MBO should be considered as a top-management planning and control approach. This is the "systems management-oriented" conceptualization of MBO, in which MBO becomes an outcomes-oriented system that stresses specification of objectives and organization of resources and energy around their achievement. Personnel appraisal, motivation, and behavior understanding are not neglected but are considered to be major dimensions in the operation of complex organizations. Most major organizations are too large and complex for a single executive or other individual to direct all activities. But, to quote Odiorne once again, if the executive "can control *results* he indeed can manage even the largest" of organizations. (Italics in the original.)[8] MBO becomes a "general system of management" or part of the "systems approach to administration" in this conceptualization. According to Odiorne, "in systems terms, MBO is a system which begins by defining outputs and applies these (output statements) as criteria to judge the quality of activity (behavior) and to govern the release and effectiveness of the inputs."[9] (Parentheses in the original.) Again, the individual is helped to understand his unique position objectives and, it is hoped, improves his performance thereby. But the systems management-oriented conceptualization of MBO looks at the total organizational picture in "a direct attempt to build into management systems an unremitting attention to purpose."[10] Success is defined in terms of specific outcomes or products. This puts a high priority on defining organizational objectives and communicating them to all people within the organization.

The word *management* in MBO applies to the total organization, not simply its personnel, in the systems-oriented conceptualization. This interpretation of MBO brings it into harmony with PPB. The stress placed on objectives in MBO and PPB in this interpretation reaches a higher degree of similarity in giving more precise direction to organizational activities and above all relating resources to results. This in turn raises the question of whether MBO is a subset of PPB or vice versa. There are writers on both sides of this issue. I prefer to consider MBO (in its broadest or systems management-oriented conceptualization) as contributing to a fully operational PPB system. In other words, operating in the MBO mode contributes to the effectiveness of program budgeting.

MBO may be perceived as a management system that endeavors to stimulate change and improvement in an organization by focusing on desirable results. In other words, it is not simply the identification of objectives but the generation of a particular set of objectives that will bring about movement from existing levels of productivity to higher levels. In a sense, it becomes a kind of accountability technique for holding persons responsible for results. PPBS is consistent with this interpretation of MBO as well. In a sense PPBS may be viewed as one of the many techniques in a comprehensive educational accountability system. It is imperative to define accountability more precisely.

Accountability in Education

Accountability is not a new idea. It is at least as old as the Bible; in Romans 14:12, the Apostle Paul writes that "every one of us shall give account of himself to God." Even when applied to secular behavior within educational institutions, accountability cannot be considered a concept of very recent origin. Early in the 1900s it meant that money raised for a given purpose had to be allocated to satisfy that purpose and not switched to others. Thus, courts declare that school tax funds dedicated to educational functions cannot be diverted to other purposes, however worthy, such as the construction of roads or social activities unrelated to education. There were further legal limitations on the use of educational resources. This necessitated the design of a control system to ensure that each constraint was honored. For most of this century accountability was fulfilled by handling educational resources in a disciplined manner.

Present day emphasis on accountability calls for more than safeguarding inputs for assigned uses. It includes specification of responsibility for outputs to maximize products. (PPBS also focuses on maximizing outcomes.) The novel aspect of the current interpretation of accountability is its stress on the systematic means of clarifying what is to be accomplished (specifying objectives) and then identifying the inputs required to achieve the specific outputs. Accountability moved away from the simple and narrow concept of safeguarding inputs for assigned uses to measuring the impact of inputs on stated and measurable objectives of the institution.

Accountability may be defined as a system of operation based on determination of desirable and measurable outcomes and the assignment of responsibility for achievement of such objectives to members of the organization. It implies a set of procedures to ascertain whether assigned responsibilities or objectives have been satisfied. In an operational accountability system every person or group in the organization is answerable or responsible to some degree to another person or position for some thing or objective—expressed in terms of performance levels, results, or achievements—to be realized within certain constraints such as a specific time period or stated financial limits. This is shown in figure 5-1. In essence the system specifies who is answerable to whom and for what. Accountability, therefore, is a goal-referenced term.

Figure 5-1. Operational accountability system

Every person (or group)
↓
Answerable (to some degree)
↓
To another person (or position)
↓
For something (objectives)
↓
Expressed in performance terms
↓
Within specified constraints (time, money)

As conceptualized here, accountability is not an end in itself; its fundamental purpose is to optimize relationship between resources and results. PPBS is concerned with a similar problem and, therefore, may be construed as an instrument within an operational accountability system. Accountability improves resource use patterns and provides better information on the performance qualities of personnel and teachers as they relate to organizational objectives. An accountability system gives administrators and policy makers an important new capability by providing them with data necessary to make more definitive judgements on how well or poorly the organization's resources have been used to achieve stated purposes. Again, a similar outcome can be expected from operating in the PPB mode.

An operational accountability system demands clarification of whether personnel will be held responsible for the execution of a process or for the development or achievement of a product. Thus, teachers may be held accountable for teaching, that is, the execution of an instructional process or activity with so many pupils and so many classes per day over so many months in a school year. The traditional teaching contract is a "performance contract," but the performance is stated in service terms. Similar service performances are specified for a physician, lawyer, architect, or television repairman. Teachers may also be held accountable for results, that is, the increase of pupil knowledge to a previously specified level. This is accountability for a product or outcomes as opposed to execution of a process. The so-called performance contracts in education, which attained a measure of recognition around the beginning of this decade, are more accurately described as variable payment contracts for the fulfillment of instructional outcomes. Payments are not fixed but related to the outcome level satisfied. Clearly then, the so-called performance contract in education did not introduce accountability per se but did switch the focus from accountability for instructional inputs and processes to accountability for instructional outcomes. PPBS did not originate the concept of accountability, but does contribute to the fulfillment of some of the accountability demand.

An accountability system demands careful specification of objectives, assignment of responsibilities, and subsequent measurement of achievements. Here is where such a system comes close to MBO, for MBO is also a way to manage more effectively by stressing outcomes. Clearly, operation in an MBO mode is also an accountability technique. Obviously, the success of this system depends in part on the sharing of common goals by all personnel. It will not work if the administrator has one set of objectives and the teachers another.

Designing and implementing a system of educational accountability that is meaningful, flexible, economical, and simple to operate is easier to talk about than to execute. Simplistic pronouncements obscure the fact that it is a complex undertaking demanding the formulation of an accountability game plan. It is not a panacea, and its use does not ensure the dawning of the millenium in education. Administrators charged with translating rhetoric into reality will have a higher probability of achieving accountability when the system is seen as one demanding careful specification of objectives, more precise assignment of responsibility, subsequent appraisal of achievements, and more prudent resource allocation.

The development and implementation of output-oriented management systems such as PPBS can do much as part of an overall strategy for the implementation of an accountability system. PPBS stresses performance and achievement of objectives rather than promises or inputs alone. For this reason PPBS is one of the means used to bring greater accountability into the operation of educational systems.

Relating MBO to PPBS

The broader conceptualization of MBO as a top-management planning and control system, or systems management oriented approach, brings it into close relationship to PPBS. Both MBO and PPBS call for better integration of objectives throughout the organization, its subunits, and its individuals. Operation in an MBO mode can enhance the implementation of PPBS.

It must be emphasized that MBO and PPBS demand that objectives be formulated or written in a manner that will clarify intent and indicate directions for actions. Poorly stated objectives formulated through questionable procedures may doom operations before they start. Drucker very early condemned the "search for the one right objective" as being as "unproductive as the quest for the philosopher's stone" and "certain to do harm and misdirect."[11] In the opposite vein, Schleh warned that "too many objectives tend to take the drive out of an objectives program."[12] He offered a rule that *"no position should have more than two to five objectives."* (Italics in the original.)[13]

An operational PPB or MBO system demands specification of objectives written in terms that are understandable, behavior oriented, measurable, operational, challenging, and realistic. It is also imperative that they be significant, developmental, comprehensive, accurate, balanced and brief.

Twelve criteria for assessing the quality
of objectives and goals for PPBS

1. Understandable: clear, unambiguous language.
2. Behavior-oriented: describes behavior expected.
3. Measurable: outcomes assessment is feasible.
4. Operational: defined in terms of operations.
5. Challenging: stimulates higher level of behavior outcomes.
6. Realistic: achievable in terms of resources, time, talents, and techniques available.
7. Significant: spells out important or relevant outcomes.
8. Developmental: continuity of growth over time and in different contexts.
9. Comprehensive: embraces all important outcomes.
10. Balanced: priorities set for multiple objectives.
11. Accurate: reflects true intent of the organization.
12. Brief: uses as few words as possible to communicate.

Each of these twelve criteria for assessing the quality of an objective deserves further expansion. The first criterion, "understandable," implies that clear, unambiguous language must be employed, leaving no doubt in the minds of the readers about what outcomes are expected. Clarity and specificity are important. Terms whose antecedents are not clear or whose implications are in doubt must be avoided. Operational definitions are preferred to increase the probability of more precise comprehension of what is involved.

"Behavior-oriented" terms describe outcomes as a particular set of behaviors expected to be obtained at the completion of a set of activities or use of specific resources. It suggests what a person should be able to do, that is, what new skills or skill levels he should have attained when the objective is satisfied.

The criterion, "measurability," cannot be overemphasized in the assessment of an objective. The ultimate goal is to develop capability among administrators to generate measurable objectives describing outcomes in terms that indicate to what degree a behavior has been performed. The least that should be expected is that the assessment of outcomes is feasible. Objectives in nonmeasurable terms are of little value to outcomes-oriented management systems such as PPB or MBO.

The "operational" criterion was partially defined in the previous paragraph describing what is meant by behavior-oriented terms. It implies that concepts communicate the substance of the objective.

Goals or related outcome statements are future oriented. They reveal the basic values and priorities of an organization. They may serve as guiding stars providing the bearings needed to steer a course of action. Goals can be used to motivate action, but when they are satisfied, they motivate no more and loose their status as goals. To be a challenge, an objective must demand more than what presently exists. The "challenging" criterion suggests that the objective define how much more is to be done.

By the same token the new demands should be "realistic" in terms of resources and constraints. What is called for should be feasible, that is, achievable within the limits of the time, talents, techniques, and technology available to the organization. To expect more than can be delivered could destroy rather than generate initiative. In other words, objectives should be reasonable.

Meaningful objectives should address themselves to the major areas of responsibility or social concerns of a school system, that is, they should focus on the "significant" problems confronting the institution. Therefore, the objective spells out the desired or important behavior outcomes, that is, those highly relevant to the person or the organization.

Objectives should also be "developmental," that is, conceived in terms of continuity of growth over time and in different contexts. This development can focus on products as well as process.

The "comprehensive" criterion is an expansion of the previous one calling for objectives to focus on those matters of great relevance or significance to the organization. It seeks to include all important behaviors or outcomes for a person or level of operation. It applies to a total statement of objectives rather than to any single one.

The next point calls for "accuracy," namely that the statement reflects the true intent of the organization. Objectives should not be a flowery mask for the real intentions of an organization.

The "balanced" criterion sets a perspective. Multipurpose institutions, by definition, pursue many outcomes and require a priority system to sort out matters of high concern. The justification of an objective may be based on what it contributes to balance within the organization. Tradition has it that effective administration begins with a clarification of objectives to be achieved. This assumes, however, that such outcome statements are homogeneous and never in conflict. The truth of the matter is, however, that most organizations, and particularly educational institutions, pursue multiple objectives because they are multipurpose institutions. There is a distinct possibility that not all purposes can be satisfied with the resources at hand and some may conflict with others. As Drucker noted, "in addition to balancing the immediate and the long range future, management also has to balance objectives."[14]

Lastly, it is recognized that "brevity" is desirable; when preparing a statement of outcomes, the law of parsimony should prevail, that is, each objective should be expressed in as few words as is possible to communicate meaning and still remain understandable, behavior oriented, significant, measurable, operational, challenging, realistic, developmental, and accurate. This does not mean that an objective should not exceed an absolute number of words. The number of words will vary, but the goal is to use as few as possible to communicate the substance of the objective.

Implementation of MBO within PPB

Some objectives may focus on a product such as the more effective learner. Others derive their importance from the fact that the system producing the product has needs of its own, and resources must be allocated to keep it operating at the same if not improved levels of performance. In short, not all objectives focus on the end product. Some are required to design new systems approaches. Still others help to develop satisfactory environmental relations or to sense changing social demands on the system.

As stated earlier, management by objectives from the human relations point of view analyzes the impact of objectives in terms of their impact on people. More specifically, it examines (a) how the generation of objectives may help motivate people, (b) how it helps them to fit in the organization by relating personal goals to those possessed by the organization, (c) how it gives them a sense of direction, (d) how it enables them to make a commitment to the organization, and (e) how it may be useful in appraising individual efforts. Clearly, the establishment of objectives and the specification of activities needed to achieve them make up the total work plan. This work plan, or progress during it, is evaluated by relating actual results to those rejected when the objectives were generated.

Management by objectives from the systems point of view analyzes the impact of objectives in terms of how they relate to the planning and control of organizations. In addition, the interpretation perceives objectives as means for generating improvement. Again, a purpose satisfied no longer motivates. The challenge lies in going beyond the present level of accomplishments, and the continuing need for revising outcome statements is obvious.

From a conceptual point of view, management by objectives, whether interpreted from the human relations or systems point of view, is not very profound. Nonetheless many have stumbled at various points in seeking to implement an approach that does not seem to be too complex. One common failure can be traced to the generation of objectives that fail to meet most of the tests of quality suggested earlier.

To illustrate, the administrator may (1) fail to revise a goal that has already been satisfied or set the goals too low to challenge; (2) fail to clarify common objectives or relate organization-wide objectives to individual units, divisions, and departments; (3) set the goals so high that they overload individuals with challenges that are either inappropriate or impossible to achieve in light of resources and capabilities; (4) fail to establish a monitoring system to reveal when the individuals in the organization are off target; (5) accept the easy way to get agreement by accepting pious and vaguely defined goals to save time and the possible conflict of generating meaningful and measurable outcomes; or (6) fail to translate a statement of objectives into the tasks required and resources demanded to fulfill its demands.[15]

On the more positive side, it is evident that one test of an administrator's leadership capabilities is whether he can stimulate the development of significant and measurable outcomes statements. The *problems, pressures,* and *aspirations,* or PPA, approach was designed by the writer to help overcome the feelings teachers and administrators often have of being overwhelmed by the magnitude of the

Figure 5-2. The PPA approach to objectives determination

1. What are the major problems?
    • Willingness to admit problem exists
    • Ability to recognize a problem when you see one
    • Ability to define problems with clarity
2. What are the major pressures?
    • From the community
    • From parents
    • From students
    • From employers—professional and others
3. What are the major aspirations?
    • Anticipation of concerns before they become full-blown problems or pressures
    • Long-range needs
    • Professional contributions

task or the frustration of a boring and tiring year devoted to meaningless activity. It is not imperative to identify all the objectives of an organization at one time. Relevant objectives should grow out of needs being experienced at a given point in time. A need is defined as a gap, i.e., the discrepancy between what is and what is desired. A starting point in assessing needs and developing objectives is identification of *problems* recognized by teachers, students, administrators, etc., or the *pressures* felt from community, legislative, or federal agencies. To this could be added concerns that could some day become full-blown problems and pressures but which at present could be identified as *aspirations* of the professional. The lists of problems, pressures, and aspirations could be screened to identify those of great and common concern as opposed to those of narrower and unique focus.

Figure 5-3. An operational strategy for formulating objectives

1. List of problems and pressures identified by
       Teachers   Other administrators
       Students   Board members
       Principals   Community groups
                          ↓
2. Screening of lists to determine commonly recognized concerns vs. those unique to particular groups
                          ↓
3. Setting priorities to determine which comes first

The next step in the preparation of measurable objectives as related to the definition of needs is to establish the base case; specify what new performance levels are desired and by what target date; assess the available or procurable resources and capabilities needed to satisfy new performance levels; and incorporate a self-correcting mechanism, such as recycling to assure the continuing revision of objective statements.

Figure 5-4. Defining objectives in measurable terms

| | The base case (present conditions) | The desired status sought | |
		Next year	Five years from now
List of problems of common concern			
Drug abuse	10 percent of students on hard drugs; 50 percent experimenting with alcohol; 40 percent trying marijuana	Reduction in use by 25 percent	Reduction in use by 50 percent
Vandalism	Window broken somewhere every 12 hours	Breakage reduced by 50 percent	No malicious window breakage
List of pressures of common concern			
List of aspirations			

This deserves a more practical illustration. High school dropouts may be listed as a serious problem (need), and there are pressures on the schools to do something about it. The base case describes the magnitude of high school dropouts in the school system. Assume that the data collected show that at this time 28 percent of those enrolled at the fifth grade level in the district terminate their education prematurely and do not earn a high school diploma. The next step is to specify what reduction in dropout rate is desirable and feasible. This begs the measurable question of reduction of how much and by what time? It may be determined by involvement of many in the system that the dropout rate could be reduced realistically to 20 percent within five years and to 25 percent within two years.

The next issue is whether the school has the money and a set of strategies it is willing to apply to move from a dropout rate of 28 percent at present to 20 percent within five years. If this is a realistic challenge, the administrator establishes the goal of reducing high school dropout rates by 8 percent over a five-year period. A task analysis is made to bring meaning and substance to these objectives. At the end of stated periods a self-correcting mechanism operates. There is monitoring, appraisal, and subsequent recycling to revise the objectives necessary to arrive at the desired state of affairs five years hence.

The procedures outlined can be generalized to other problems and pressures. The trick is to focus on those demanding immediate attention, not *all*. This is a test of administrative judgment and skills in separating the most pertinent from those of lower priority.

In reviewing the soundness of a statement of an objective, the answers to these questions should be sought:

1. Does this express a major or important concern for the school system?

2. Could a better statement of intent be generated if better or different data were available?

3. Have the gaps between actual and desired performance levels been identified with the clarity and preciseness needed?

4. Is the attainment of the objective feasible, that is, is it within the realm of capability of the organization to influence or close the gap stated in the performance objective?

General MBO Model

A general MBO model with check points and recycling is presented in figure 5-5. This rather comprehensive conceptualization brings it very close to the major dimensions of PPB. It starts with a definition of organizational goals, followed by the identification of performance indicators and standards for these goals. Objectives are then set for each division or executive consistent with such goals to discover whether or not these objectives are being satisfied. Again, performance indicators and standards must be set to determine the degrees of achievement. This is followed by the assignment of responsibility to units, departments, or individuals. Once again, setting the performance standard requirement for each is demanded. The figure shows only the assessment of Objective B in terms of times and costs, but the same procedure would apply to all objectives.

If, as is shown in the figure, it is not feasible to reach Objective B,

Figure 5-5. General MBO model

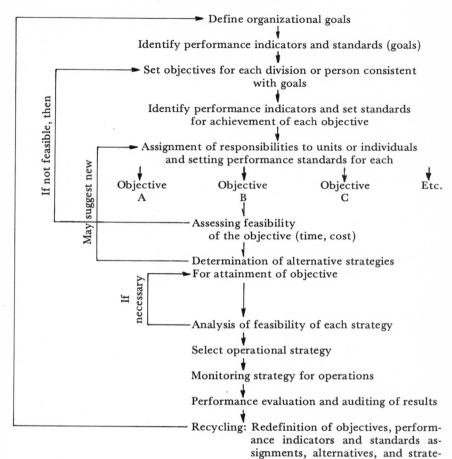

efforts are made to redefine the objectives for each division to identify those that may be feasible. Likewise, if the determination of alternative strategies demonstrates that Objective B was assigned to the wrong unit, reassignment is necessary. This general model of the systems management-oriented interpretation of MBO may be applied to all types of organizations.

Operating in the MBO mode from the systems point of view is

consistent with and facilitates the implementation of PPBS. It is a disciplined approach and requires far more than meets the eye. It is also an attitude or a frame of mind. Such disciplined approaches do not come naturally; history shows the propensity of managers to ignore the generation of or living by objectives. A disciplined approach does take time to perfect, but it can and must be perfected if there is to be any hope of operating in the program budgeting mode.

Summary

Decisions enable the decision maker to arrive at some future desired state of affairs: his objectives. There can be no operational program budgeting system without specification and clarification of organizational outcomes. PPB may be called "budgeting by objectives."

Management by objectives, MBO, also stresses the importance of objectives raising the question of its relationship to PPBS. Drucker and McGregor helped to popularize MBO during the 1950s. It is sometimes called management by results because of its focus on outcomes rather than activities per se.

There are two basically different interpretations of the substance of MBO. The first is human relations oriented and is considered to be the original and narrower of the two. It has four subsets. The initial subset stresses "management personnel evaluation by objective." It is a personnel appraisal approach that focuses on results achieved rather than characteristics or behaviors demonstrated. A step away is the view of MBO as a way to motivate personnel to increase productive capabilities. MBO becomes a leadership style that develops self-directed personnel. A third viewpoint of MBO stresses more broadly conceived management training programs. The fourth subset gets close to what others call "sensitivity training," an effort to gain a deeper understanding of human behavior and values. These are all conceptualizations from the behavioral scientist's point of view.

A broader interpretation of MBO emerged during the 1960s. This interpretation of MBO as a top level management planning and control approach is identified as the systems management oriented conceptualization. Personnel appraisal, motivation, and behavior understanding are not neglected but are considered a major single dimension in the operation of organizations. MBO becomes a way to manage by identifying objectives and applying them as criteria to judge the quality and effectiveness of inputs and activities. A high priority is placed on defining organizational objectives and com-

municating them to all personnel. The "systems management oriented" conceptualization of MBO is much closer to PPBS than is the
human relations based interpretation. MBO is considered to be a
subset of PPB: an approach that facilitates the realization of a
comprehensive PPB system.

Accountability is a much heard term in the early 1970s. It is an
old concept that has had its fundamental meaning changed from the
traditional safeguarding of inputs to assigned uses to the optimizing
of the relationship between resources and results. Accountability is a
system of operation based on the determination of measurable outcomes and the assignment of responsibility for achievement of objectives to members of the organization. In the system every person is
answerable to someone for some things expressed in performance
terms and within specified constraints. Accountability is a goal-
referenced term.

PPBS is concerned with optimizing relations between resources
and results as is accountability. PPBS and MBO can be considered as
important instruments within a comprehensive educational accountability system. All three demand careful specification of objectives,
assignment of responsibilities, and subsequent measurement of
achievements.

The quality of objectives statements is important to PPBS. Likewise, MBO is not to be construed as simply management by any type
or quality of objectives. Criteria have been developed to assess the
quality of objective statements. Objectives should be written in terms
that are understandable, behavior oriented, measurable, operational,
challenging, and realistic. They should also be significant, developmental, comprehensive, accurate, balanced, and as brief as possible.

Although many have urged managers to define objectives, few have
developed meaningful statements. It is easier to talk about the
definition of objectives or MBO than it is to implement it. Goals are
future oriented. They may motivate action. A satisfied goal, however, no longer challenges.

Educational institutions are multipurpose institutions. Goal conflicts are not uncommon. There is a need to balance or establish a
statement of priorities where multiple objectives must be satisfied.
Some objectives deal with a product. Others focus on what is
necessary to make the system operate, change, or relate to its
environment.

A general MBO model based on the systems management point of
view is useful in implementing PPBS. It is a disciplined approach that
requires time and practice for perfection.

Notes

1. D. W. Miller and M. K. Starr, *The Executive Decisions in Operations Research* (Englewood Cliffs, N.J.: Prentice-Hall, 1960), p. 33.

2. P. F. Drucker, *The Practice of Management* (New York: Harper & Row, 1954); D. M. McGregor, *Human Side of Enterprise* (New York: McGraw-Hill, 1960).

3. G. S. Odiorne, "Management by Objectives," *College and University Journal* 10, no. 2 (March 1971): 13.

4. Ibid.

5. McGregor, *op. cit.*

6. H. Levinson, "Management By Whose Objectives," *Harvard Business Review*, July-August 1970, pp. 125-34.

7. R. A. Howell, "A Fresh Look at Management By Objectives," *Business Horizons,* fall 1967, pp. 51-58.

8. Odiorne, *op. cit.*, p. 13.

9. Ibid.

10. Ibid.

11. Drucker, *op. cit.*, p. 62.

12. E. C. Schleh, *Management By Results* (New York: McGraw Hill, 1961), p. 22.

13. Ibid.

14. Drucker, *op. cit.*, p. 86.

15. Adapted by E. C. Schleh, *op. cit.*, chap. 3.

Selected References

Drucker, P. F. *The Practice of Management.* New York: Harper & Row, 1954.

Howell, R. A. "A Fresh Look at Management By Objectives." *Business Horizons,* fall 1967.

Levinson, H. "Management By Whose Objectives." *Harvard Business Review,* July-August 1970.

Odiorne, G. S. "Management By Objectives." *College and University Journal* 10, no. 2, March 1971: 13-15.

Schleh, E. C. *Management By Results.* New York: McGraw-Hill, 1961.

6. Programming and generating programmatic formats for educational institutions

The first long step on the journey toward implementing PPBS is to produce a statement of objectives. One of the important changes stimulated by program budgeting is the switch in focus from inputs and activities, such as personnel salaries and support services, to outputs or end products. Much of the potential of the PPB system depends on the quality and significance of outcomes declarations.

Objectives determinations represent the initial phase of program budgeting. They may serve as beacons to guide the future destiny of an organization and may motivate employee performance, but they are not self-executing. To fulfill the demands of an objective, an organization requires resources and a strategy, that is, a set of unified activities likely to facilitate goal attainment. Through the programming process, activities and the resources consumed in them are clustered around objectives. This phase of PPBS is every bit as challenging as determining directions and priorities.

Although related in sequence to planning, and an outgrowth of it, programming is a strange and often misunderstood process in educational circles. There is little confusion about the importance of clarifying objectives. Confusion sets in at the next step: the translation of objectives into meaningful operations. In PPBS the term *programming* is used in the noncomputer sense. Programming a computer means inserting a program or set of instructions in a language the electronic device understands so that the data will be received, processed, and reported according to those instructions. Programming in PPBS is the translation of a plan of action based on objectives into a series of activities and necessary resources required to achieve those objectives. Roles and functions are clustered on the basis of output-oriented activity. The program spells out who should do what and when. Business and industry, and to some extent the federal government, prefer to identify an administrator as a program manager, or officer if he is responsible for the integration of all activities necessary for successful mission accomplishment. The emphasis is not on location of a set of functions. A principal in the building, therefore, would not be a program manager, and neither would a department head concerned with an instructional area such as mathematics. The closest an educational institution comes to the concept of program manager is the project director. The use of a title such as project officer or program manager does not imply automatically that the organization is structured along program lines.

The purposes in generating programs and structures to facilitate their attainment are to illuminate the significance of one or more objectives and to display the resources and activities that facilitate the realization of the end products. Unfortunately, there is no single definition of a program or generally accepted set of techniques for generating a program in a given field.

Many definitions of programs exist in the literature on PPB. The following represent only a sample:

1. To program, in the program budgeting sense, is to cluster activities and related inputs around each of the many missions of an organization.[1]

2. The basic principle of an objective-oriented program structure is the grouping of activities that serve the same purpose.[2]

3. With the RAND Study for the Defense Department, however, the term program came to mean the ultimate goal of many interdependent activities.[3]

4. Program categories are groupings of agency programs (for activities or operations) which serve the same broad objectives (or mission) or which have generally similar objectives.[4]

5. A program is a set of activities, a social enterprise, with certain inputs of resources and conditions, certain ways of organizing those resources and conditions and establishing relations among them and certain outputs with standards for evaluating them.[5]

6. We prefer the following formal definition of a program: an organized response to eliminate or reduce one or more problems where the response includes one or more objectives, performance of one or more activities and expenditure of resources.[6]

7. In the context of the program budget structure, programs are defined as: "A broad category of similar services for an identifiable group or segment of the population for a specific purpose."[7]

8. A program is a collection of activities that have the same purpose or that function together to produce the same outputs.[8]

The common thread running through the various definitions of a program is that there must be a declared or implied objective to serve as a unifying point for organizing resources and activities. By definition, then, there can be no program or program structure developed *before* objectives have been defined and clarified. This obvious fact is stressed because some launch into program development before objectives are known. It may be easier to think of the term in its verb form *to program* or *programming* rather than in the noun form. Programming, in the verb sense, implies translating time-phased plans into action by relating resources and activities to stated objectives. In the RC–ASBO report it is stated: "Programming, another process in an ERM system, is defined as the process of developing program plans consisting of interrelated learning activities and support services with each plan representing a design for attaining educational objectives."[9]

The school science program may or may not be a "program" in the PPB sense. More often than not it describes the subject matter content of a discipline without implicitly or explicitly stipulating measurable science outcomes to be achieved at various learner levels. It would fail the test implied in most of the definitions of *program* in the PPB sense if the objectives of that which is called school science are not known or are vaguely phrased in nonperformance terms.

Purposes of Developing a Program Structure

Programming is a means to an end. It is part of the structural dimension of PPBS, that is, the implementation of PPBS calls first for the statement of desired outcomes and then for the design of a programmatic structure for achieving these outcomes. The purposes of such a program structure are

1. to serve as a means of integrating all other PPBS components
2. to give explicit attention to objectives, that is, using objectives as focal points in clustering activities and resources
3. to facilitate analysis of activities by organizing costs and other input data to include all relevant concerns
4. to group activities of an organization in a meaningful way so that costs can be assigned to each function or activity
5. to display data on objectives and evaluation information that is meaningful to administrators and useful in decision making

6. to identify possible trade-offs and alternatives

7. to facilitate subsequent systems analysis

8. to reveal gaps in programs or new alternatives not considered previously

Hierarchy of Program Aggregations

A program structure is output oriented. More than that, it modifies the traditional way of looking at an organization in terms of activities or inputs to one that places such activities in a perspective of the outputs to be generated and the resources to be consumed in the process. The total work of a multipurpose organization often is comprehensive and complex. The basic framework for planning, programming, and budgeting processes is established by a program structure of varying degrees of abstractness.

Schick concludes that "the case for PPB rests upon the assumption that the form in which information is classified and used governs the action of budget-makers, . . . Take away the assumption that behavior follows form and the movement for PPB is reduced to trivial manipulation of techniques."[10] Although as Merewitz and Sosnick put it, "no empirical evidence has been offered to support the proposition that more desirable decisions—or even different decisions—will emerge," as a result of the manner in which information is presented to a decision-maker, many intuitively feel that it may.[11]

The Bureau of Budget's Bulletin 66-3 of October 12, 1965, recommended a program structure for use in the federal government. The hierarchy of program aggregations recommended included (1) program categories, (2) program subcategories (packages), and (3) program elements.

The broad program objective is the basis for generating a program category. Thus, in the Coast Guard, "Search and Rescue" represents a program category, and in the Forest Service "Outdoor Recreation" represents another. In the federal government, higher education is also an illustration of a program category, that is, a cluster of activities identified as being part of higher education concerned with a broad objective, such as improvement of higher education through increasing the preparation level of professors, building better libraries, or supporting outstanding scholars with doctoral or post-doctoral study grants.

An elementary school reading program or a high school mathematics program may or may not be a program category. Much the same thing can be said for vocational education. These familiar terms in the subject matter curricular organization could be simply convenient groupings for a set of traditional activities, that is, a way of classifying expenditures to identify the salaries paid to specific kinds of teachers or for the purchase of particular kinds of books and materials. If, in addition, such inputs are related to a measurable output, such as increasing the reading skills of all students in grades 1-6 by one grade level for one year of instruction, it can be said that a program category has been produced. The crucial point in designing a program structure is the relationship between the educational activities identified as a program category and the outputs or objectives to be satisfied as a result of the activities.

All efforts to classify programs in terms of institutional scope, that is, level of operation, are meaningless unless there is an objective to unify and give meaning to a cluster of activities. Some writers speak of Level 1 programs as programs that are districtwide in scope or summarize the program resource allocations to obtain a district total. In the next breakdown, or Level 2, the resources are grouped for the next broadest function, such as instruction. The subdivision continues to show cost breakdowns for a specific kind of instruction with Level 3 being "regular instruction," "special education instruction," etc. "Regular instruction" may be subdivided further to identify resources allocated for each of the subject fields within it. Thus, mathematics for grades K-12 would be at Level 4, as would science, language arts, and any other recognized discipline. Specific subject costs, such as those for Algebra 9, would be included as Level 5. These levels can be summarized as follows:

Program level	Program description
1	Districtwide summary of all educational activities
2	Instruction (all instructional costs)
3	Regular instruction
4	Mathematics
5	Algebra 9

The above so-called program structuring is highly suspect even though it appears to be commonly used in education at this point in time. To begin with, it is a very old cost classification scheme, one that has been in use for most of this century and cannot by any stretch of the imagination be called new simply because the noun *program* is attached to it. It should be recognized for what it is: a device to summarize costs incurred for a specific subject, a given discipline, a type of instructional activity, all instruction, or all educational purposes in a district. It presents cost breakdowns by institutional levels, not program levels. This seemingly popular "hierarchical program classification scheme" is a snare and delusion. It does little restructuring. The traditional subject matter curriculum is continued without any effort to reveal objectives to be satisfied. It presents or categorizes only inputs, without so much as a suggestion about the outputs to be realized from any discipline or subject for a learner at a particular stage of maturity. Without outcomes specification, the assignment of costs to pursue broadly defined, or even specific activities questionably referred to as "program levels," the related "program descriptions" become merely the old and traditional exercise in cost accounting or unit cost analysis. Such cost classification systems are much more closely related to performance budgeting than to program budgeting, as will be described in greater detail in the next two chapters.

It cannot be overemphasized that a program structure cannot be developed simply by grouping instructional costs either by subject area, target area, grade level, grade span, building, or some larger unit. The crux of the issue in an output-oriented system, such as PPBS, is to identify the objectives to be satisfied by instructional activities or within attendance centers. This is what is new in program budgeting, that is, what has been ignored in previous years. Cost accounting in education by subject areas, grade levels or attendance centers is over fifty years old. The utility of such approaches in improving decision making among administrators is open to serious question. It has severe limitations, and many problems may be created when such data are released to the public, which is not likely to study the figures carefully. Over fifty years of experience has demonstrated that knowledge of unit costs alone will not facilitate appraisal of whether the expenditures were prudent or whether other resource allocation schemes might have been more meaningful.

It has been argued that what some educators call "program categories" or "program levels" do not satisfy the tests suggested for federal agencies in the Bureau of Budget's Bulletin 66-3. The program aggregations recommended in the bulletin continue from program categories to program subcategories; these are subdivisions within a program category. The basis for this grouping is a more specific or narrower set of objectives than those used to generate the program category. As stated in the bulletin, "Program sub-categories are sub-divisions which should be established within each program category, combining agency programs (or activities or operations) on the basis of narrower objectives contributing directly to the broad objectives for the program category as a whole." To illustrate, there may be a general program category calling for "the improvement of educational administrators" or "an increase in the number and types of specialists within medical colleges." The program subcategory for the first could be "improvement of instructional leadership competencies of educational administrators" or "developing skills in the implementation of output-oriented management systems." A program subcategory for the second general category could be "a 25 percent increase in hospital administrators." In the field of elementary and secondary education, improvement of reading skills for those involved in compensatory educational programs could be identified as a program subcategory. The objective is more specific. The next step is definition of how much improvement, over what period of time, within what constraints, and for what target group. Subcategories are sometimes referred to as "program packages," but whatever the title, it is a further breakdown within a program category.

A program element is the next level of breakdown, that is, it is a "subpackage" of a program subcategory. It is comprised of specific products to be expected, such as goods and services used in the attainment of objectives. Referring to Bulletin 66-3 as the authoritative source for such definitions, "Each program element is an integrated activity which combines personnel, other services, equipment and facilities." A program element is related to a highly refined objective. This could be illustrated as "the number of educational administrators in higher education to be trained to acquire a high level of concept understanding and managerial skills in implementing PPBS." In the medical school illustration, it would be the number of medical practitioners prepared in space medicine or in pediatrics. Once again, the basic characteristic of a program—whether it be a program category, program package, or program element—is determined by objectives of varying degrees of specificity and the resources and activities consumed to achieve the objectives. In short, the basic test of a program is the ease with which objectives within it may be identified and their achievement measured, not whether cost data alone may be conveniently clustered within it.

Steps in Programming and Program Plan Development

The basic steps in programming suggested by Newman and Sumner are:[12]

1. Divide into steps the activities necessary to achieve the objectives.

2. Note the relations between each of the steps, especially any necessary sequences.

3. Decide who is to be responsible for doing each step.

4. Determine the resources that will be needed for each step.

5. Estimate the time required for each step.

6. Assign definite dates for each part.

These delineations are necessary for smooth and efficient operations.

One source identified "in a broad sense" the "educational program information included in the programming process" as including (1) objectives; (2) resource requirements; (3) procedures for transforming inputs into outputs; (4) alternative ways of achieving objectives; (5) anticipated effectiveness resulting from the utilization of resources; and (6) criteria to be used for program assessment.[13] Obviously, this description of the process is so broad as to encompass all dimensions of the PPB system, not simply programming. The first three steps above would more narrowly define the process, with the last three being related more closely to other dimensions of program budgeting.

In the federal government the "program memorandum" is the end product of the programming process; it describes the various program categories. The Research Corporation of The Association for School Business Officials prefers to call it the "program plan document" and states that it describes "in detail the related components of each individual program included in the program structure for achieving the goals of the school district."[14] It could include information related to (1) identifying description, e.g., name and code number; (2) performance objectives and subobjectives; (3) student target populations; (4) content; (5) organization; (6) procedures, e.g., learning experiences and service activity procedures; (7) sequence of activities; (8) interprogram relationships; (9) operating procedures; (10) resource requirements; (11) performance criteria; (12) projected effectiveness; (13) time factors; and (14) other information deemed appropriate, e.g., recommendations and suggestions for the implementation of the program.[15]

This same source indicates the sequence of program plan development in the following manner.[16]

Program plan development states

Stage	Definition
1. Exploratory plan	A program plan designed to explore the potential of a means for achieving a desired objective

2. Prototype plan	A program plan designed to test the accumulated evaluations of exploratory plans
3. Interim plan	A tentative program plan designed to test the general advisability of prototype plan evaluations
4. Operational plan	A program plan designed to put into practice interim plans which have been evaluated to be effective

Programming is not a rigid approach to goals to be realized. It should include generation of alternative courses of action. The top executive is responsible for this activity. Likewise, no program structure remains static for long. As new objectives emerge for an organization, a force is created to generate new sets of programs designed to satisfy these objectives. It may call for the elimination of other programs that no longer satisfy objectives or serve objectives assigned to other institutions. In short, there is no single set of eternal programs, and there are no programs that fit all types of educational institutions at grades K-12 or the university level. The dynamic quality of programming is one of the reasons why PPB has so much to offer during times of rapid change.

Program activities may cover a time span no longer than a single year or may encompass two to five fiscal years. Exhibits in budget documents must be designed in a program format covering a specified time period to facilitate identification of fundamental program purposes.

Early writers in programming sought to develop a number of criteria for program operations. One important criterion was that the program structure should permit comparison of alternative methods for pursuing a policy objective. Another is related to time span over which expenditures are made. Programming thus became an activity-grouping technique aimed at optimizing the use of the resources required to develop a final product or goal. On occasion the programs cut across service or departmental lines. In this sense program concepts served as instruments of coordination for various organizational services or functions. The more diverse, complicated, and amorphous the objectives of a given institution, the more difficult it is to develop a programmatic structure for it. Educational institutions at the elementary-secondary, vocational-technical, or higher levels are complex organizations pursuing multiple objectives. It is very difficult and most challenging to develop a programmatic structure for educational institutions. It is unrealistic to expect to accomplish this for the institution as a whole in anything less than ten years!

Programs include a number of complementary components, none of which can be effective without the others. Thus, an educational program requires the right proportions of administrators, teachers, and buildings. A separate program may be designed when one part of an organization supplies services to others. For example economies are more likely to be realized if a single agency controls computer operations rather than allowing each department in a building to share responsibility for it. It must be emphasized that the popular reference to such things as a "school building program" or a "campus development program" is not likely to meet the tests of program in the PPBS sense unless it has a specific set of objectives or services to supply to other program operations.

The need for programming arises from the effort to overcome human limitations facing the obstinacy of the physical environment and limited resources. The process is best attacked by establishing what writers in this field call optimizations and suboptimizations. Furthermore, since results cannot be achieved instantaneously in complex institutions, long times are involved. Once resources are committed to a purpose, it is difficult to transfer them elsewhere. Programming helps to determine in advance what needs to be done to overcome the problems cited above. It is sometimes expedient to differentiate between final and intermediate programs of an organization. Final programs contribute directly to achievement of general objectives. Intermediate programs are characterized by operations that contribute to a final program in the immediate or remote future.

The revision of any element within a program may call for a review of others. The structuring of activities into a program implies some loss of flexibility. Once adopted, however, the program reduces the organizational freedom to do something different in future years. This dilemma can be partially resolved by expressing program functions in ranges rather than set and narrow limits.

Programs are formulated by those in authority to do so and remain under the direction of a responsible authority. The limits of responsibility of an executive department are determined program criteria.

Illustrations of Program Formats in State and Federal Government

Programs are time-phased plans for allocating resources and specify successive and interrelated activities required to achieve stated objectives. They focus on one or more problems and seek to eliminate or reduce those problems. Brown suggests that "programs are thus defined in terms of what services are provided for a group with similar disabilities, needs or attributes, or what is done for whom?"[17]

On the statewide level, Wisconsin designed the basic program structure for the Department of Natural Resources as follows:[18]

DEPARTMENT OF NATURAL RESOURCES

(A) [GENERAL] DEPARTMENT OBJECTIVES

> To guide the protection, development and use of Wisconsin's natural resources, to provide a system of recreational facilities and to enhance the economic development of the state through tourist promotion and private recreational assistance.

(B) PROGRAM DESCRIPTIONS

Program I: Fish and Game—Management of our wildlife resources for sustained recreational use and the preservation of valuable wildlife species.

Program II: Forestry—Management of our forest resources for the protection of the land, the preservation of the species and sustained optimum use.

Program III: State Parks—Management of a park system for optimum educational and recreational use and to protect outstanding scenic, historic and ecologic features.

Program IV: Tourism and Information—Management of a public education system in conservation needs, objectives and progress and promotion of vacationing and travel in Wisconsin.

Program V: Environmental Protection—Development of plans and enforcement of standards required to preserve and enhance the quality of the water and air resources of Wisconsin and the appropriate disposition of the solid wastes of our society.

Program VI: Trust Lands and Investments—Management of school trust lands and investments to provide a continuing source of support for public education.

Program VII: Outdoor Recreation (ORAP)—Development of a broad system of public recreational facilities. This program is shown primarily as a summary of the activities which constitute the Outdoor Recreation Act Program. All expenditures shown under this program are reflected in other programs of the department and the Historical Society and the Department of Transportation except debt service costs for recreational facilities which are only reflected under this program.

Program VIII: General Services—Management of the housekeeping functions for overall administration of the Department of Natural Resources, including clerical, finance, legal, personnel, engineering, real estate, research, data systems, and planning and aids, and to provide these services for the operating bureaus of the department.

(C) [SUBPROGRAMS FOR PROGRAM FOR] ENVIRONMENTAL PROTECTION

1) Program Objectives

To manage the waters of the state and to protect and enhance the quality of Wisconsin's water, air and land resources.

2) Subprogram Descriptions

The program is administered through five major subprograms described below:

   a) *Water Supply and Pollution Control*—Assures proper design, construction and operation of potable water treatment and supply systems and of sewage and industrial waste treatment and collection facilities and administers the state aid for pollution control facilities program.

   b) *Pollution Control Aids: Bond Retirement*—Debt service costs associated with the $144 million, ten-year bonding program for construction of municipal treatment plants.

   c) *Water and Shoreland Management*—Regulation of the use and development of state navigable waters, regulation of floodplain and shoreland management, comprehensive water resources planning and regulation of private water supply.

   d) *Water Standards and Surveys*—Evaluation of the surface water quality of the state in comparison with established standards, coordination of water research efforts and supervision of aquatic nuisance control.

   e) *Air Pollution and Solid Waste Disposal*—Establishment of statewide air quality standards, evaluation of air quality, licensing and regulation of solid waste disposal sites.

   f) *Field Operations*—Maintain district offices in support of the four central bureaus.

3) [Illustration of Subprogram Objectives—] Water Supply and Pollution Control

To protect the public from disease due to contaminated water and to protect the state's surface waters from pollution due to inadequately designed, constructed or operated water, sewage or industrial waste treatment plants.

   a) *1971-75 Anticipated [Water Supply and Pollution Control] Subprogram Developments*

   It is estimated that the state bonding program for pollution control facilities as well as increased federal participation will cause a significant increase in the plan review requests made to the bureau in order to qualify for aid funds. Additionally, population growth and economic development will increase the need for public water supply systems. The following table shows the estimated increases in the various types of plans which are submitted to the department.

   b) *Performance Indicators*

      1. Extensiveness

      Tables I and II show the actual number of plans reviewed, operators certified, and waterworks and treatment plants supervised. In addition, projected workloads through 1975 are shown. Table I indicates the breakdown of the plans reviewed by type. [Tables not shown in this publication]

In addition to the above extensiveness indicators, in 1969, Wisconsin did not have a single case of disease attributable to contaminated drinking water. Also, the population of the state not served by private water supplies or private sewage treatment plants (approximately 70%) was served by public treatment plants and waterworks which were all directly operated or supervised by certified operators.

Approximately 70% of municipal sewage treatment plants provide secondary treatment (biological removal of organic matter) while 15% of these provide tertiary treatment (nutrient removal). The pulp and paper industry continues to discharge 900,000 pounds of biochemical oxygen demand per day into Wisconsin's surface waters.

2. Efficiency
The average time lag between receipt of plans and final action (either approval or disapproval) has been 130 days. Recent legislation requires that all plans be reviewed within 90 days of submission except where an extension is approved by the owner of the plans.

The cost per water treatment or sewage disposal plant plan has average $115. It is estimated that this cost figure will remain about the same if additional positions are authorized to handle increased workload. If not, consulting engineers will have to be utilized in order to meet statutory deadlines resulting in increased review costs per plan.

State costs per applicant for waterworks and sewage treatment plant operator certification has averaged $15. This cost is based on one man-year for administration of the program. Facilities, materials and instruction are covered through an application fee.

Cost of annual inspections of waterworks and sewage treatment plants has averaged $15. This cost is expected to remain at the $15 level. However, total inspection costs will approximately double in 1971-73 due to a doubling in the frequency of inspections.

4. Program Benefit
Surface water as a resource for public water supply will be enhanced. In addition, a better quality surface water will benefit all citizens in recreational, aesthetic and economic terms.

Hatry suggests criteria with the following general properties for the program analysis:[19]

1. Each criterion should be relevant and important to the specific problem for which it is to be used. (This will depend on the fundamental objectives to be satisfied.)

2. Together the criteria used for specific problems should consider all major effects relative to the objectives. Enough criteria should be evaluated to cover all major effects.

3. Each of the criteria ideally should be capable of meaningful quantification.

In practice, however, "it is very difficult, and probably impossible, to meet all three of these ideal properties of criteria."[20] For example, purely qualitative criteria may be necessary when quantitative data are difficult to obtain. He indicated as well that "realistically most governmental problems involve the major objectives of a non-dollar nature."[21] This introduces the matter of value judgments, and, inevitably, value judgments about what the final program will look like rest with the administrator.

The following illustrative list of criteria for the evaluation of proposed programs is an abbreviated list proposed by Hatry in the areas of personal safety and intellectual development.[22]

I. Personal safety
   Objective: To reduce the amount and effects of external harm to individuals and in general to maintain an atmosphere of personal security from external events.
   a. Law enforcement
      Objective: To reduce the amount and effects of crime in general and to maintain an atmosphere of personal security from criminal behavior. (To some persons the punishment of criminals may be an important objective in itself as well as means to deter further crimes.)
      1. Annual number of offenses for each major class of crime (a reduction from the base in the number of crimes).
      2. Crime rates, as for example, the number per 1,000 inhabitants per year, for each major class of crime.
      3. Crime rate index includes all offenses of a particular type (e.g., "crimes of violence," or "crimes against property"), perhaps weighting as to seriousness of each class offensive, etc.
   [Items 4-10 omitted.]
II. Intellectual Development
   Objective: To provide satisfactory opportunities for intellectual development to the citizenry.
   1) Annual number and percent of persons satisfactorily completing various number of years of schooling.

2) Annual number and percent of dropouts at various educational levels.

3) Annual number and percent of each group enrolled in educational institutions.

4) "Intellectual development attainment" measures, such as performance on various standardized achievement tests at different ages and educational levels. Major educational areas, for example, reading skills, reasoning skills, and general knowledge, might be measured.

5) Performance on the achievement test indicated in criterion as related to intelligence tests (to indicate attainment relative to capacity).

6) Annual number and percent of students continuing their education at posthigh school educational institutions.

7) Participation in selected cultural and civic activities (and perhaps the number of persons who read newspapers or at least read certain parts of them).

Hatry also presents the following outline of an illustrative PPB system government structure:[23]

ILLUSTRATIVE PPB SYSTEM GOVERNMENT PROGRAM STRUCTURE

Summary

I. Personal safety
II. Health (physical and mental well-being)
III. Intellectual development and personal enrichment
IV. Satisfactory home and community environment
V. Economic satisfaction and satisfactory work opportunities for the individual
VI. Satisfactory leisure time opportunities
VII. Transportation-communication-location
VIII. General administration and support

Notes

1. This program structure is for illustrative purposes only. Its underlying framework is the identification of the needs of the individual citizen.

2. It is not a complete program structure. More detail is used in some areas than others; many categories have not been categorized sufficiently. Each individual government jurisdiction needs to specify the primary governmental objectives of its activities and based on this formulate its own specific program structure. The lower-level program categories particularly are difficult to structure without reference to the specific governmental jurisdiction and its problems.

3. It is highly desirable to have a statement of objectives, in as specific terms as possible, for each element of the program structure.

4. Such activities as planning, research, and experimentation

should be included with the program structure category to which they apply. If applicable to a whole program area (i.e., I through VIII above), it might be included under an "unassignable" category as shown below.

5. Categories shown in brackets are those which seem to fall readily into more than one location of the program structure. The brackets indicate the "secondary" location for these categories to avoid double counting when grand totals are prepared.

6. In many cases, it will be appropriate to include subcategories which distinguish particular "target groups." For example, consideration should be given to identification of certain programs by age, race, income level, geographical location, type of disability, etc. One illustration is shown under category IV(A). For the most part, however, this program structure does not identify target groups.

7. The lowest level categories, not illustrated here, should identify the specific programs or activities.

I. Personal safety (protection from personal harm and property loss)

    A. Law enforcement (i.e., crime prevention and control)
        1. Crime prevention
        2. Crime investigation
        3. Judging and assignment of punishment
        4. Punishment and safekeeping of criminals
        5. Rehabilitation of criminals
            a. Probation
            b. Parole
            c. Rehabilitation while confined
    B. Traffic safety
        1. Control
        2. Judging and punishment
        3. Accident prevention
    C. Fire prevention and firefighting
        1. Prevention
        2. Fighting
    D. Safety from animals
    E. Protection from and control of the natural and man-made disasters
        1. Civil defense
        2. Flood prevention and control
        3. Miscellaneous emergencies/disaster control
            a. National Guard
            b. Emergency rescue squads
            c. Other
    F. Prevention of food and drug hazards, nonmotor vehicle accidents, and occupational hazards
    G. Unassignable research and planning, personal safety
    H. Unassignable support, personal safety

II. Health (physical and mental well-being)

  A. Physical health
    1. Preventive medical services
      a. Chronic diseases
      b. Communicable diseases
      c. Dental disorders
      d. Other
    2. Treatment and rehabilitation
      a. Communicable diseases
      b. Dental disorders
      c. General
      d. Other
  B. Mental health
    1. Mental retardation
      a. Prevention
      b. Treatment and rehabilitation
    2. Mental illness
      a. Prevention
      b. Treatment and rehabilitation
  C. Drug and alcohol addiction prevention and control
    1. Drug addiction
      a. Prevention
      b. Treatment and rehabilitation
    2. Alcohol addiction
      a. Prevention
      b. Treatment and rehabilitation
  D. Environmental health (included under IV(C)-(G))
  E. Other
  F. Unassignable research and planning, health
  G. Unassignable support, health

III. Intellectual development and personal enrichment

  A. Preschool education
  B. Primary education
    1. Education for special groups
      a. Handicapped
      b. Culturally deprived
        1) Tutorial assistance
        2) Family orientation
        3) Mass media
    2. General education
  C. Secondary education
  D. Higher education
    1. Junior colleges
    2. Liberal arts colleges
    3. Universities
    4. Specialized professional schools other than 5

5. Medical and dental schools training functions (included under II)
E. Adult education
   1. General
   2. Adult vocational education (included under V(B))
F. Public libraries (included under VI(C)(2))
G. Museums and historical sites (included under VI(C)(1))
H. Vocational education other than III(E) (included under V(B))
I. Other
J. Unassignable research and planning intellectual development and personal enrichment
K. Unassignable support, intellectual development and personal enrichment

IV. Satisfactory home and community environment (creation of a livable and pleasant environment for the individual)

A. Provision of satisfactory homes for dependent persons
   1. Children
   2. Youth
   3. Aged
   4. Other dependent persons
B. Provision of satisfactory homes for others
   1. Upgrading existing housing
   2. Satisfactory supply of homes for low-income persons
   3. Information and counseling to home dwellers
   4. Enforcement of housing standards
   5. Land-use regulation
C. Maintenance of a satisfactory water supply
   1. Water supply
   2. Water sanitation
   3. Storm drainage (this category might also be included under I(E)(2))
D. Solid waste collection and disposal
   1. Garbage
   2. Refuse
E. Maintenance of satisfactory air environment (including air pollution control)
F. Pest control
G. Noise abatement
H. Local beautification
I. Intercommunity relations
J. Homemaking aid and information
K. Other
L. Unassignable research and planning, satisfactory home and community environment
M. Unassignable support, satisfactory home and community environment

V. Economic satisfaction and satisfactory work opportunities for the individual

A. Financial assistance to the needy (other than for homes, which is included in IV(B), (C))
   1. Aid to the blind
   2. Aid to the disabled
   3. Aid to the aged
   4. Aid to families with dependent children
   5. Aid to the unemployed (other than above)
   6. Programs to reduce the cost of living
B. Increased job opportunity
   1. Job training
   2. Employment services and counseling
   3. Job creation
   4. Combinations of 1, 2, and 3
   5. Equal employment opportunity
   6. Self-employment assistance
C. Protection of the individual as an employee
D. Aid to the individual as a businessman, including general economic development
   1. Support for individual industries
   2. General community promotion
E. Protection of the individual as a consumer of goods and services (other than food and drug hazards contained in II(A)(1)(c))
F. Judicial activities for protection of both consumers and businessmen, alike
G. Other
H. Unassignable research and planning, economic satisfaction and satisfactory work opportunities for the individual
I. Unassignable support, economic satisfaction and satisfactory work opportunities for the individual

VI. Satisfactory leisure time opportunities

A. Provision of outdoor recreational opportunities
   1. Parks and open space
   2. Athletics and playgrounds
   3. Zoo
   4. Other
B. Provision of indoor recreational opportunities
   1. Recreation centers
   2. Other
C. Cultural activities
   1. Museums and historical sites
   2. Public libraries
   3. Theaters
   4. Music activities
   5. Other
D. Leisure time activities specifically for senior citizens
E. Other
F. Unassignable research and planning, leisure time opportunities
G. Unassignable support, leisure time opportunities

VII. Transportation-communication-location

    A. Motor vehicle transport
        1. Highways
        2. Streets
        3. Traffic safety (included under I(B))
        4. Parking
    B. Urban transit system
    C. Pedestrian
    D. Water transport
    E. Air transport
    F. Location programs
    G. Communications substitutes for transportation
    H. Unassignable research and planning, transportation-communication-location
    I. Unassignable support, transportation-communication-location

VIII. General administration and support

    A. General government management
    B. Financial
        1. Expenditures
        2. Revenues
        3. General
    C. Unassignable purchasing and property management
    D. Personnel services for the government
    E. Unassignable EDP [Electronic Data Processing]
    F. Legislative
    G. Legal
    H. Elections
    I. Other

Novick indicates the following as major programs in the Department of Defense's program budget structure.[24]

MAJOR PROGRAMS IN THE DEPARTMENT OF DEFENSE PROGRAM BUDGET STRUCTURE

Program I. Strategic Retaliatory Forces: the forces that are designed to carry out the long-range strategic mission and to carry the main burden of battle in general. They include the long-range bombers, the air-to-ground and decoy missiles, and the refueling tankers; the land-based and submarine-based strategic missiles; and the systems for their command and control.

Program II. Continental Air and Missile Defense Forces: those weapon systems, warning and communications networks and ancillary equipment required to detect, identify, track, and destroy unfriendly forces approaching the North American continent.

Program III. General Purpose Forces: the forces relied on to perform the entire range of combat operations short of general nuclear war. These include most of the Army's combat and combat support units, virtually all Navy units, all Marine Corps units, and the tactical units of the Air Force.

Program IV. Airlift and Sealift Forces: those airlift and sealift forces required to move troops and cargo promptly to wherever they might be needed. Included in the airlift forces are both the MATS transports and the Air Force Tactical Air Command troop carrier aircraft. The sealift forces include the troop ships, cargo ships, and tankers operated by MATS and the "Forward Floating Bases."

Program V. Reserve and National Guard Forces: equipment, training, and administration of the Reserve and National Guard personnel of the several services.

Program VI. Research and Development: all research and development effort not directly identified with elements of other programs (i.e., where there has been no decision to produce for inventory).

Program VII. General Support: support activities of the several services and the agencies that serve the entire Department of Defense. It constitutes an "all other" or residual category of activities or programs and includes all costs not capable of being directly or meaningfully allocated to the other major programs.

Program VIII. Military Assistance: equipment, training, and related services provided for armed forces of allied and friendly nations.

Program IX. Civil Defense: federal assistance for fallout shelters, warning and radiological monitor systems, training and education for emergency preparedness, etc.

Program elements in Program I would include:[25]

Program elements: Program I—Strategic Retaliatory Forces
1. Aircraft forces
   B/EB-47
   RB-47
   B-52
   AGM-28A1B
   GAM-87
   B-58
   KC-97
   KC-135
   RC-135
2. Missile forces, land based
   Atlas
   Titan
   Minuteman

    3. Missile forces, sea based
       Polaris system
       Regulus system
    4. Command control, communications and support
       SAC control system (465L)
       PACCS (KC-135-1B-47)
       UHF emergency rocket communications system
       Base operating support
       Advanced flying and missile training
       Headquarters and command support

Illustrations of Programs in Education

Present program structures for K-12 or university systems tend to follow identification of grade levels K-12 in schools and under-graduate and graduate level studies in universities. However, the reader should keep in mind the warning cited earlier that grade level and subject designations may or may not serve as program categories. This approach to program structure may be little more than a continuation of the traditional classification of activities for inputs without any relationship to the desired level of outcomes to be pursued. The following is an illustration of a program description for a K-12 school system. The district is not identified, but the structure of the program is typical. *It should not be construed that this program presentation is worthy of emulation.* It merely indicates the state of art in programming in K-12 districts.

Happy County School District program structure

I. Regular programs
  A. Elementary instruction
    1. Kindergarten
    2. Primary
    3. Intermediate
    4. Supplementary services
    5. Co-curricular
  B. Middle-junior high instruction
    1. Art
    2. Business education
    3. Foreign language
    4. Home economics
    5. Industrial arts

      6.   Language arts
      7.   Mathematics
      8.   Music
      9.   Physical education
      10. Science
      11. Social studies
      12. Vocational training
      13. Co-curricular
   C. Senior high instruction
      (Same items as shown in B(1)-(13) above)
   D. Adult instruction
II. Special program
   A. Compensatory
   B. Children of migrant laborers
   C. Drug abuse
      1. Instruction
      2. Program development
      3. Staff development
   D. Exceptional children
      1.   Emotionally disturbed
      2.   Hearing impaired
      3.   Homebound/hospital
      4.   Learning disabilities
      5.   Mentally handicapped
      6.   Physically handicapped
      7.   Speech therapy
      8.   Socially maladjusted
      9.   Visually handicapped
      10. Program development
   E. Reading remediation
   F. Summer instruction
III. Support programs
   A. Auxiliary services
      1. Food services
      2. Transportation
   B. Instructional support
      1. Educational media
      2. Pupil personnel services
      3. Instructional administration
      4. Staff development
      5. Program development
      6. Program evaluation

C. Facilities support
  1. Plant operations
  2. Plant maintenance
  3. Plant construction
  4. Plant security
  5. Plant management
D. Administrative services
  1. Business services
  2. Financial services
  3. Information services
  4. Personnel services
  5. Management services

There is a real danger that unless this classification is supported by measurable objectives for each year of instruction, little will be gained that can be of value to decision makers on the optimum use of resources. It is also evident from this illustration that it is easier to develop a program structure for a relatively new thrust than for a continuing program in a school system.

Table 6-1 is an illustration of a program structure in a "program budget" at the university level. Once again, it can very quickly describe more traditional approaches and end up as a cost-accounting exercise rather than PPBS.

Educational Programs and Related Objectives

An educational program structure can be organized around objectives written in terms of the tasks of the schools. The four major dimensions of the task of the schools are:[27]
  1. Intellectual dimension
    a. Possession of knowledge: concepts; a fund of information
    b. Communication of knowledge: skills; to acquire and transmit
    c. Creation of knowledge: habits; discrimination and imagination
    d. Desire for knowledge: values; a love for learning
  2. Social dimension
    a. Man to man: cooperation in day-to-day relations
    b. Man to state: civic rights and duties
    c. Man to country: loyalty to country
    d. Man to world: wider relationships of people
  3. Personal dimension
    a. Physical: bodily health and development

Table 6-1. Five-year program budget: growing state college example[26]

	1970	1971	1972	1973	1974
Enrollment, FTE*					
Liberal arts (40%)	2,050	3,001	4,393	6,432	9,417
Business (60%)	820	1,200	1,677	2,413	3,447
Engineering	1,230	1,180	2,516	3,619	5,170
	—	—	200	400	800
Cost per FTE					
Liberal arts	800	800	800	800	800
Business	1,400	1,400	1,400	1,400	1,400
Engineering	1,900	1,900	1,900	1,900	1,900
Average	1,160	1,160	1,194	1,206	1,223
Total budget	2,378,000	3,481,000	5,244,000	7,757,000	11,516,000
Output					
FTE student years	2,050	3,001	4,393	6,432	9,417
Degree productivity index	.48	.48	.48	.48	.48
Degree equivalents (four year)	246	360	527	772	1,130
Cost per degree equivalent	9,700	9,700	9,900	10,000	10,200

*FTE: full-time equivalent.

  b. Emotional: mental health and stability
  c. Ethical: moral integrity
  d. Esthetic: cultural and leisure pursuits
4. Productive Dimension:
  a. Vocation-selective: information and guidance
  b. Vocation-preparative: training and placement
  c. Home and family: housekeeping, do-it-yourself, family life
  d. Consumer: personal buying, selling, investment

An "educational task-oriented" program format can be shown based on only one objective (it would be more precise to call it a goal or a mission statement) as follows:

OBJECTIVE I: To promote one year of educational growth and development for each year of school attendance in each of the school experiences offered. The programmatic format for this would be as follows:[28]

Program A: Experiences to continue intellectual growth of all pupils equal to one year as measured by existing evaluative instruments, possession, communication, creation, and desire for knowledge

  Subprogram 1: For Client Service Unit P—primary units for children under five (target population identification)

  Program subcategory a: Developing the ability to think and communicate clearly for all pupils

  Program subcategory b: Developing the desire for knowledge in all pupils

  Program subcategory c: Acquiring pertinent quantitative knowledge for all pupils

  Program subcategories d-n: Other specific objectives promoting intellectual growth on a regular and sequential basis

  Program activity 1: Direct instructional services
    Program element a: Teacher salaries
    Program element b: Instructional supplies
  Program activity 2: Special instructional services
    Program element a: Counseling salaries and other inputs
    Program element b: Psychological testing and related services
  Program activity 3: Administrative services
    Program element a: Principal salaries, supplies, etc.
    Program element b: Supervisory salaries, supplies, etc.
    Program element c: Central office salaries, supplies, etc.

Program activity 4: Instructional facilities procurement, maintenance, and/or operation

Program activity 5: Innovations and pilot projects

Subprogram 2: For Client Service Unit E—elementary units for pupils in K-6 (Target Population Identification)

(Program subcategories as above modified to relate to pupils of this level of development)

(Program activities and elements as shown above)

Subprogram 3: For Client Service Unit J—junior high or middle school units (Target Population)

Subprogram 4: For Client Service Unit S—senior high students (Target Population)

Subprogram 5: For Client Service Unit C—community college students (Target Population)

Subprogram 6: For Client Service Unit A—adult units (Target Population)

Subprogram 7: For Client Service Unit X—exceptional student units (Target Population)

Program B: Experiences to continue social development for all pupils equal to one year of growth as measured by existing instrument

(Subprograms, program subcategories, program activities, and program elements developed similarly to those shown for Program A)

Program C: Experiences to continue personal development—physical health and development, emotional health and stability, ethical and esthetic development

(Subprograms, program subcategories, program activities, and program elements developed similarly to those shown for Program A)

Program D: Experiences to continue developing the productive capabilities of individuals—vocational selection, vocation preparation, home and family life, and consumer skills and insights

(Subprograms, program subcategories, program activities, and program elements developed similarly to those shown for Program A)

OBJECTIVE II: To provide compensatory experience for all pupils one year or more below peers and to ensure completion of educational opportunities for at least 90 percent of those entering grade 9.

Program A: To minimize the number of students who terminate
their education prematurely—dropout prevention
Subprogram 1: For pupils in elementary or middle school client
service units
Program subcategory a: To identify potential dropouts
Program subcategory b: To design compensatory programs
Program subcategory c: To provide a pattern of home and
family counseling
Program subcategory d: To provide job opportunities and sti-
pends to students
Subprogram 2: For senior high students
(Program subcategories similar to those above)
Program B: To reduce learning deficiencies among students
(Subprograms and program subcategories similar to those above)
OBJECTIVE III: To maintain system support services at efficient
levels and design new system approaches
Program A: Improving staff rapport and staff negotiations
Program B: Operating an efficient transportation system for cli-
ents served
Program C: Ensuring system security
Program D: Evaluating system operations and designing new ap-
proaches
Program E: Managing with efficiency the system's fiscal and ma-
terial resources
OBJECTIVE IV: To develop satisfactory environmental relations
and to sense changing social demands on the system
Program A: Improving parent and community relations
Program B: Developing more effective state and federal relations
Program C: Meeting the standards of accrediting agencies
Program D: Meeting attacks on schools

Obviously the objectives are stated in very general terms and lack
more specific criteria for measurement. Thus, for Program A, subprogram 3, it could be stated that by the end of junior high school
65 percent of the students will be able to read English-language
magazines or newspapers with the degree of comprehension
equivalent to the ninth-grade norms as measured by a valid and
reliable standardized reading comprehension achievement test.
Programs have a time dimension. The program categories noted in
the previous illustration will be formulated in chapter 8 (pp. 133-34)
to show the dimension in future years.
The illustration does not follow subject matter lines completely as

suggested in other program illustrations. Expenditures for various subject matter areas would be clustered around each of the objectives indicated rather than separate from them. In this manner a decision maker has a better display of what resources are consumed to satisfy the tasks of the school in the intellectual, social, and personal dimensions, as well as the productive dimension.

Programmatic Curriculum In Education

The school curriculum has been defined by many writers as a set of learning experiences sponsored by an educational organization. Such a definition tends to emphasize the content rather than the objectives of learning experiences. How these experiences are organized is a matter of growing concern. By far the most popular format for organizing the curriculum, that is, the learning experiences, is the subject matter format. It includes a listing of the various disciplines subdivided into the subjects to be taught within each discipline. Thus, in the science discipline subjects such as biology, chemistry, and physics are organized as learning experiences for students of various age levels. The broad fields approach, the fused curriculum, and the so-called experience curriculum have been discussed, but relatively few schools have actually implemented these curricular organizations in spite of all the shortcomings and the many criticisms of the subject matter curriculum. The subject matter curriculum organization continues to dominate the field of education at all levels, but the stress remains on content and activities rather than outcomes.

There are other ways of organizing the curriculum. It can be based on the "individually guided" educational approaches that have appeared and gained some degree of popularity during the past decade. The author suggests that the programmatic curriculum format is consistent with the individually guided educational approaches and with PPBS. The programmatic curriculum organizes sets of learning experiences offered within an educational institution around objectives to be satisfied rather than subject matter. It calls for the programming of learning experiences, that is, clustering the activities pursued by students around stated objectives to be attained in the short run as well as in the long run. It can be called the "learning-by-objectives" or "teaching-by-objectives" approach. Teaching and learning are viewed as two sides of the same coin, assuming that teaching has as its purpose the stimulation and guidance of more productive learning among students.

Learning-by-objectives demands identification of goals, missions, general objectives, performance objectives, and target population objectives. Many of the instructional systems developed during the past decade, such as individually guided education (IGE), individually prescribed instruction (IPI), programmed instruction (PI), and computer-assisted instruction (CAI), demand that performance objectives be specified with a high degree of clarity before the learning activity can be designed and implemented. These approaches also demand the use of criterion-referenced evaluation. Criterion-referenced evaluation focuses on objectives and might be called "evaluation-by-objectives."

The generation of the programmatic curriculum is consistent with the efforts during the past decade to develop new instructional systems. It may require that places where learning activities occur be renamed "learning progress centers" rather than the traditional "classroom." The eggcrate classroom structure is being challenged by the "open concept," where large clusters of learners are formed into "units" as noted in the multiunit elementary and secondary schools.

It is the author's contention that new capabilities will emerge within the programmatic curriculum format. Such a format may provide better direction for relating resources to instructional activities. It provides an improved basis for evaluation of instructional outcomes; it may give the administrator a better basis for making more prudent resource allocations; and it is consistent with the goals of PPBS.

Obviously, there will be problems in generating a programmatic curriculum format that stresses learning-by-objectives. The long-established subject framework will not give way easily. No curricular revolution can be accomplished in a relatively short period of time. Those who have grown up within the subject matter format and have skills for operating within this mode must change their perspectives as well as develop new skills.

Perhaps, the biggest point to be made here is that PPBS demands the attention of curriculum and instructional specialists as well as top-level executives and school business officials. As stated previously, the initial step in generating PPB is to identify and clarify institutional objectives. Likewise, there can be no program budget without generating a programmatic framework for education. This implies that the educational experiences will have to be reorganized into a programmatic mode as implied in the previous discussion on the programmatic curriculum. This is a plea for curriculum and instructional specialists to obtain a greater understanding of PPBS so that their much needed services can be used in generating a learning-by-objectives format in education, which will facilitate a development of program budgeting. Curriculum planners face the challenge of moving the organization from its subject-centered programs to those that are more closely oriented to the needs of learners and the objectives of society. There is a very close relationship among curriculum, instruction, and PPBS, a fact which unfortunately has been overlooked for too long by those who view PPBS as a matter of primary concern only for school business officials. This is a most unfortunate interpretation of the system.

Synthesis of Planning and Programming

Planning and programming are interrelated processes. Programs depend on mission definition. One output of planning is clarification of the natures of missions and the resources required to achieve them. There can be no effective implementation of PPBS without a creation of a program structure in education. This does not and should not imply simply specifying in accounting classification terms the amounts spent for mathematics, science, reading, or other instruction. One of the prime mistakes some school systems make in seeking to establish PPBS is the attempt to force the traditional interpretation of program into the PPBS mode; the two do not fit. The potential of this decision technology in education will never be realized without a more sophisticated interpretation of programming. A program format for education must be built around stated objectives, that is, around the development of a programmatic curriculum rather than traditional subject matter and subject discipline designations.

Various illustrations of program structures for education have been indicated. Another may be illustrated by the goal of minimizing the number of high school dropouts. This objective would be the basis for clustering activities and identifying resources required for its achievement. Generating alternatives for reaching it would follow. Dropouts could be reduced by expanding counseling services, reducing class size, or designing new instructional strategies to increase the probability of learning success. These would be program subcategories. Teachers must be identified and trained for program purposes. Other program elements would be space and equipment allocated to the school. Note that mathematics instruction, sometimes called a "math program," is at best a program subcategory element, not a program in the PPBS sense. This type of structure would cut across existing organizational lines in education. It could be a task calling for the efforts of administrators of all levels, not simply the school business official. Designing accounts and budget documents to identify inputs to this and other programs would be one contribution of the school business officer.

The development of a program structure for some aspects of either the K-12 or the university level of education will consume at least two years if not five. Again, this suggests that one does not insist today that tomorrow the school system will employ PPBS across the board. A period of preparation is required. During the transition period new emphasis must be placed on planning a new perspective of programming as well as a new approach to budgeting. In addition, a staff with analytical capabilities (to be indicated subsequently) will be required to help the chief executive determine the courses of action that will maximize the use of resources allocated to various programs.

In brief, planning and programming are important and complex activities that precede the implementation of PPBS in educational institutions. No educational executive working alone can generate the format. Executives at all levels must pool their resources to clarify the goals and priorities and to interpret the programmatic significance of planning in the educational institution. It is an exercise in futility for the educational institutions fiscal officer to modify existing budgetary and accounting classifications systems without a prior determination of purposes and program structures and subsequent analysis by qualified personnel.

PPBS can be seen as a conflicts resolutions device. There is a disparity between what is demanded of education and what can be done with the resources at hand. The planning and programming processes help to frame the issues and strategies for subsequent fiscal and systems analysis. It also sets the stage for accountability for results.

Implementation of Programmatic Formats for PPBS

A supplement to the Bureau of the Budget's Bulletin 66-3 outlines the types of documents necessary to implement the system. One is called the Program Memorandum (PM), which is prepared annually for each of the program categories to be included in the program and financial plan. It has a specific format and a given length and outlines the methods of achieving goals as well as the legislative implications of programs. This is accompanied by a Program and Financial Plan

(PFP), which indicates program output and program costs. Also outlined is the Special Studies document, which constitutes the analysis of program operations.

Although in 1971 the federal government scaled down its requests for these documents, they can still be applied to educational institutions.

Initially, and subsequently for all new programs, the administrator may call for program memoranda to identify the program, the objectives to be satisfied, the target population served, the alternatives, approaches to the satisfaction of these objectives, and the various resource requirements. A memorandum may indicate how the new program departs from existing programs and whether there are likely to be any duplications of ongoing activities. This basic document can be filed and serve as the justification for continuing the activities in the long range as well as the short range. It may also be useful when program modifications are requested. It is not recommended that program memoranda be submitted each year for all activity. This would place a tremendous burden on the staff and could literally drown the executives in data each year.

Developing programmatic formats in education requires a team effort. Top-echelon administrators must stimulate development of this effort, as well as appraise and approve new programs. A sample document providing the data necessary to interpret the quality of program plans follows. It is called simply the Program Planning Document and can be adapted to satisfy special local needs.

Program Planning Document

(Request for Program Modification, Extension, or Introduction)

(School) _____   _____ (Grade, area, or other subdivision)

1. Purposes: Modification or extension of existing educational programs and the introduction of new program dimensions that call for additional resource allocations must be justified. One purpose of this document is to provide decision makers with data helpful in arriving at decisions to approve or disapprove program changes.

2. Program title (Identification data)

3. Estimated starting date

4. Estimated termination date

5. Major program objectives (State in performance and measurable terms.)

6. Outline of program strategies (Briefly describe what strategies, techniques, and procedures will be followed to fulfill each objective.)

7. Anticipated program outcomes (Describe what improvements or end products are likely to result at various points in time during the program.)

8. Target populations and learner levels to be served (Indicate numbers, types, and maturity levels to be influenced.)

9. Relationships to existing programs, if any (If none, indicate. Demonstrate likelihood of duplications.)

10. Program locations (Where will program actually be in operation?)

11. Resources requested over life span of the program

Identification of inputs requested	Amounts requested					
	Current year	2d year	3d year	4th year	5th year	Total for all years
Numbers and types of inputs						
Personnel needs						
Types and specialization						
Professional						
Others						
Numbers						
Professional						
Others						
Space demands						
Types of spaces						
Numbers						
Total area						
Special design problems						
Equipment needs						
Materials						
Fiscal resource demands						
Salary and benefits payments						
Space rental, construction, or remodeling costs						
Equipment rental or purchase expenditures						
Materials costs: texts and supplies						

Identification of inputs requested	Amounts requested					
	Current year	2d year	3d year	4th year	5th year	Total for all years
Other costs: overhead etc.						
Total fiscal resources						
Revenue sources						
Local						
State						
Federal						
Foundation or other						
Total revenues anticipated						

12. Program director

Submitted by   Approved or disapproved

Date   Date

Summary

Clarifying objectives is an initial step toward PPB and is followed quickly by programming. Objectives are not self-executing but demand resources and a strategy for their fulfillment.

Programming is a frequently misunderstood process in the educational field. What this means in computer-based information systems is not the same as what it means in PPBS. In program budgeting it calls for the translation of a plan of action based on objectives into a series of activities and related resources to achieve the objectives. Program officers are not uncommon in government and business, yet they are relatively rare in education.

A program structure illuminates objectives and the resources and activities necessary to facilitate the realization of outcomes. There is no single program definition or generally accepted set of techniques for generating a program for a given field. A common thread running through various conceptualizations of program is that objectives serve as the unifying peg around which to organize resources and activities. Comprehension of this concept is easier in the verb form *to program* or *programming* than in the noun form. A school's "science program" may be little more than a description of the substantive concepts of a discipline if measurable performance in understanding or using science concepts are neither implicit nor explicit.

Programming as a means to an end is part of the structural dimension of PPBS. Its purposes are to integrate all other PPBS components, to use objectives as focal points, to facilitate analysis of activities, to serve as a basis for grouping costs around activities, to display data in a meaningful way for decision makers, to identify trade-offs, to facilitate systems analysis, and to reveal program gaps.

PPBS rests on the assumption that classification of information will influence decision makers. Bulletin 66-3 suggests a hierarchy of program aggregations, including program categories, program sub-categories and program elements. The first is based on rather broad objectives and the last on more specific definition of the same outcomes. The crucial point in designing a program structure is the relationship between outcomes satisfied by a set of activities.

Efforts to classify expenditures by so-called program levels, such as district-wide, instruction, regular instruction, a given discipline, and a specific subject field, are highly suspect. The so-called levels are not related to program in the PPBS sense and do little more than revive old cost-accounting practices for inputs.

Programming starts with dividing into steps the activities needed to achieve objectives and ends with assignment of dates for completion of each part. It is not a rigid approach. It is a top-executive responsibility. No program structure remains static for long; as new objectives emerge, a force is created to generate new sets of program. Program activities may cover a time span of many years. Exhibits in budget documents must be designed in a program format covering a specified time period to facilitate identification of program purposes. Programs may cut across previously drawn service or departmental lines. The more diverse, complicated, and amorphous the objectives, the more difficult it is to develop a programmatic structure for an institution. Revision of any element within a program may necessitate review of all others.

Programs are time-phased plans for allocating resources; they specify successive and interrelated activities required to achieve stated objectives. Programmatic formats have been developed for some departments in the federal government and in some state governments. Criteria have been developed to aid educational institutions as well, although most continue traditional classification systems such as the subject matter curriculum. The developments in education are still in a rudimentary stage, because it is often difficult to identify supporting and measurable objectives behind so-called program activities.

The school curriculum is the set of learning experiences sponsored by an educational organization. The most popular format for organizing the curriculum is by subject matter. The emphasis is on content and activities rather than outcomes. Other curricular organizations are needed. A programmatic curricular format calling for the programming of learning experiences around objectives rather than subject matter is suggested. It can be called the "learning-by-objectives" or "teaching-by-objectives" approach. It is consistent with the other efforts to develop new instructional systems. The format may give administrators a better basis for making more prudent resource allocation and is compatible with PPBS. It is imperative that curriculum and instructional specialists give attention to and develop skill in PPBS. Program budgeting will remain ineffective until these specialists contribute their skills to the generation of programmatic formats.

The development of a programmatic format will take at least two if not five years. It requires a team effort. The planning and programming processes help frame educational issues and strategies for subsequent fiscal and systems analysis. A sample Program Planning Document is presented to collect data on new or modified program plans, which decision makers need to make more prudent resource allocation decisions.

Notes

1. S. J. Knezevich, ed., *Administrative Technology and the School Executive* (Washington, D.C.: American Association of School Administrators, 1969), p. 90.

2. State and Local Finances Project, *PPB Note 5* (Washington, D.C.: George Washington University, 1967), p. 6.

3. V. Held, "PPBS Comes to Washington," *The Public Interest* no. 4 (summer 1966): 102-15.

4. Executive Office of the President, Bureau of the Budget, *Bulletin #66-3*, October 12, 1965, p. 4.

5. F. W. Neal, quoted in O. L. Deniston and I. M. Rosenstock, "Relating Program Evaluation to Planning," *Public Health Reports* 85, no. 9 (September 1970): 836.

6. Ibid.

7. P. L. Brown, "Establishing a Program Structure," in *Planning-Programming-Budgeting*, 2d ed., ed. F. J. Lyden and E. G. Miller (Chicago: Markham Publishing Co., 1972), p. 190.

8. L. Merewitz and S. H. Sosnick, *The Budget's New Clothes* (Chicago: Markham Publishing Co., 1971), p. 16.

9. W. H. Curtis, Project Director, *Educational Resources Management System*, prepared by the ASBO Research Staff on a Planning-Programming-Budgeting-Evaluating System (Chicago: Research Corporation of the Association of School Business Officials, 1971), p. 73.

10. A. Schick, "The Road to PPB: The Stages of Budget Reform," in *Planning-Programming-Budgeting*, p. 48.

11. Merewitz and Sosnick, *op. cit.*, p. 24.

12. W. H. Newman and C. E. Sumner, Jr., *The Process of Management* (Englewood Cliffs, N.J.: Prentice-Hall, 1961), pp. 415-16.

13. W. H. Curtis, *op. cit.*, p. 73.

14. Ibid., p. 75.

15. Ibid.

16. Ibid., p. 77.

17. P. L. Brown, "Establishing a Program Structure," in *Planning-Programming-Budgeting*, p. 190.

18. Bureau of Budget and Management, *Sample Program Budget, 1971-73 Biennium* (Madison, Wis.: Department of Administration, March 1970), pp. 4, 8-10.

19. H. P. Hatry, "Criteria for Evaluation in Planning State and Local Program" in *Planning-Programming-Budgeting*, p. 197-98.

20. Ibid., p. 199.

21. Ibid.

22. Ibid., pp. 200-204.

23. Ibid., pp. 212-20.

24. D. Novick, "The Department of Defense," in *Program Budgeting*, ed. D. Novick (Washington, D.C.: Government Printing Office, 1964), pp. 59-61.

25. Ibid., p. 61.

26. J. Former, *Why Planning, Programming, Budgeting Systems for Higher Education?* (Boulder, Colo.: Western Interstate Commission for Higher Education, 1970), p. 11.

27. L. M. Downey, *The Task of Public Education* (Chicago: University of Chicago, Midwest Information Center, 1960), pp. 22-26.

28. S. J. Knezevich, ed., *Administrative Technology and the School Executive* (Washington, D.C.: American Association of School Administrators, 1969), pp. 92-95.

Selected References

Brown, P. L. "Establishing a Program Structure." In *Planning-Programming-Budgeting*. 2d ed. Edited by F. J. Lyden and E. G. Miller. Chicago: Markham Publishing Co., 1972.

Curtis, W. H. *Educational Resources Management System.* Chicago: Research Corporation of the Association of School Business Officials, 1971. Chapter V.

Hatry, H. P. "Criteria for Evaluation in Planning State and Local Program." In *Planning-Programming-Budgeting*.

Knezevich, S. J., ed. *Administrative Technology and the School Executive.* Washington, D.C.: American Association of School Administration, 1969.

Neal, F. W. Quoted in article by O. L. Deniston and I. M. Rosenstock, "Relating Program Evaluation to Planning." *Public Health Reports* 85, no. 9 (September 1970): 835-40.

State and Local Finances Project. *PPB Note 5.* Washington, D.C.: George Washington University, 1967.

7.   Budgeting and the budget document

In contrast to planning and programming, budgeting is the most familiar process in the PPB system as far as most administrators in educational institutions are concerned. It is also a process that is likely to be practiced, and with some degree of skill, in many types of organizations. Although fairly common, budgeting is a complex concept. It is one of the several fiscal dimensions of PPBS. There are a number of phases in the budgetary process. The output of budgetary activities is the budget document. The budget document may be designed in many ways and have a variety of functions within an organization.

This chapter and the next are dedicated to a description of the impact of the PPB system on the budgetary process and the role assigned to budgets. But first it is imperative to examine the history of budgeting and to probe more deeply into the contributions of this process to the management of institutions. Budgeting, as far as governments in the United States and educational institutions are concerned, is a twentieth-century development. During its relatively brief history of about a half century, a continuing number of reforms have been recommended in governmental and educational budgeting. Program budgeting represents one of the more recent of these efforts. In the previous chapter Schick was quoted as saying, "the case for PPB rests on the assumption that the form in which information is classified and used governs the action of budget-makers."[1]

Before describing the manner in which information is organized or the changing roles of budgeting in PPBS it is necessary to lay the conceptual framework. The budgeting process will be reviewed. The budget document will be defined and analyzed. This, in turn, will be followed by a review of the budgetary reforms introduced by PPBS.

Budgetary Process: History and Basic Concepts

The practice of budgeting was developing in England for several hundred years before its introduction into the United States federal government. Budgeting may be construed as part of an evolutionary movement that established representative or popular control over the sovereign or governing authority.[2] Although the process of budgeting can be said to have had its rudimentary beginning at the time of the Magna Carta, it was not until 1822 that it was formally implemented in the British government.[3]

Historically, the establishment of budgeting at the national level in the United States came with the passage of the Budget and Accounting Act of 1921. This took place about 100 years after the adoption of governmental budgeting in Britain. In general, it can be said that whenever a fiscal crisis hit a nation, the hue and cry grew louder for greater economy and efficiency in government. This reinforced the movement toward formal establishment of budgeting.

Before 1920 local school budgets "were relatively under-developed and non-standardized."[4] Improvements were relatively slow in coming. As late as the 1930s public school budgetary practices in most school systems left a great deal to be desired. It is a matter of historical record that educational budgeting lagged behind the development of budgeting in other levels of government, business, and industry. To illustrate, studies of school expenditure decisions showed that before 1920 they were based on a hit or miss policy, rather than disciplined budgeting. During the 1920s budget preparation, presentation, and execution practices were of a low order. Budgeting inadequacies continued to plague many school systems during the 1950s.

Budgets describe the hopes and aspirations of people and help to identify the resources required to translate these desires into reality. However base money may appear to the romantics, it is a truism that sooner or later everything desired must be translated into its dollars and cents equivalent. Clearly then, budgets for public education, as for government in general, are more than arithmetic and financial data exhibited in an imposing report that relates proposed expenditures to anticipated receipts during a given period of time. In educational institutions, "the budget must be regarded as the fiscal translation of the educational program."[5] In England under the leadership of Prime Minister Gladstone, the maxim that "expenditure depends upon policy" gained wide favor. This conceptualization may well be considered the rudimentary beginnings of program budgeting, which likewise calls for relating resources to hoped for results. In PPBS expenditures are derived from educational policies (or objectives). Along the way the more mechanistic conceptualizations of the budget won out over the broader conceptualizations of it as the way of expressing the values people attach to competing objectives in a multipurpose institution, that is, how they allocate their limited resources among competing ends.

In more formal and traditional terms, a budget has been defined as:

1. a plan for financial operation which includes an estimated proposed expenditures for given period of time and a proposed means of financing expenditures
2. a systematic plan for the efficient utilization of manpower, materials or other resources
3. a financial plan which serves as a pattern for and control over future operations of an institution[6]
4. a specific plan for implementing organizational objectives, policies, and programs for a given period of time[7]

Writers in a United States Office of Education publication viewed the budget as follows:[8]

A school budget is an official statement of the anticipated revenues and expenditures of the school district for a definite period. Through the budget, the board of education, the school administration and the people of the community reach agreement on the financing of the educational program. In other words, the annual budget is the educational plan of a school district for a school year expressed in dollars.

From these definitions it should be apparent that the budget document is a statement that is future oriented and concerned with what resources are available and how they shall be allocated among the competing purposes of an institution. It is a mechanism for systematically relating expenditures to accomplishments or planned objectives. "The more complex the institution the more imperative it becomes to develop a plan which will identify human, financial, and material resources necessary and are available to pursue varied missions."[9] The budget, as an instrument of fiscal responsibility and control, is a disciplined way to manage expenditures.

Budgeting is a time-consuming process with specific phases of a cyclical nature related to its development. The budgetary process, or budget cycle as it is called by some, includes:

1. *Preparation* of the budget document; usually an executive responsibility
2. *Presentation* of the prepared document usually to a regulative or legislative body such as a school board or board of trustees; submission of the plan for resource procurement and expenditures for a given fiscal period is likewise an executive function
3. *Adoption or authorization* for implementation of the budget; typically a function of a board of control or legislative body, but such legislative actions are not meaningful until appropriations are made for each segment of the budget and approval registered for the revenue or resource procurement plan
4. *Administration or execution* of the authorized budget; an executive act
5. *Appraisal* of the budget document; a combined executive legislative activity with primary responsibility resting with the legislative body, which assesses how well the resource procurement plan was fulfilled and how carefully resource expenditures followed those planned earlier and approved

As will be described in greater detail in subsequent paragraphs, the emphasis attached to each phase of the budget cycle has varied throughout history. The differing emphases reveal the evolution of reform efforts in the budgeting process and uses to which the budget document is put.

The budget may be perceived as one of the important instruments of fiscal management which includes the accounts, pay roll procedures, purchasing practices, the audits, and financial reporting. A diagram of the fiscal management cycle for institutions is shown in figure 7-1. "The budget, however, deserves recognition as the very heart of fiscal management."[10] The process seeks to describe "what goals will be accomplished rather than simply as a record of things and service to be permitted next year."[11] In PPBS, as will be elaborated on in subsequent paragraphs, the budget is more than simply a fiscal instrument. It becomes "an instrument which helps relate objectives to resources required to maximize achievement of the objectives."[12]

The budget document is a synthesis of three significant factors. This is demonstrated by figure 7-2.

Figure 7-1. The fiscal management cycle

The base of the "budget triangle" is the educational plan. The educational plan is an expression of educational objectives to be satisfied and related activities. Unfortunately, most educational budgets ignore or at best severely limit the description of the educational plan. Where it does exist, the tendency has been to describe activities and inputs rather than performance outcomes. In most educational institutions, the base of the budget triangle is missing or very weak. PPBS reemphasizes the base and demands planning and programming to produce an educational plan.

Figure 7-2. The budget triangle

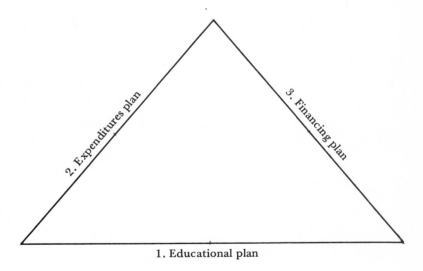

Organizations that pursue objectives consume resources, that is, expenditures must be made for the time and talents of personnel and for materials, equipment, and space. The realization of the educational plan calls for the generation of an expenditures plan. To reduce expenditures within a budget document means a concommitant reduction in educational services or, in the PPBS sense, satisfaction of a lower number or level of educational outcomes. PPBS has been identified as part of what was called public expenditures economics. This side of the budget triangle is subjected to systematic analysis where PPBS prevails.

The third side of the budget triangle is the financing or revenue plan. Resources must be procured to liquidate liabilities incurred in the expenditure process. The general hope is that the revenues will equal or, better, exceed the expenditures to produce a "balanced" budget. PPBS offers less on the revenue or financing side than it does to the other two. Public finance and taxation policies have more to offer this dimension of the triangle.

This is not to suggest that the three dimensions of budgeting pictured in the budget triangle are pursued independently; there is a continual interplay among them. While preparing a budget document, the administrator keeps a wary eye on the resource constraints and attempts to tailor the expenditures related to a given educational plan to the realities of resources available.

The budget calendar is the time plan and strategy for producing the budget document. It is the period of time alloted for the completion of a budget cycle. It ranges from six months to a year or more of preparation before adoption and execution of the budget. It may involve teachers and professors in contributing ideas and cost estimates as well as department heads, central office executives, and fiscal officials. Expenditure requests or plans may bubble up from operational levels to executive levels of an organization or vice versa. If operational personnel participate in the preparation of future year expenditures, such estimates may have to be sent back down again for further thinking and revisions and then move up the hierarchy once more before the finished document satisfies all constraints.

How the proposed expenditure plan is organized and when it must be presented are important decisions. Usually the budgetary expenditure classification designations follow the agreed on or mandated financial accounting approach. In some cases state laws may stipulate the budget form and exhibits, the date by which it must be adopted, and the start of the fiscal year during which the budget document will prevail. Where legal budgeting requirements prevail, educational institutions are given little leeway, and the forms, procedures, and dates must be satisfied or the document has little standing in the eyes of the law. Where program budgeting is said to exist there is frequent reference to the generation of program accounts or accounting. These may or may not differ from traditional classification. Program budgeting and accounting will be explored in greater detail in the next two chapters.

Budget Reform Movements

Budgeting in government has never remained static for very long. As Jernberg put it, "history of budgeting in the United States is a history of reform."[13] As stated earlier, PPBS is only one of the more recent and controversial approaches to budgetary reform. Program budgeting is neither the first nor is it likely to be the last effort to modify substantially the roles and relationships of participants in the budgetary process, the way information is organized, the methods employed in decision making, and the anticipated outputs.

The budget document came into being in response to public pressures for improved efficiency in governmental operations. Held defined the budget as "the central expression of how the government's finite resources will be allocated, the terms of the annual cease-fire, as it were, within the executive branch, between the competing claims of different advocates for more money for defense, or agriculture, or new welfare programs."[14]

Stedry perceived the budget "as a *plan*" and "as a *control*," but these functions were not mutually exclusive, and it was not unusual for both to be represented in a "single document." (Italics in the original.)[15] The traditional function of the budget was to serve as an instrument of control. It was a disciplined way of handling expenditures over a period of time. The administrator assigned responsibility for the execution of the formally approved budget—supported by necessary appropriation and revenue acts—must follow the plan without major deviation. Expenditures may be made without prior approval of the legislative authority if they are incorporated and approved in the formal budget document. When extra budgetary expenditures are contemplated, the administrator must seek the formal approval of the board of control or legislative authority before incurring any liability for such extrabudgetary expenditures.

How well the budget has controlled the pattern of expenditures during a fiscal period is ascertained at its conclusion, usually through the audit function. Typically an independent authority with special expertise verifies whether the expenditures made were consistent with the plan approved earlier. In short, the control function of the budget ensures that expenditures are made according to a predetermined plan.

There are many types of budgets within an institution. Some cover current expenditures; others are confined to large capital outlays for buildings and equipment; still others focus on rather special projects. Legal procedures may constrain some or all types of budgets. There is evidence to suggest that some "legal controls governing school budgets" may "hamper school official's intent to develop adequate educational programs."[16]

The narrow interpretation of the budget as an instrument in administration for purposes of control has prevailed through much of history. It has given the budget an image of being a mechanistic instrument where cold budgetary data are compiled for the benefit of accountants and bookkeepers rather than the man in the street. There are writers who argued that the school budget "is a living thing the purpose of which is to implement social process."[17] The budget in this light would enable schools to (1) give an account of financial stewardship; (2) facilitate the control of expenditures; (3) identify key elements in the management of funds, facilities, and personnel; (4) appraise the operation of the school program; and (5) specify educational objectives in financial plans.

The budget conceived primarily as an instrument of financial control for a given fiscal period demands specification of the objects for which expenditures are made, such as salaries of personnel, numbers of personnel employed, materials procured, or miles of transportation completed. The typical "line item" budget is written in terms of the objects of expenditure. It can be said that all expenditures in the last analysis are for a set of objects used in functions. The important factor is how objects are grouped. In a "control" budget document objects are identified as ends in themselves.

Schick identified three successive stages of budget reform.[19] The first placed emphasis within the budget on developing an adequate system for controlling expenditures. The other dimensions were not absent but the matter of highest priority was "called a reliable system of expenditure accounts."[20] It was indicated that administration or execution of the budget was the fourth phase of the budgetary process. The execution phase receives the greatest priority when the budget is perceived as primarily a disciplined system for controlling expenditures within an organization.

The second reform stage had its origin during the 1930s and is identified with the New Deal. It changed the image of budgeting to include a "reform of the appropriations structure, development of management improvement work measurement programs, and the focusing of budget preparation on the work and activities of the agency."[21] About a decade later performance budgeting was spawned from this reform effort. The expenditure control emphasized detailed tabulations of the objects of expenditures. In performance budgeting there is less emphasis on the objects of expenditures and more on the functions supported by the expenditure, that is, the character of the expense. It is a matter of historical record that even before the adoption of the federal Budgeting and Accounting Act of 1921 there were those who favored "functional" budgeting over "object" budgeting, even though the initial emphasis was on the object of expenditure appropriations.

Although budgeting in the federal government continued to follow the object of expenditure classification system in most agencies until at least 1950, public budgeting in elementary and secondary schools (where it existed) tended to be based on the functional-character system of accounting for expenditures. In other words the kind of work, or function, helped along by the expenditure, its financial character, dominated educational institution accounting rather than the actual thing bought or service obtained in education. It can be said that educational budgeting and accounting followed at least part of the spirit of performance budgeting (not to be confused with program budgeting) several decades before it was recommended for the federal government.

According to Schick, the third phase of budget reform, "the full emergence of which must await the institutionalization of PPB, can be traced to earlier efforts to link planning and budgeting as well as to analytic criteria of welfare economics but its recent development is a product of modern informational and decisional technologies such as those pioneered in the Department of Defense."[22] The planning function is emphasized in this third phase. Once again, the first step of the budgetary process or cycle is *preparation*. In reality most of the PPBS processes are started before the traditional preparation stage. It can be said that PPB focuses more on the "pre-preparation" phase than on execution. This should not be interpreted to imply that the budget as a control vehicle or a disciplined way of handling expenditures is ignored in PPB. Far from it. Rather, another function is added to the control function and given even greater emphasis. It is an expanded conceptualization of the budget as a strategic instrument for planning optimum use of resources by stressing objectives and alternative means of attaining objectives. In the program budget the institutional outputs gain primacy along with planning. As Novick put it, "the program, therefore, is the end object and is developed or budgeted in terms of all elements necessary to its execution."[23] A more detailed description of the essential elements of performance budgeting and program budgeting are reserved for the next chapter.

Relationship between Budgeting and Other Fiscal Instruments

The budget is one of many fiscal devices needed to achieve fiscal accountability. It is an essential element that has an impact on all other dimensions of the central fiscal apparatus. As a matter of fact, all other fiscal operations are harnessed to it in some way. The functional-character classification used in accounting for school expenditures, developed in the late 1920s and early 1930s, is also used in budgeting. This scheme, with some variations from state to state, has long dictated the school budget format. Planned expenditures for relatively short fiscal periods such as one year were related to instruction, administration, plant operation, maintenance, and other processes. The emphasis was on fulfilling administrative demands. Activities and functions were used instead of end products because it was easier to define and measure inputs than outputs. It was hoped that specific functions would inevitably lead to desired outcomes. When the educational institution took on new responsibilities, separate functional budgetary classifications had to be created. Thus, what was once called "auxiliary services" became separate account classifications for attendance services, food services, transportation, and community services. These changes appeared after World War II as relatively new budgetary classification. Outputs of the educational organization were implied but not made explicit in the budget document, and there were no hard data on the degree to which an objective was to be realized through expenditure of resources. The point is that classification of fiscal transactions in the budget was the same as that used for expenditure accounting. These will be described in greater detail in chapter 9. The budgetary cycle of events was often conceived in mechanical and fiscal terms. There was a fairly close matching of receipts and expenditures for a given year. Hope was expressed for a surplus of resources at the end of the relatively short fiscal planning period. To promote this budget planners tended to *overstate* expenditures and *understate* receipts.

Budgeting was an art with little science to support it. Few budget documents contained educational justifications for expenditure requests. Objectives were implied but related only indirectly to resources. Past practices were continued into the next fiscal period with minor modifications. The typical "budget planning" procedure was to publish actual expenditures in a given budget classification for the previous years, to indicate the amount requested for the next year, and to show the size of the increase over the past and future requests. There was little justification of the increases on ground other than vague allusions to "need." What gains in effectiveness could be expected in performing the function or fulfilling an educational goal for additional sums requested were not likely to be indicated.

Administrative decision about how to allocate scarce dollars among many different educational programs was not facilitated by the traditional budgeting approaches. It was difficult to do otherwise, because educational goals were not stated in operational terms and outcomes were difficult to measure. Review of the budget document alone may not reveal all essential data on resource allocation practices. The manner in which data are organized for the budget document may influence the ease with which certain types of decisions can be rendered. As will be demonstrated subsequently, something more than an approach to organizing information in a budget is necessary in the total system. With traditional budget formats it is all but impossible to determine whether a unit increase in resources allocated to a given purpose will result in increasing the effectiveness or enhancing the quality of performance levels to some degree.

The complexity of educational institutions, the scarcity of resources available for educational programs, and the growing public demand for evidence of what results can be expected for increased fiscal inputs calls for the creation of a new vehicle. Program budgeting is an attempt to relate inputs to outputs to improve decision making about resource allocation among various competing educational purposes and activities. As late as 1968, school budgeting was relatively untouched by PPBS, and there were comparatively few pressures to reform the budget classification system to facilitate analysis of alternative means of achieving a goal. More states are now passing laws to increase such pressures. To date there has been a PPBS void in the Office of Education's financial and accounting manuals, even in those of recent vintage. However, some research and development grants were awarded in 1968 to adapt PPBS to education, and the new manuals hold promise of rectifying this situation.

Summary

Budgeting is more familiar and more commonly implemented than other processes in the PPB system. It is one of several fiscal dimensions of program budgeting. The manner in which the budgeting process is executed influences its contributions to PPBS.

Budgeting is a complex process and, for the United States government and schools, a twentieth-century development. During its relatively brief history a number of reforms have been recommended. Budgeting existed in Britain 100 years before its introduction to the United States in the Accounting Act of 1921. Educational institutions lagged behind other government agencies in the use and sophistication of budgeting. Inadequacies continued to plague schools in the 1950s, although they were less intense than in previous years.

Budgets go beyond matters of arithmetic and touch the hopes and aspirations of people. In education the budget is often referred to as the fiscal translation of the educational program. The maxim that "expenditure depends upon policy" gained favor as far back as the days of the English Prime Minister Gladstone. Program budgeting is consistent with the spirit of this maxim.

Various definitions of a budget stress its future orientation, concern for systematic planning, and the allocation of resources among competing purposes.

The budgetary process consists of preparation, presentation, adoption, execution, and appraisal. The chief school executive plays a key role in practically all phases. The output of the process is the budget document. It is one of the important instruments in fiscal management. The budget document is a synthesis of three significant factors: the educational plan, the expenditures plan, and the financing plan. The base of the "budget triangle" is the educational plan, which unfortunately is poorly developed or at best simply describes inputs rather than outcomes. PPBS reemphasizes the importance of this base and demands that planning and programming be instituted to produce an educational plan. The three dimensions are not mutually exclusive; rather, there is continual interplay among them.

The budget calendar is the time plan and strategy for producing the budget document. Expenditure requests may bubble up from operational levels or maximum expenditure levels may filter down from top executive levels. State laws may stipulate the budget form, calendar, and procedures. Budgetary expenditure classification systems follow previously agreed on or mandated financial accounting systems.

Budgeting in government has never remained static for long. PPBS is only the most recent reform effort. Traditionally, the budget has been perceived as an instrument of control, that is, a disciplined way to handle expenditure requests. In such cases the execution stage of the budgetary process is emphasized. Performance budgeting and program budgeting, the substance of the next chapter, seek to expand the budget image to incorporate additional dimensions.

Notes

1. A. Schick, "The Road to PPB: The Stages of Budget Reform," in *Planning-Programming-Budgeting*, 2d ed., ed. F. J. Lyden and E. G. Miller (Chicago: Markham Publishing Co., 1972), p. 48.

2. S. J. Knezevich and J. G. Fowlkes, *Business Management of Local Schools* (New York: Harper & Row, 1960), p. 18.

3. J. Burkhead, *Government Budgeting* (New York: John Wiley & Sons, 1956), p. 2.

4. Knezevich and Fowlkes, *op. cit.*, p. 19.

5. Ibid., p. 17.

6. Ibid.

7. L. Ovsiew et al., "Budgeting," in *Theory and Practice of School Finance*, ed. W. E. Gauerke and J. R. Childress (Chicago: Rand McNally, 1967), p. 209.

8. B. K. Adams et al., *Principles of Public School Accounting*, OE22025 (Washington, D.C.: Government Printing Office, 1967), p. 37.

9. S. J. Knezevich, ed., *Administrative Technology and the School Executive* (Washington, D.C.: American Association of School Administrators, 1969), p. 64.

10. Knezevich and Fowlkes, *op. cit.*, p. 17.

11. Knezevich, ed., *op. cit.*, p. 64.

12. Ibid.

13. J. E. Jernberg, "Information Change in Congressional Behavior: Caveat for PPB Reformers," in *Planning-Programming-Budgeting*, p. 102.

14. V. Held, "PPBS Comes to Washington," in *Planning-Programming-Budgeting*, p. 13.

15. A. C. Stedry, *Budget Control and Cost Behavior* (Chicago: Markham Publishing Co., 1967), p. 3.

16. Ovsiew et al., *op. cit.*, p. 210.

17. Ibid., p. 218.

18. Ibid.

19. Schick, *op. cit.*, pp. 30-31.

20. Ibid.

21. Ibid.

22. Schick, *op. cit.*, p. 30.

23. D. Novick, *Which Program Do We Mean in Program Budgeting* (Santa Monica, Calif.: RAND Corp., 1954), p. 17.

Selected References

Burkhead, J. *Government Budgeting.* New York: John Wiley & Sons, 1956.

Knezevich, S. J., and Fowlkes, J. G. *Business Management of Local Schools.* New York: Harper & Row, 1960.

Ovsiew, L. et al. "Budgeting." In *Theory and Practice of School Finance.* Edited by W. E. Gauerke and J. R. Childress. Chicago: Rand McNally, 1967.

Schick, A. "The Road to PPB: The Stages of Budget Reform." In *Planning-Programming-Budgeting.* 2d ed. Edited by F. J. Lyden and E. G. Miller. Chicago: Markham Publishing Co., 1972: 26-52.

Stedry, A. C. *Budget Control and Cost Behavior.* Chicago: Markham Publishing Co., 1967.

8. Budgeting in transition: evolution of performance and program budgeting

A budget was recommended as a government management tool in England almost 150 years before the inception of program budgeting in United States agencies. In PPBS an existing and important fiscal process is recast to perform additional and new roles. In the previous chapter, the budget document was perceived in its traditional role of fiscal control. To fulfill such demands the focus was on objects of expenditures and, therefore, on the execution phase of the budgetary cycle.

During the 1940s and 1950s greater attention was directed to another budget function, namely, its contributions to the efficient management of the organization. This type of fiscal instrument became known as the performance budget. During the 1960s another important step in the evolution of budgeting took place with the advent of PPBS. Control and efficiency in management continue to receive emphasis, but the budget is also asked to play its part in strategic planning.

Each of these new budget images will be explored. The first in time sequence is performance budgeting; the second program budgeting. Although more closely related in spirit to program budgeting than others, "zero-base budgeting" is a general approach that can be applied to any interpretation. It will be described in the final portion.

Performance Budgeting

Performance budgeting as a concept was identified in the Hoover Commission's report of 1949. It called for a reform in budgeting to permit "alterations in budget classifications consonant with management orientation."[1] What other reformers referred to as "functional" or "activity" budgeting, that is, classifying expenditures by the function or kind of work helped along, acquired a new label: "performance budgeting." In all fairness it must be stated that more was involved than functional accounting classifications for budgets. To add to the confusion certain writers for the Hoover Commission preferred the term "program budgeting" to identify what others called performance budgeting. Their conceptualization was not consistent with what Novick refers to as "program budgeting." In this book the fiscal management modifcation called for by the Hoover Commission will be referred to as performance budgeting.

Performance budgeting is different from PPB. To quote Schick, "performance budgeting is management oriented; its principle thrust is to help administrators to assess the work efficiency of operating units by (1) casting budget categories in functional terms and (2) providing work-cost measurements to facilitate the efficient performance of prescribed activities."[2] It seeks to identify how well the work process was accomplished. It is retrospective, whereas PPBS is prospective, that is, it looks to the future. Performance budgeting stresses work measurement and is related closely to the scientific management spirit of Frederick W. Taylor. Cost accounting and unit cost analysis seek to establish what resources are consumed to complete a given *activity*. As a matter of fact, performance budget formats and major exhibits look like an exercise in unit cost analysis. Some schools that purport to implement PPBS are actually much closer to performance budgeting.

The output of a budget format that yields data on activity costs would be costs per pupil for instruction in vocational education versus cost per pupil in nonlaboratory or "academic" courses such as mathematics or English. Institutions of higher learning could have performance budgets designed to indicate the cost of a university education for each four-year bachelors degree graduate in the liberal arts. Additional data may show that the costs are less for four-year liberal arts graduates than for engineering or biological science graduates. These kinds of data were available in K-12 school districts in the early part of this century. Misinterpretations of such statistical

information lead to some unfortunate recommendations and controversy. A renewed emphasis on some types of unit costs may
rekindle similar objections at this point in time.

There is a propensity to confuse budgets that permit unit cost
analysis with PPBS. Novick made it clear that "program budgeting is
not cost accounting, although a great many people have fallen into
this trap."[3] Performance budgeting emphasizes work or service to be
accomplished; PPBS stresses objectives or purposes to be fulfilled by
the investment of public funds. Obviously, the collection of performance data may call for a program classification, but this does
not make it a "program" budget in the PPB sense. Performance
budgeting moves control budgeting a step beyond accounting for
receipts and expenditures to the next level, namely, management
concern for efficiency of work processes and, therefore, the unit
costs of activity done. It does not yield a method of making choices
among alternative objectives, but concentrates on efficiency or
"alternative means of performing a stated task."[4]

As indicated in the previous chapter, educational institutions are
more prone than other governmental organizations to use the
functional-character clarifications for receipts and expenditures. The
functional-character classification of budget and financial accounts
groups objects of expenditure around selected activities or work
processes. Such a classification system is necessary for implementation of the performance budgeting recommended by the
Hoover Commission in 1949. This was relatively new for the federal
government but not for educational institutions.

Even though performance budgeting was recommended by the
Hoover Commission, it never really got off the ground. The PPBS
introduced in the federal government in the 1960s actually replaced
conventional government accounting and control budgets rather than
performance budgeting.[5] If and when PPB supplants existing budgeting in education, it will replace procedures that are more akin to
performance budgeting than the fiscal practices that exist in the
federal budget. Perhaps one reason why school budgets purporting to
be in the PPBS mode look more like performance budgets is that it is
not too difficult to modify the common functional-character fiscal
accounting practice into performance budgets. It is argued that if the
information or output of a mode of budgeting is nothing more than
unit costs for various instructional processes, the organization is
operating in the performance rather than the program budgeting
mode.

Table 8-1 presents a budget document for a school seeking to

Table 8-1. Midwestern city school district, summary of program
budgets, 1973-74 estimated program costs

I. Elementary educational programs—grades K-6
Kindergarten	$ 244,320
Grade 1	611,585
Grade 2	554,989
Grade 3	533,070
Grade 4	571,425
Grade 5	561,701
Grade 6	488,893
Title I	132,275
Elementary educational general	811,013
Total	$ 4,509,271

II. Secondary education programs—grades 7-12
Agriculture	$ 13,002
Business education	184,199
Co-curricular activities	24,173
Distributive education	14,229
Driver education	127,557
English	726,605
Foreign languages	278,142
Guidance services	326,756
Health instruction	21,816
Home economics	152,797
Humanities	5,945
Industrial education	379,374
Mathematics	553,833
Music co-curricular activities	5,547
School newspaper	14,240
School yearbook	1,441
Sciences	526,746
Social sciences	697,082
Athletic co-curricular activities	162,740
General education secondary 7-12	553,636
Total	$ 4,769,860

III. Programs related to instruction—grades K-12
Art	$ 313,494
Audio-visual services	134,949
Health services	33,856
Instructional materials centers (IMC)	30,443
Instruction & curriculum coordination and supervision	255,018
Intramurals	90,871
Library services	480,738
Music	497,932
Physical education	499,318
Planetarium	25,604
Reading	426,269
Resource centers	212,311

Special education		622,491
Summer school instruction		230,675
Total		$ 3,853,969
IV. General program areas—K-12		
Community and recreation services		$ 34,200
Noon supervision		33,250
Substitute teachers		135,000
Transportation		640,960
Operation and maintenance of plant		2,754,530
Fringe benefits and insurance		596,200
Debt service fund		2,100,900
Total		$ 6,295,040
V. Programs at _____ area vocational institute		
Vocational programs for secondary students		
Pre-vocational programs	$ 42,350	
Continuing education center	21,750	
	$ 64,100	
Regular Vocational Programs		
Agriculture	21,406	
Business & office education	151,846	
Health occupations	125,612	
Home economics	48,691	
Technical education	94,724	
Trades & industry	112,954	
Vocational food training	17,048	
Multimedia resource center	15,900	
Work study	2,400	
General administration & services	92,961	
Maintenance—operation of plant	89,150	
	$772,692	
Adult evening programs		
Adult basic education	14,761	
Classes for persons with special needs	34,925	
General adult education	16,500	
Adult evening vocational	51,900	
	$118,086	
Total	$954,878	
VI. Districtwide general support services		
Board of education		$ 34,600
Superintendent		54,554
Assistant to superintendent		35,415
Business office		179,182
Data processing		67,600
Personnel office		53,573
Public information		13,500
Student accounting office		37,000
Total		$ 475,424
Total budget		$20,858,442

implement PPBS. The school is in its first year of switching from a traditional budget format and calls the present effort a "program-oriented budget." The Summary of Program Budgets shown in table 8-1 was preceded by almost 100 pages including statement of objectives, program descriptions for grade levels and subject, number of students served (enrolled) by the program, and allocated direct expenditures. The manner in which the objectives were stated made it difficult to measure outcomes and, therefore, difficult to relate them to expenditures. Nonetheless, it demonstrates the backup data needed to present the budget in a programming format. The illustration fails to show a multiyear time frame.

A university illustration of a so-called program budget is shown in table 8-2. The emphasis placed on cost accounting suggests that a better case might be made for identifying it as performance budgeting. The value of formatting such data for top level administrators is not as great as for others. Performance budgeting, with its focus on cost accounting and scientific management procedures, "is chiefly relevant to the problems of lower and middle echelons of an administrative hierarchy."[6]

No cost data were inserted in the illustration shown. The significant factor is the classification system. Other functional breakdowns could be added beside the four shown, and subcategories, such as instructional media, can be subdivided into expenditures for library, audio-visual materials, and computer services. Only data for undergraduate programs are illustrated, but a similar approach may be used for graduate level and special studies. This illustration also fails to show a multiyear time frame.

This is a more complex program budget than the one developed by the Western Interstate Commission for Higher Education (WICHE).[7] Again, it bears repeating that the format shown, as well as that depicted in the WICHE illustration, are exercises in cost accounting and unit cost analysis and come closer to performance budgeting than to program budgeting.

There are other practical illustrations that come closer to program budgeting than to performance budgeting. Thus, a large university is preparing to use a program budgeting format for its 1973-75 biennial budget. To move in this direction, a large volume of data was demanded to support expenditure requests, including data for the following program categories: (1) instruction; (2) research; (3) public service; (4) academic support (media, computing, and other services); (5) student services; and (6) instructional support. A report is prepared by each department and college for each of these program

Table 8-2. Program budget at ICU (by colleges and department—undergraduate and graduate programs)

Expenditures by function (at undergraduate levels)

| By location of programs | Direct instruction | Instructional support | | | Central univ. adm. | | Physical plant | Totals | Unit cost major | Proj. degree unit cost |
		Dept. adm.	Student services	Instr. media	Campus adm.	Univ. sys. adm.				
Liberal arts college depts.										
Chemistry										
Physics										
Mathematics										
Sociology										
German										
History										
Etc.										
Subtotal—all liberal arts										
College of Education										
Elem. educ.										
Sec. educ.										
Behavioral disabilities										
Educ. psych.										
Etc.										
Subtotal—all college of educ.										
College of medicine										
Pediatrics										
O.B.G.A.										
Etc.										
Subtotal—all college of medicine										
Other										
Totals for university										

categories. Each report includes (1) an introduction (mission statement, program evaluation procedures to be used, and base budget review procedures); (2) evidence of effective resource use in the previous fiscal period; (3) goals and objectives for continued use of current base budget in the next fiscal period; (4) a statement of anticipated new demands for the next fiscal period; (5) program adjustments planned for the next fiscal period; and (6) a productivity improvement program. To facilitate the preparation of a budget in a programmatic format, guidelines are issued to facilitate priorities determination, effectiveness and program benefits demonstration, clear objectives statement development and meaningful performance indicator identification. This is an impressive array of data and comes much closer to the spirit and substance of PPBS than is evident in most other existing or planned budgetary approaches.

Program Budgeting

Schick argued that "program budgeting (PPB) is planning oriented; its main goal is to rationalize policy-making by providing (1) data on the costs and benefits of alternative ways of attaining public objectives, and (2) output measurements to facilitate the effective attainment of chosen objectives."[8] It completes the evolution of budgeting from control device, to middle management tool for assessing work efficiency of operating units, to instrument of strategic planning. In the last step of reform the budget emerges as an instrument of strategic importance that can enhance the decision-making capabilities of top-echelon executives.

This can be called the "budgeting-by-objectives" approach. It should be recognized that the objectives themselves are subject to scrutiny; through analysis a new statement of desired outcomes may be demonstrated. "In program budgeting the objective itself is a variable."[9] In this sense the budget becomes an instrument of policy making, identifying objectives to be satisfied and the resources and activities dedicated to such purposes. As such the budget document concentrates on "expenditures aggregates" rather than specific objects. It becomes more than a model to facilitate efficiency. Novick noted that "program budgeting is not . . . performance budgeting."[10]

In 1940 V. O. Key reported on the lack of budgetary theory to facilitate the determination of whether "to allocate X dollars to activity A instead of activity B."[11] PPBS comes to grips with this problem and suggests the use of economic analysis—particularly the principle of marginal utility—to furnish the objective criteria to facilitate the optimal allocation of public funds among competing goals. At least this is the hope of the branch of economics known as welfare economics. As suggested in a previous chapter, PPBS is a subset of public expenditure economics, which in turn is a subset of the newly developed welfare economics.

However, Schick observes that "in terms of its direct contribution to budgetary practice, welfare economics has been a failure. It has not been possible to distill the conflicts and complexities of political life into a welfare criterion or homogeneous distribution formula."[12] Smithies proposed instead a budget rule that "expenditure proposals should be considered in the light of objectives they are intended to further, and in general final expenditures decisions should not be made until all claims on the budget can be considered."[13]

Had PPB been attempted twenty-five years ago, it might not have succeeded for lack of the technology to accomplish its demanding purposes. As Schick observes, "without the availability of decisional informational capability provided by cost-benefit systems analysis it is doubtful that PPB would have been part of the budgetary apparatus today."[14] Computer-based information systems and new quantitative analysis techniques make it possible for PPB to deliver on some of its promises.

The development of measurable objectives with a related programmatic structure and economic analysis are significant dimensions of program budgeting. These processes enable budget reform to go beyond the simple cost analysis suggested in the performance budget for purposes of control. PPBS demands organization of fiscal information and program data in a format based on output categories rather than simple description of inputs. More will be said about the generation of alternatives and the analysis of each in terms of costs and benefits in chapters 10 and 11.

Another very important dimension of PPBS is multi-year costing of program and financial plans. Program budgeting helps to minimize the danger of deceptively low expenditures during the first fiscal year of a new program. In other words, it illuminates the long-range cost implications of proposals. The program budget format requires objectives to be achieved through a programmatic format and exhibited in a multi-year time frame. Merewitz and Sosnick point to a limitation; according to them "multi-year costing has been helpful only when a commitment is being created or when current expenditures find justification in benefits that are products of both current and future expenditures, since these are the two kinds of decisions for which future expenditures would be predicted."[15] Obviously, complex problems are not likely to be resolved in a single fiscal period. By the same token, computing future implications of current decisions generates a cost of its own. Perhaps this is the reason the federal government in 1971, "restricted multi-year costing and benefit cost analysis to expenditures that would represent new policy decisions."[16]

Table 8-3 illustrates a summary program budget exhibit in a programmatic format with long-range costing, typically a five-year period (assume FY 1974 to be the present fiscal period). It demonstrates the many important characteristics of a program budget, including specification of objectives, programs that are not bound to subjects taught, identification of target populations, and a multiyear time frame. Expenditure estimates for FY 1979 will obviously be less accurate and subject to continuing revision of the "long-range period" than those for FY 1975. Totals are computed for each "program category" or objective, as well as for combined programs. Not shown are the backup or detailed descriptions of specific programs or the analysis of alternatives leading to the selection of the one presented in the document.

To summarize, the distinguishing features of a program budget are the following:

1. Explicit statements of desired outcomes (objectives) are an integral part of the budget document.

2. Budget exhibits are organized around major programs of the organizations, that is, there is a programmatic format with activities clustered around objectives.

3. Expenditures or operating costs are aggregated around program elements, subcategories, or categories rather than around inputs unrelated to measurable outcomes or subject matter disciplines and instructional functions where objectives are nonexistent or obscure at best.

4. Benefits as well as costs are exhibited for major programs.

5. There is a multiyear costing framework projecting new program resource demands for at least the next five years.

6. Data are organized to facilitate resource allocation decisions by executives.

In PPBS the budget does more than control expenditure decisions and assess efficient work procedures. It becomes an instrument for strategic planning, that is, a process for deciding on objectives, priorities, resources needed to attain outcomes, and policies governing use and disposition of resources.

Table 8-3. Multiyear financial plan based on a program format—a program budget document

| | Estimated program expenditures for fiscal year | | | | | | |
Program categories	1974	1975	1976	1977	1978	1979	Total 1974-79
Objective I: Educational growth and development							
Intellectual growth							
Primary client service centers							
Elementary client service centers							
Middle school client service centers							
Senior high client service centers							
Community college and adult client service centers							
Exceptional student client service centers							
Social development (Details omitted for program subcategories)							
Personal development (Details omitted for program subcategories)							
Productive development (Details omitted for program subcategories)							
Total for all Objective I programs							

Table 8-3. Multiyear financial plan based on a program format (continued)

Program categories	Estimated program expenditures for fiscal year						Total 1974-79
	1974	1975	1976	1977	1978	1979	
Objective II: Compensatory experiences							
Dropout prevention							
Among elementary and middle school students							
Among senior high students							
Reducing learning deficiencies							
Total for all Objective II programs							
Objective III: System maintenance and design of new systems							
Staff rapport and negotiations							
Transportation							
System security							
Evaluation of system operations and design							
Fiscal and material resource management							
Total for all Objective III programs							
Objective IV: Environmental relations							
Parent and community relations							
State and federal relations							
Accrediting agencies							
Attacks on schools							
Total for all Objective IV programs							
Grand total for Objectives I-IV							

Summary of Various Budget Types

A summary of the essential features of traditional, performance, and program budgets is presented in table 8-4. It relates to what Schick refers to as "basic differences between budget orientations."[17] Each of the three types of budgets is contrasted in terms of approximate starting date, primary mission, primary concern of budget officers, perceptions of the budget as a fiscal instrument, prime roles for budget agency, budgetary process emphasized, fiscal elements of major importance, basic classification unit, duration of budget period, budget execution emphasis, operational skills emphasized, implementation skills stressed, disciplines contributing the most to the budget, information focus within the budget, approach used to arrive at new budget estimates, planning emphasis in budget development, budget output, criteria for appraising budget decisions, and relationships of prime concern. To illustrate, line 3 of the table shows that the primary concern of budget officers in traditional budgeting practices is to safeguard funds for assigned uses; in performance budgeting practices it is gathering data on costs incurred for the execution of various functions; and in program budgeting practices it is determining the relationship between objectives and expenditures. There is some degree of overlap among the nineteen characteristics cited.

Zero-Base Budgeting

The usual method or set of procedures used to arrive at estimated expenditure figures for a future budget fiscal period is to start by placing the actual expenditures incurred in the previous year for each classification category in the first column. This is followed by a second column in which are placed the estimated expenditures for each budget classification for the present year. In a third column are the estimated expenditures for the next or future fiscal period. This is computed by assuming that expenditures will increase or decrease by a given incremental unit over that of the present fiscal period. This may be shown in a fourth column and indicated as a percent or actual dollar increment over the present period. This is known as the incremental approach to budgeting, because it assumes a base period figure and the program's continuation with an incremental change. If the increment is zero, the program will consume the same amount of resources as were allocated for the present period.

Table 8-4. Comparison of essential characteristics of three types of budgets

Essential characteristic (criterion)	Traditional budget 1920	Performance budget 1935	Program budget 1960
1. Approximate starting date of budget practice			
2. Primary mission of the budget	Disciplined expenditures control	Work-cost data accumulation and expenditure control	Fiscal implications of objectives attainment data and expenditures control
3. Primary concern of budget officers	Safeguarding funds for assigned uses; stewardship and protection of fiscal resources	Gathering information on costs of various functions or work processes in organization	Determining relationship between objectives and expenditures for each alternative
4. Perceptions of the budget as fiscal instrument	Instrument for fiscal control	Instrument for cost-analysis and efficiency promotion	Instrument for planning and analysis needed for resource allocation decisions
5. Prime roles for budget agency and officials	Fiduciary-fiscal tool developments; responsibility for fiscal control operations or items	Maintenance of efficiency of processes, activities, or work	Fiscal policy development and definition of purposes of resources allocated
6. Budgetary process(es) stressed	Execution and appraisal	Preparation and execution	"Pre-preparation," preparation, and appraisal
7. Budget or fiscal elements of major importance	Uniform classification of receipts and expenditures	Prorating procedures: cost accounting systems and unit-cost analysis; what it "costs" to furnish services	Cost-effectiveness analysis; benefits received for resources consumed
8. Classification unit basic budget emphasizes	Expenditure objects; line items	Costs organized in terms of functions or activities	Fiscal data organized in terms of programs; programmatic structures related to objectives or target groups

9. Duration of budget period	One fiscal period only (single fiscal year planning)	One fiscal period only (single fiscal year planning)	At least one and as many as five fiscal periods (multiyear fiscal planning)
10. Budget execution emphasis	Tactical-operational activities	Tactical-managerial functions	Strategic planning and administration
11. Operational skills emphasized	Technical fiscal operations (accounting and auditing)	Supervisory activities for 2d- and 3d-echelon officers (cost accounting and efficiency determination)	Leadership and executive (top-echelon) level skills in program planning
12. Focus on implementation skills	Accounting and auditing activities	Efficiency computations; unit cost analysis studies	Economics and systems analysis techniques (quantitative analysis)
13. Disciplines contributing most to budget development	Accounting	Engineering (efficiency) or administration	Economics and systems analysis
14. Information focus or important units within budget	Items of expenditures	Processes or work functions	Performance or measurable objectives
15. Approach used to arrive at new cost estimates	Incremental (amount requested over previous year's budget)	Incremental	Zero-base (justification of total new resource requests)
16. Planning emphasis in budget development	Assuring that estimated expenditures do not exceed estimated receipts for fiscal period; "balanced budget" concept	Ascertaining unit costs for various functions or work; costs of work accomplished	Developing expenditure proposals in light of objectives
17. Budgeting output	Fiscal control	Work efficiency determination	Prudent resource allocation decisions

Table 8-4. Comparison of essential characteristics (continued)

Essential characteristic (criterion)	Traditional budget	Performance budget	Program budget
18. Criterion used for appraisal of budget decisions	How resources planned for various activities actually used	Frequency of use of most efficient functions or lowest cost activities	Quality of alternatives generated and frequency of selecting desirable alternative as determined by cost-effectiveness analysis
19. Relationships of prime concern	Between planned and actual expenditures and receipts	Between activity accomplished and costs incurred for doing work	Between programs (activities related to objective) and fiscal implications

This approach's heavy emphasis on the magnitude of previous expenditures and the probability of continuing expenditures for programs that might well be eliminated has aroused considerable criticism. Criticisms of this type are not new; they started when budgeting began to be used in governments. As early as 1924, one writer said that taking last year's estimates for granted as the base and modifying it by a given increment for the future period might be the easy way out, but it was wasteful, extravagant, and a trap to perpetuate obsolete expenditures.[18] Others joined in castigating the incremental, fragmented, and sequential approach. Maurice Stans, budget director under President Eisenhower, declared that "every item in a budget ought to be on trial for its life each year and matched against all the other claimants to our resources."[19]

Zero-base budgeting is an alternative to incremental budgeting. Wildavsky and Hammann refer to this alternative as "comprehensive" budgeting. Although historically the incremental approach has been subjected to much criticism, it was not until the 1960s that an agency in the federal government dared to subject the zero-base budgeting concept to a comprehensive test in practice. This was done in 1962 in the Department of Agriculture. The experiment demanded that each agency program justify from zero, rather than the previous year's level of expenditures, its reason for continuing. It called for reconsidering the basic funding level for each program within the agency, as well as any proposed incremental change. Orville Freeman, then secretary of agriculture, demonstrated considerable interest in this budgeting approach. What began in 1962 as a zero-base budget was to take effect in fiscal year 1964.

The heart of the approach is the consideration of the need for a given program in the first instance. Only after this is ascertained can a recommended magnitude of expenditures for a fiscal year be developed. To illustrate, simply because the program in the Department of Agriculture was demanded by statutory law was not considered to be sufficient grounds for its continuance. It had to be demonstrated that the program objectives could satisfy today's problems or needs. Obviously, this places a tremendous burden on agency personnel to review each program from the ground up rather than simply in terms of increments or other changes recommended for the future budget year. Keep in mind that the focus is on total program expenditures, not simply on elements or items within the program.

Preparation for the zero-base budget in the Department of Agriculture required the agencies to make three major types of calculations: (1) justification of the need for agency activities in programs without reference to congressional mandate or past practice; (2) justification of the requested level of expenditure (fund obligations) based on needs; (3) justification of the cost of the needed program from the ground up.[20]

The essential differences between the traditional or incremental approach to budgeting and the novel comprehensive or zero-base approach is summarized in table 8-5.

Table 8-5. Comparison of incremental and zero-base budgeting

Incremental or traditional budgeting	Zero-base budgeting
1. Changes in amounts based on increments differing from prior appropriations only	1. Review and justification for *total* expenditures (not just incremental changes) for each program
2. Justification of magnitude (amount) of increment only	2. Justification from zero for every program, reconsidering basic funding for programs and any incremental changes for next fiscal year
3. Reference frequently made to base case or previous level of appropriation	3. No base case: defense of entire budget request, not simply changes from previous level of appropriation, must be reference point
4. All programs perpetuated unless clear and dramatic evidence suggests abolition from budget	4. Continuation of each program questioned and must be documented: this approach encourages reallocation of funds to new programs when old program cannot be fully justified or better use of resources is identified

The concept of zero-base budgeting has considerable intellectual appeal; its rationality cannot be questioned. Serious problems have been encountered in its implementation, however. As Wildavsky and Hammann point out

all agencies had serious difficulty in conceptualizing circumstances in which there were no legislative mandates, no past commitments, no consideration of items to be included because other participants in the budgetary process would demand it, no programs for which support could not conceivably be expected; in a word no history or learning based on that history.[21]

In the Department of Agriculture there was resistance to implementing the concept on practical grounds, because it seemed unrealistic, if not ridiculous, to some agency heads to assume that an executive department could question whether Congress had a right to pass laws mandating specific agricultural programs. There were also complaints about the fantastic work load generated in collecting and processing data to justify all programs at one time for every fiscal period. This calls for a mode of behavior which is clearly atypical. No one appears to question the major purpose of zero-base budgeting, "to examine all programs at the same time and from the ground up to discover programs continuing through inertia or design that did not warrant being continued at all or at their present level of expenditure."[22] What some executives objected to was the futility of questioning what the law demands and the tremendous expenditure of resources demanded for the process of justification.

This experience with zero-base budgeting cannot be considered to be positive and complete support for the approach. Nearly half of the executives commented favorably after it was over. They felt that budgeting was finally proceding in a rational manner.[23] It did, however, consume a tremendous amount of resources while budgeting for only a single fiscal period. A conservative estimate was that one thousand administrators in the Department of Agriculture spent an average of thirty hours per week for six weeks in producing data that some felt did not make any difference when it was all over, that is, did not significantly affect outcomes.[24] Wildavsky and Hammann conclude that the procedure might be justified and useful every five years and that "no one suggested that the zero-base approach be followed every year."[25] They added, however, that zero-base budgeting "vastly overestimates man's limited ability to calculate and grossly underestimates the importance of political and technological constraints."[26]

Merewitz and Sosnick are more direct and state unequivocally, "We will show that zero-base budgeting makes an impossible demand of these men, provides no help in deciding whether the allocation of funds could be improved, and tells them to discard some information that might help."[27] They argue that (1) "it is not possible to justify a program's appropriation"; (2) "zero-base budgeting provides no help for agency heads in deciding whether the allocation of funds could be improved"; and (3) "to exclude reference to previous years of appropriations is self-defeating."[28] They conclude that the department's experience could be extrapolated and that "zero-base budgeting is not likely to produce a better allocation of funds."[29]

Although the intent of zero-base budgeting is clear, Merewitz and Sosnick are of the opinion that the approach "does not provide any basis for judging what is appropriate nor any impetus to reallocation."[30] They consider zero-base budgeting one of the "distinguishing features of PPB," because it calls for the "defense and review of the total expenditure proposed for a program, instead of the *changes* from its previous appropriation."[31] It is interesting to note that in the Department of Agriculture's experiment, zero-base budgeting was not a part of PPBS, which had been implemented earlier in the Department of Defense but not in the Department of Agriculture. Some writers consider zero-base budgeting essential to operation in the PPBS mode. In reality, program budgeting is more concerned with identifying and clarifying objectives, organizing programs around objectives, relating resources to program objectives, and systematically analyzing program alternatives than with zero-base budgeting per se. Not all writers equate zero-base budgeting with PPBS, although the spirit of focusing on something more than changes from the preceding year's budget is implied in PPBS.

As an alternative to zero-base budgeting, Merewitz and Sosnick offer "the idea . . . that each official in the budget making hierarchy would inform his superior as to what would be gained or lost if his agency appropriation were expanded or contracted by selected amounts."[32] They suggest consideration of three expenditure levels in a budget called "the same dollar amount," "the same performance amount," and "the recommended amount." The justification comes from communicating what would be lost if zero dollars or the same dollars appropriated in previous years were continued instead of the dollars needed to sustain the same performance amount. This could be called "alternative expenditure planning" budgeting. Their recommended "alternative expenditures" budgeting and that of zero-base budgeting focus on the same goal of encouraging officials to curtail or eliminate obsolete programs. Merewitz and Sosnick's approach "does not throw away information about last year's appropriation and does not demand justifications that cannot be given."[33]

Zero-base budgeting is surrounded by a romantic appeal suggesting that it is a rational approach for deciding how resources will be allocated among the many programs and activities of an organization. Its failures arise from the difficulties of implementing such a scheme. This is particularly true in view of the tremendous resources demanded and the generation of the seemingly unreal assumption that what the law demands can be ignored in school budgeting. At this time, most school systems and universities lack the manpower and fiscal resources to implement zero-base budgeting on an annual and continuing basis. Whether state political agents seeking to stimulate the practice in educational institutions will provide the necessary resources to bring it into being remains to be seen. It is not realistic, however, to assume that there should be periodic reviews of a given set of programs calling for a rethinking of basic purposes and magnitude of resources consumed. No administrator should be forced to perpetuate questionable programs simply because the same level or only a limited increase of resource expenditures is indicated. In short, zero-base budgeting is easier to talk about than it is to implement.

Summary

Budgeting was not invented by the originators of PPBS. PPBS does demand that the budget be recast to perform important functions in addition to its traditional functions.

Performance budgeting came on the scene in the 1940s and was talked about even more in the 1950s. Interest in it was fanned by the Hoover Commission's report of 1949. It called for a budget reform and alterations in budgetary classifications of value to management in the pursuit of more efficient operations. Budget categories were cast in functional terms to facilitate work-cost measurements. The traditional budget emphasized objects of expenditures and "line items" rather than functions. Performance budgeting is related to the scientific management spirit suggested by Frederick W. Taylor. A sound cost-accounting base and unit cost analysis studies are essential to it. Program budgeting is not cost accounting, but performance budgeting is more closely related to cost accounting. Performance budgeting emphasizes work to be accomplished; PPBS emphasizes purposes or objectives to be fulfilled.

Performance budgeting moves control budgeting closer to managerial concern for efficiency. It calls for the functional-character budgetary accounting classification system. This classification was relatively new in the federal government budgets that focused on objects. Schools had a tendency to emphasize functional accounting classifications for almost fifty years.

Performance budgeting never gained much of a foothold in governmental operations. PPBS replaced the control and line items budget rather than performance budgeting in the federal government. If PPBS gains popularity in education it will replace a system more like performance budgeting. Many of the school districts and universities that now claim to operate in the PPBS mode are actually following the precepts of performance budgeting. They tend to equate unit cost analysis data in budget documents with indicators of PPBS, which is erroneous.

Program budgeting emerged in the 1950s and was practiced in the federal government in the 1960s. It continues the budget reform efforts toward the use of the budget as an instrument of strategic planning. Its main purposes are to make policy making more rational by providing data on benefits and costs of various alternatives. It can be called "budgeting-by-objectives." PPBS has been facilitated by the availability of computer-based information systems and new quantitative analysis techniques.

The distinguishing features of a program budget are: statements of objectives within the budget document, a programmatic format for budget exhibits; expenditures aggregated around program elements and categories, benefits and costs exhibited for major programs, multiyear costing of new program expenditures, and data organized to facilitate resource allocation decisions.

Expenditure estimates for next year's budget usually are derived from the present and previous years patterns. In traditional or incremental budgeting, an increment may be added to last year's base to obtain an estimated expenditure figure for the next fiscal year. This approach has been criticized almost since the beginning of budgeting in government as tending to perpetuate obsolete activities.

Zero-base or comprehensive budgeting is an alternative to incremental budgeting. It is an approach considered by some, but by no means all, as an essential feature of PPB. It demands that previous budgetary allocations be ignored and that every program document its reasons for continuing before any consideration is given to allocating resources to it for the next fiscal period. In making next year's budget, you literally start from zero and justify the total resources, not just incremental changes.

The idea of zero-base budgeting impresses many with its rationality, but it was given a trial until 1962 in the Department of Agriculture, which was not operating in the PPBS mode at that time, although the Department of Defense was. The results of the experiment showed zero-base budgeting rested on some unrealistic assumptions, made great time demands on executives, and offered few significant changes in outcomes from the more traditional incremental approach. It is considered a more feasible idea applied periodically rather than annually.

One set of writers accuses zero-base budgeting of making impossible demands and calling for the discard of possibly useful information. They agree with its purposes of eliminating deadwood from continuing budgetary support but question its ability to aid in more prudent resource allocations. They suggest an alternative based on information spelling out the consequences of eliminating, sustaining, or increasing the same amounts for programs or performance levels. At this time, most educational institutions lack the resources to implement zero-base budgeting.

Notes

1. A. Schick, "The Road to PPB: The Stages of Budget Reform," in *Planning-Programming-Budgeting,* ed. F. J. Lyden and E. G. Miller (Chicago: Markham Publishing Co., 1971), p. 37.

2. Ibid., p. 38.

3. Quoted in Research Corporation of the Association of School Business Officials, *Report of the First National Conference on PPBES in Education* (Chicago: The association, 1969), p. 22.

4. Ibid., p. 21.

5. L. Merewitz and S. H. Sosnick, *The Budget's New Clothes* (Chicago: Markham Publishing Co., 1971), p. 21.

6. Ibid.

7. R. H. Huff, *Program Budgeting at Micro-U* (Boulder, Colo.: Western Interstate Commission for Higher Education, 1970); see also chap. 6 of this book.

8. Schick, *op. cit.,* p. 38.

9. Ibid.

10. Research Corporation of the Association of School Business Officials, *op. cit.,* p. 21.

11. V. O. Key, "The Lack of a Budgetary Theory," *American Political Science Review* 34 (1940): 1138.

12. Schick, *op. cit.,* p. 45.

13. Ibid.

14. Ibid.

15. Merewitz and Sosnick, *op. cit.,* p. 41.

16. Ibid., p. 302.

17. Schick, *op. cit.,* p. 50.

18. A. Wildavsky and A. Hammann, "Comprehensive vs Incremental Budgeting in the Department of Agriculture," in *Planning-Programming-Budgeting,* p. 141.

19. Ibid., p. 142.

20. Ibid., p. 144.

21. Ibid.

22. Ibid., p. 150.

23. Ibid.

24. Ibid.

25. Ibid., p. 156.

26. Ibid., p. 157.

27. Merewitz and Sosnick, *op. cit.,* pp. 62-63.

28. Ibid., p. 63.

29. Ibid., p. 64.
30. Ibid., p. 65.
31. Ibid., p. 59.
32. Ibid., p. 65.
33. Ibid., p. 70.

Selected References

Key, V. O. "The Lack of a Budgetary Theory." *American Political Science Review* 34 (1940): 1138-46.
Merewitz, L., and Sosnick, S. H. *The Budget's New Clothes*. Chicago: Markham Publishing Co., 1971, chap. 5.
Schick, A. "The Road to PPB: The Stages of Budget Reform." In *Planning-Programming-Budgeting*. Edited by F. J. Lyden and E. G. Miller. Chicago: Markham Publishing Co., 1971, pp. 26-52.
Wildavsky, A., and Hammann, A. "Comprehensive vs Incremental Budgeting in the Department of Agriculture." In *Planning-Programming-Budgeting*, pp. 140-62.

9. Cost accounting and unit cost analysis in education: additional fiscal dimensions of PPBS

Program budgeting is goal oriented. The attainment of stated outcomes, however, demands resources and a plan of action. PPBS is identified as a resource allocation decision system, that is, an approach that attempts to optimize the relationship between resources and results. Merewitz and Sosnick considered program accounting, "the first distinguishing feature of PPB and multi-year costing its second."[1] During the late 1960s a number of independent efforts in education were concerned with what some called "program accounting," others "program-oriented" budgeting or "program-oriented" accounting, and still others "PPBS accounting."[2]

The fiscal dimension of PPBS includes a new format and capabilities for the budget document to relate expenditures to program categories, subcategories, and elements. It also demands improved cost accounting and unit cost analysis for programs. The next chapter begins the development of the kinds of economic analyses that require such organization and costing. This chapter focuses on the data base required for operation of a PPB system. Particular emphasis is placed on classification systems for expenditure accounts, cost accounting systems, and unit cost analysis approaches, which are essential parts of a PPB system.

School Accounting Developments

A program, as defined in previous chapters, is a clustering of activities and resources grouped around one or more objectives or focused on the production of similar outputs. The importance of defining objectives and activities in measurable and operational terms will not be pursued further in this chapter. Primary emphasis shall be on how records are kept of resources consumed to reach the objectives of a program. Therefore, program accounting by definition is a system of identifying, collecting, and classifying fiscal resources consumed in the pursuit of program objectives. But first of all let us look at the basic facts of school accounting.

Enke indicated that, "PPB has been a disappointment to many people" for in his mind "proponents of this approach often overlook the raw material of decision making—information."[3] He defined "an approach to PPBS" as an "information system concept which emphasizes the need for information to illuminate policy decisions."[4] PPB in this light made contributions by "presenting information in more useful formats, presenting information not previously available, and providing a data base for special analyses."[5] The perception of PPB as a unique and powerful management information system necessitated:

1. Classifying the costs of government by program structures with common goals or objectives
2. Attempting to find quantitative and qualitative measures of program outputs and collecting these on a regular basis
3. Projecting program financial cost inputs and service outputs several periods into the future
4. Identifying special problem areas and using analytical techniques to appraise solutions
5. Attempting to integrate this information into the regular budgetary process so that it is considered systematically as part of the on-going process of government financial management [6]

Various writers concerned with the practical aspects of implementing PPB recognize the importance of the financial accounting classification system. As stated earlier, the decision maker needs information and demands that it be organized in a particular way to facilitate selection of the most prudent course of action. PPB rests in part on an accounting base, but the system is far more than another approach to accounting. The contributions and limitations of this fiscal dimension of PPB need further elaboration.

Accounting is basically a record-keeping procedure. The records kept deal with financial transactions, such as collecting, expending, and reporting on fiscal resources required to pursue organizational objectives. It calls for classification of resources expended, such as money, in a significant manner and interpretation of results. Financial accounting is specialized record keeping based on classifying quantitative fiscal data. The manner in which data are classified enables accounting to serve as an information system furnishing data of significance to decision makers. This chapter deals with how financial data are processed and presented in program budgets and in program accounting classification approaches.

First some basic definitions are in order. An *account* is a specific financial record containing information on a resource or a financial transaction related to a specific asset, liability, fund balance, revenue, expenditure, or budgetary item identified within its title. It was stipulated in the previous chapters that expenditures accounting in most school systems followed the functional-character system for classifying fiscal transactions. Ever since 1909, the Office of Education, in cooperation with other national and state organizations, has sought to stimulate the use of a uniform set of recording and reporting procedures for educational financial transactions. For the purposes of a book devoted to PPBS as a subset of public expenditures economics, only expenditure accounts will be reviewed. The reader is referred to more comprehensive books on business management of local school systems or universities for more comprehensive and detailed information on other aspects of accounting such as receipts accounting or encumbrance accounting. In 1948, the recommended main headings for expenditure account headings for K-12 educational institutions were: (1) Administration (formerly called "general control"), (2) Instruction, (3) Auxiliary Services, (4) Operation of Plant, (5) Maintenance of Plant, (6) Fixed Charges, (7) Capital Outlay, and (8) Debt Service.

What in previous years were identified as Coordinate Activities and Auxiliary Services became simply one heading of Auxiliary Services. It included the three major items of School Services (health and school lunches), Transportation, and Community Services (public libraries and community recreation services under the control of a school board). In 1957 the Office of Education substantially revised these major expenditure account classifications.[8] The publication containing these revisions is commonly referred to as Handbook II. It recommends the following major headings for school expenditure of accounts:

1. Account Series 100—Administration

2. Account Series 200—Instruction
3. Account Series 300—Attendance Services
4. Account Series 400—Health Services
5. Account Series 500—Pupil-Transportation Services
6. Account Series 700—Operation of Plant
7. Account Series 700—Maintenance of Plant
8. Account Series 800—Fixed Charges
9. Account Series 900—Food Services
10. Account Series 1000—Student Body Activities
11. Account Series 1100—Community Services
12. Account Series 1200—Capital Outlay
13. Account Series 1300—Debt Service from Current Funds
14. Account Series 1400—Outgoing Transfer Accounts

Several items should be noted. First the number of major headings
increased from eight in 1948 to fourteen in 1957 reflecting the
greater complexity of educational services. Most of the increase can
be traced to what happened to the account classification for Auxiliary Services. Thus, activities previously grouped under Auxiliary
Services were split into five different special account headings for
Health Services, Pupil Transportation Services, Food Services, Student Body Activities, and Community Services.[9] Second, these major
headings document the propensity of schools to use functional
groupings rather than objects of expenditures alone. For example,
Administration and Instruction represent functions, but Student
Body Activities and Outgoing Transfer Accounts do not qualify as
functions.

At this writing Handbook II has been revised but has not come off
the press. Its publication is scheduled for late 1972. The first draft of
what can be called Handbook II, Revised was made available to the
author for inspection.[10] One of its unique features is the grouping of
several major expenditure accounts into four broad functions. The
first grouping is Instruction; the second Supporting Services; the
third Community Services; and the fourth Non-programmed Costs.
The four broad groupings and the specific major expenditure accounts as summarized from the forthcoming revised handbook are
shown in table 9-1. Certain definitions should be kept in mind in
reading this table.[11]

1. A *function* is one of a major group of related actions that
contributes to a larger action.

2. A service area is a major division of a school system operation
consisting of activities that may have the same several operational
objectives.

Table 9-1. Summary of expenditure accounts for K-12 school systems
recommended in Handbook II, revised

Account code	Function
100-299	*Instruction* (broad functional classification)
	(Major account heading by scope of service)
110	Regular Education
120	Occupational Education
130	Special Education
140	Continuing Education
300-699	*Supporting Services* (broad functional classification)
	(Major account heading by function or service)
300	Pupil Personnel Services
310	Attendance
320	Guidance
330	Health
340	School Psychological
350	Social Work
400	Instructional Support
410	Instructional Media (e.g., school library, ETV, CA1)
420	Instructional Administration (e.g., service area direction, curriculum and instruction improvement)
430	Research, Planning, Development, and Evaluation
500	General Support
510	Board of Education
520	Data Processing
530	Facilities Acquisition and Construction
540	Fiscal Services (e.g., budgeting, payroll, purchasing)
550	Food Services
560	General Administration (superintendent's office)
570	General Services (e.g., warehousing, printing)
580	Information Services (e.g., public information, community relations)
590	Operation and Maintenance of Plant (care and upkeep of building, grounds, and equipment)
600	Pupil Transportation Services
610	School Administration (principal's office)
620	Staff Services (e.g., recruitment, in-service training)
630	Statistical Services
690	Other
700-799	*Community Services* (broad functional classification)
	(Major account heading by function)
710	Community Services (e.g., community recreation, public library)
800-899	*Non-Programmed Costs* (broad classification)
810	Non-Programmed Costs
811	Payments to Other Governmental Units
812	Transfers to Other Funds

3. An area of responsibility is a subdivision of a "service area" consisting of activities that relate directly to the operational objectives of that "area."

The revised handbook also identifies accounting for specific objects of expenditures. An object is the specific service, item or commodity obtained as an outcome of making a specific expenditure. The objects of expenditures are grouped under the major functions shown in table 9-2.

The accounting recommendations in the revised handbook are similar to those in the final report of the Midwestern States Educational Information Project (MSEIP).[12] The MSEIP report does not employ the four broad groupings. It recommended accounting by area of responsibilities, subject area, activities, and object expenditures. A summary of the major expenditure account classification by area of responsibility is presented in table 9-3. Note the use of the old term General Control for expenditures in the Board of Education and Superintendent Offices. Instructional Administration covers expenses of the principal's office and instructional administration in general. Likewise, there is no propensity to aggregate the functional headings into broader packages, such as Instruction and Support Services, as in the revised Handbook II.

Lindman proposes a "three-dimensional account classification system" for public schools.[13] It calls for two expenditure groupings on the basis of instruction and support services. The following is his listing of "objects of expenditures" under the major category of Instruction and a set of functions under the other major category of Support Services.

    A. Instruction
        1. Principals' and Supervisors' Salaries
        2. Classroom Teachers' Salaries
        3. Other Professional Salaries
        4. Clerical and Paraprofessional Salaries
        5. Books
        6. Instructional Supplies
        7. Instructional Equipment
        8. Other Cost of Instruction
    B. Support Services
        1. Administration
        2. Operation of Plant
        3. Maintenance of Plant
        4. Pupil Transportation

Table 9-2. Classification of objects of expenditures
recommended in Handbook II, revised

Account code	Major object categories and subdivisions
100	*Salaries*
110	Regular Salaries
120	Temporary Salaries
130	Overtime Salaries
200	*Employee Benefits*
300	*Purchased Services*
305	Professional and Technical Services
310	Communication
315	Travel
320	Transportation
325	Advertising
330	Printing and Binding
335	Insurance and Bond Premiums
340	Public Utility Services
345	Repairs and Maintenance Services
350	Rentals
355	Tuition
360	Other Purchased Services
400	*Supplies and Materials*
410	Supplies
420	Textbooks
430	Library Books
440	Periodicals
450	Warehouse Inventory Adjustment
460	Other Supplies and Materials
500	*Capital Outlay*
510	Land
520	Buildings
530	Improvements Other than Buildings
540	Equipment
550	Vehicles
560	Other Capital Outlay
600	*Other Expenses*
610	Redemption of Principal
620	Interest
630	Housing Authority Obligations
640	Dues and Fees
650	Judgments against the School System
660	Miscellaneous Expense
700	*Transfers*
710	Transfers
720	Other Charges

Table 9-3. Summary of major account classifications by area of
responsibility recommended in the MSEIP report

Account code	Function
100-199	*Instruction*
101	Instructional Services, General
111	Classroom Teaching
121	Library Services
131	Computer-Assisted Instruction
141	Educational TV Services
151	Audio-Visual Services
161	Homebound Teaching and Other Teaching
200-249	*General Control*
201	General Administration
206	Board of Education
211	Business and Finance
216	Data Processing
221	Legal Services
226	Personnel Administration
231	Warehousing and Distribution
236	Centralized Printing and Publication Services
241	Other General Control
250-269	*Instructional Administration*
251	Instructional Administration, General
256	Administration of a School
261	Improvement of Curriculum and Instruction
266	Other Instructional Admin.
270-299	*Research and Development*
271	R & D, General
276	Research
281	Development
286	Evaluation
291	Statistics
296	Other R & D Services
300-349	*Facilities, Maintenance, and Operation*
301	Plant Maintenance and Operation, General
311	Site Maintenance
316	Site Operation
321	Building Maintenance
326	Building Operation
331	Built-in Equipment, Maintenance
336	Built-in Equipment, Operation
341	Movable Equipment, Maintenance
346	Movable Equipment, Operation
350-399	*Facilities, Acquisition, or Improvement*
351	Plant Acquisition/Improvement, General
361	Site Acq./Improvement
371	Building Acq./Improvement

Table 9-3. Summary of major account classifications (continued)

Account code	Function
381	Built-in Equip. Acq./Improvement
391	Movable Equip. Acq./Improvement
400-499	*Food Services*
401	Food Services, General
411	Food Preparation and Serving
421	Transportation of Food
431	Other Food Services
500-549	*Pupil Personnel*
501	Pupil Services, General
511	Attendance Services
516	Guidance Services
521	Social Work Services
526	Psychological Services
531	Therapeutic Services
541	Other Pupil Services
550-599	*Health Services*
551	Health Services, General
561	Medical Services
566	School Nurse Services
571	Dental Services
581	Other Health Services
600-699	*Pupil Transportation*
601	Transportation, General
611	Vehicle Operation
621	Vehicle Servicing and Maintenance
631	Other Transportation Services
700-799	*Community Services*
701	Community Services, General
711	Recreation
721	Civic Activity
731	Public Libraries
741	Custody and Detention
751	Welfare Activities
761	Non-Public School Services
771	Other Community Services
800-899	*Outgoing Transfers*
801	Transportation within State
811	Transportation outside State
821	Tuition within State
831	Tuition outside State
900-999	*Debt Service*
911	Bond Redemption
921	Long-Term Loan
931	Short-Term Loan
941	Current Loan

     5. Other Support Services
     6. Fixed Charges
He also submits a "scope-of-service account classification" with the
following major categories: (1) The Basic Program, (2) Vocational
Education, (3) Special Education, (4) Compensatory Education, (5)
Health Services, (6) Pupil Transportation, (7) Lunch Program, and
(8) Other Supplementary Programs.

     There are similarities among the recommendations for expenditure
account changes in the proposals of Lindman, the MSEIP report, and
the 1972 Office of Education revised handbook. All of them call for
the abandonment of the nebulous category of Fixed Charges. This
has been recommended for years. The assignment of salaries for
principals is placed in Instructional Support Services, rather than
Direct Instruction. In general the revised handbook uses an additional aggregation similar to that noted in Lindman's.

     Reporting by major functions, grade levels organization and ob-
jects are at least implied in the three reports cited. This is illustrated
in figure 9-1.

Figure 9-1. Financial accounting report using three dimensions[14]

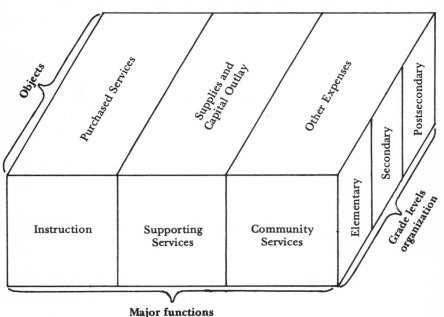

Program Accounting

Recent publications calling for revisions in school financial accounting systems depart from, but still demonstrate the influence of, the original 1957 Handbook II. Obviously, if the original handbook on financial accounting failed to group functions by programs, the modification suggested in the revised handbook cannot make a claim for program accounting. The 1972 revisions were simply more detailed, expanded, and regrouped categories of the original 1957 document.

Program accounting means the recording and classifying of resource expenditures around one or more outcomes, not a new or regrouped set of activities devoid of measurable objectives. No financial handbook can develop a program accounting, or what some prefer to call "program-oriented budgeting and accounting," system unless outcomes are explicit or implicit. Both recent and earlier editions of school expenditure classifications follow the functional-character or activity classifications for the grouping of objects of expenditures. What counts is how these functional expenditures categories are grouped within programs. A new outline of major classifications and headings of new or different activities and objects does not constitute program accounting.

What then is program accounting? By definition, it is accounting by purpose in a multiyear time frame. This means that the following criteria must be satisfied:

1. There must be programs designed at the very beginning.

2. Expenditures are clustered around activities (functions), but then the activities must be aggregated around a program and its objectives.

3. There must be a multiyear time frame for recording fiscal data. Most of the so-called program accounting efforts in education fail to meet all the above criteria. As Merewitz and Sosnick put it, "program accounting is a way of organizing information with the objective of revealing how much is being spent for each purpose."[15] The word "purpose" should be interpreted strictly as an outcome and not loosely as a function or set of inputs. They also think that this type of accounting is likely to be satisfied "by classifying expenditures in terms of programs regardless of which agencies spend the money or what kinds of things the agencies buy."[16] They recommend that the first two steps in program accounting be (1) defining the programs and (2) listing expenditures by program. It is believed that program accounting will help foster better decision making.

The traditional accounting rationale is classification of expenditure by major object category. From a managerial point of view, improvement comes when these objects were clustered around functions. This is where schools are now. Adding the word *program* to a functional accounting classification system does not magically transform it into a fiscal information pattern related to PPBS. Some schools are more modest and refer to their accounting system as "program-oriented." Again, the inclusion of the vaguely defined term "program-oriented" at the top of all school fiscal documents, such as purchase orders, budgets, and job work sheets, does not automatically yield PPBS. Program accounting calls for a three-way classification of expenditures: by object, by function, and *then by objective or purpose satisfied*. Note that the last factor was not "by program." Not all so-called programs are rooted in objectives. The organization of fiscal data to display the last of the three dimensions enables top-level executives to make more prudent resource allocation decisions. Most so-called program accounting budgeting displays in education are two-dimensional at best and omit the crucial third dimension, namely, how costs are related to results. If the executive knows the anticipated benefits or outcomes as well as the costs or expenditures, he is in a better position to make the best choice among alternatives.

Program accounting exacts a price for its benefits. Setup costs, operating costs, and revision costs "are not trivial."[18] In the first place, the program possibilities are numerous and may generate jurisdictional disputes where several departments feel they have much to contribute to realization of objectives. For at least a short period of time, books may have to be kept in conventional as well as program accounting form. The federal government was forced to increase the number of PPBS personnel by more than 1,000 in a three-year period. Likewise, in a dynamic society programs will not remain static, and this will necessitate sizable changes in organizing data in program budgets. As one set of writers put it:

> We conclude that both of the conventional ways of classifying government expenditures should be maintained, that classifying expenditures by purpose should be introduced only if reorganization along functional lines has been considered and rejected, that the case for introducing program accounting even then is not persuasive, and, finally, that the people who expect program accounting to reduce government spending are in for a big surprise.[19]

As far as this author is concerned, this is an extreme position that tends to emphasize the limitations of program accounting.

Within each of the recent recommendations for further evolution and reform of expenditure accounting classifications systems, there is an approach to the coding of each object of expenditure to facilitate the use of computer-based data processing for accounting purposes. The insertion of such coded fiscal data into an information system makes it possible to generate computer programs that will facilitate the reordering of objects purchased to satisfy a reporting of such expenditure patterns in whatever way desirable. This is to say that the technology of computer-based information systems makes it possible to obtain true program accounting classifications very quickly, but that first step of developing a programmatic format is essential if the computer processing is to have such merit. Table 9-4 is an illustration of a system for coding expenditures.

Cost Accounting

Until recently, many public educational and eleemosynary institutions felt that they were not and should not be concerned with cost of service performed. They were not pursuing a profit, many of their social contributions were intangible but "significant," and cost accounting might lead to a "cult of efficiency." This questionable tradition is being shattered by the escalating investment in education, the growing demands for accountability, and the increasing recognition that waste is not a virtue. Cost accountants are not bad guys who shatter fragile, humane values. Measuring educational performance and outcomes against resources consumed may proceed without threatening quality of service. It may actually enable the schools to contribute more with their limited resources.

"Cost accounting can be defined as that branch of accounting concerned with searching out and reporting all elements of the cost incurred in executing a specific activity or a unit of work."[20] Obviously, the important base for all cost studies is the financial accounting system used. Poorly conceptualized expenditure-accounting classifications will greatly inhibit the system's capability for generating meaningful and comprehensive cost data. Although cost accounting was generated initially to answer questions on product costs in manufacturing, the approach can be generalized to other endeavors as well.

It is essential that the expenditure-accounting system be designed in the first instance to facilitate cost accounting. This does not guarantee misinterpretation or misuse of cost data. However, it has been noted that

Table 9-4. Coding of expenditures recommended in MSEIP report[17]

Code section	A	B	C	D	E	F	G	H
Section title	Fund	Type of account	Organiza-tional unit	Area of respon-sibility	Subject area	Course	Activity	Object
Number of digits used	XX	X	XXX	XXX	XX	XXX	XX	XX

> no matter what degree of uniformity in the accounting systems in use, no matter what degree of care is taken in posting expenditures to the appropriate accounts and no matter how precise is the unit for measuring educational load the unit cost figures are subject to significant qualifications if they are not expressions of the same educational program or results.[21]

It must be established that the program outcomes among two or more school systems are very similar before there can be meaningful interpretation of cost data.

Macleod noted that although cost accounting was "an essential aid to maximizing profits," it had at least three other values important to nonprofit institutions, namely, "efficiency and cost control, planning and allocating resources of people and funds, and 'pricing' for cost reimbursement."[22] Using his practical experience in a nonprofit mental health center, he argues that in the first contribution, cost accounting helps to highlight actions of personnel who get careless and force the institution to absorb extra costs that add nothing to the quality of services. While recognizing that efficiency experts have a bad name, he maintains that "standards should be a sensible way of organizing and carrying out tasks, not a means for applying pressure to reach unnatural levels of performance."[23] The "pricing" point may seem foreign to those not in administrative posts. Yet this is what must be done to arrive at tuition rates or amounts of federal reimbursements for selected programs or services.

Macleod declares that "the principal conceptual innovation in program budgeting is disciplined thinking about what it is that an institution is producing."[24] To fulfill this mission, expenditures must be sorted out to identify accurately the costs related to programs. Without an effective cost-accounting system, valuable economic data would not be available to the executive confronted with resource allocation decisions. Macleod's recommendations to administrators of nonprofit institutions were:

> 1. Insist on knowing what the institution's programs are and who is paying for them.
> 2. Insist on analysis of the costs of proposed program changes.
> 3. Insist that the reasons for proposed changes in expenditures be stated, and in terms of output of services.
> 4. Insist on knowing what the institution is getting for its overhead.[25]

To him, cost accounting was an essential element in making program budgeting work in nonprofit institutions.

Unit Cost Analysis

Unit cost analysis is built on cost accounting. It enables the determination of the cost side of the cost-effectiveness equation to go the extra step in attempting to measure how much was to be accomplished at a given price. "Unit cost accounting attempts to determine output per standard measurable unit."[26] A meaningful cost analysis system likewise demands carefully designed and well-maintained financial records and significant units to measure outputs. In this sense, unit cost analysis is a further refinement of cost accounting.

As suggested earlier, unit cost analysis is an important aspect of performance budgeting. Its purpose is to identify the most efficient work process, and computing the resources consumed for a unit of output is essential for that purpose. Obviously, the unit selected for purposes of cost analysis is crucial in this process. Vague terms such as per pupil unit raise the question whether the reference is to per pupil enrolled, per pupil in average daily attendance, per pupil in average daily membership, or per weighted pupil. The unit employed should be meaningful to the purposes of the unit cost analysis. Services are performed and therefore related to some measure of pupils in the school system; area, such as square feet of floor space for building operational costs; or transportation, such as per pupil per bus mile computations for unit bus costs.

Another issue in unit cost analysis is the method of prorating expenditures that can be assigned to more than one account. It is not unusual to find costs that are common to several services. This is particularly true for a large number of support services that may be needed in a number of instructional programs. There must be an agreed on method of prorating such items as overhead or central office staff services. Prorating techniques are usually defined in the various handbooks on financial accounting used to enhance the accuracy of unit cost analysis for comparative purposes. The Office of Education's revised handbook devotes chapter 8 to Proration and Attribution. It defines methods of prorating based on such factors as time, hour consumption, mileage, and number of pupils.

Cost accounting or unit cost analysis is not the same as cost-effectiveness analysis. It is not unusual to find school systems claiming to operate in the PPBS mode presenting budget information based on unit costs such as proposed average expenditures per pupil enrolled.

There is nothing novel about unit cost studies in education. They have been computed for most of this century. One writer is very critical of unit cost studies completed early in this century.[27] In one school study in the early 1900s that writer reports, "of every dollar expended, 0.3% of one cent goes for Greek, while 15.6% goes for English," and an "increase of 1.7 recitations per week per teacher reduced the annual cost per pupil by $3.10. This was equivalent to a saving for the school of nearly $2,2000,000."[28] Although such facts may be interesting, they have only limited application in decision making. In all fairness it must be stated that unit cost analysis early in this century was retrospective, that is, completed after the fact. Unit cost accounting in performance or alleged program budgeting is prospective, that is, presents data on unit costs likely to be incurred in future operation.

Cost accounting and unit cost analysis have important contributions to make in PPBS, but PPBS is far more than cost accounting or unit cost analysis alone. These techniques satisfy only one dimension of the decision system. Cost accounting and unit cost analysis represent initial, not terminal, steps. A display of the kinds of data represent the beginning rather than the end of one of several processes in PPBS. Only a limited number of decisions are possible based on cost of inputs with no indicators of quality or of effectiveness. As an end in itself, unit cost analysis is of very limited value.

The test of operating in a program budgeting mode is not the ability to verbalize on the importance of objectives but the ability to find where operational behaviors in systems implementing the technology are lacking. Cost accounting data fail to generate the kinds of data the decision makers demand in assessing alternatives. As Novick states emphatically, "program budgeting is not cost accounting, although a great many people have fallen in this trap, and don't be surprised if you have."[29] He cites the case of the Canadian government that spent two years "developing what they thought was a program budget only to discover that they had a new cost accounting system."[30]

Tables 9-4 and 9-5 document the same types of errors in education. The names of the districts are withheld and only a representative sample of the total of so-called program budgets are shown. This is a very common misinterpretation and is not a reflection of the failings of only a few. In table 9-4 cost aggregations are made for broad Instructional Programs, Supporting Programs, Transfers, and Reserves. Such groupings are not evident in table 9-5. Moreover, unit cost data are not shown.

In reality a decision about whether a district or a university is

Table 9-5. Summary of budget appropriations by programs of school district X

Instructional Programs	Amount	Costs Per ADA	Percent
Schools			
Elementary (Grades K-6)	$17,197,640	$ 407.50	32.3
Junior High (Grades 7-9)	8,062,018	491.86	15.2
Senior High (Grades 10-12)	8,290,159	658.89	15.6
Special Education (All Grades)	2,699,639	1,512.40	5.1
Laboratory Schools	14,696	273.93	—
Vocational-Technical Centers	534,406	535.48	1.0
Adult Education	217,907	76.46	.4
Total Instructional Programs	$37,016,465	$ 500.50	69.6
Supporting Programs			
Instructional Services			
Administration	$ 253,800	$ 3.43	.5
Educational Services	1,715,151	23.20	3.2
Total Instructional Services	$ 1,968,951	$ 26.63	3.7
Administrative Services			
Board of School Trustees	$ 34,720	$ .47	.1
Office of the Superintendent	73,500	.99	.1
Communication Services	289,694	3.91	.5
School Facilities	92,114	1.24	.2
Personnel Services	307,106	4.15	.6
Business Services	1,440,800	19.48	2.7
Total Administrative Services	$ 2,237,934	$ 30.24	4.2

Operational Services			
Maintenance Department	$ 1,376,997	$ 18.62	2.5
Operations Department	2,367,374	32.01	4.5
Ground Services	313,586	4.24	.6
Transportation Department	1,648,723	22.30	3.1
Utilities, Insurance & Fixed Charges	4,873,380	65.89	9.2
Total Operational Services	$10,580,060	$143.06	19.9
Transfers			
Emergency Loan for Integration	$ 207,840	$ 2.81	.4
Reserve Programs			
Contingency Reserve	$ 575,625	$ 7.79	1.1
Ending Balance	600,000	8.11	1.1
Total Reserve Programs	$ 1,175,625	$ 15.90	2.2
Total Operating Budget	$53,186,875	$ 719.14	100.0

Table 9-6. Summary of program budget for school district Y

	Elementary schools	Middle schools	Senior high schools	Adult education	All schools
Regular Programs					
Elementary Instruction	$54,495,390	—	—	—	$ 54,495,390
Middle School Instruction	—	$28,704,963	—	—	28,704,963
Senior High Instruction	—	—	$27,973,538	—	27,973,538
Adult Instruction	—	—	—	$7,359,568	7,359,568
	$54,495,390	$28,704,963	$27,973,538	$7,359,568	$118,533,459
Special Programs					
Compensatory	—	—	—	$ 200,563	$ 200,563
Migrant Workers	$ 1,840,551	$ 733,158	$ 389,285	203,400	3,166,394
Drug Abuse	48,121	21,905	19,274	160,700	250,000
Exceptional Child	3,615,684	1,836,454	530,958	517,262	6,500,358
Reading Improvement	2,881,578	214,820	37,307	—	3,133,705
Summer	1,175,847	988,372	1,111,104	14,954	3,290,277
	$ 9,561,781	$ 3,794,709	$ 2,087,928	$ 1,096,879	$ 16,541,297
Support Programs					
Auxiliary Services	$ 526,890	$ 901,262	$ 1,239,207	$ 275,983	$ 2,943,342
Instructional Support	13,580,588	8,669,620	7,231,005	5,330,027	34,811,240
Facilities Support	9,212,935	4,208,338	3,617,476	2,938,320	19,977,069
Administrative Support	—	—	—	7,023,904	7,023,904
	$23,320,413	$13,779,220	$12,087,688	$15,568,234	$ 64,755,555
Total	$87,377,584	$46,278,892	$42,149,154	$24,024,681	$199,830,311

operating in the program budgeting mode calls for a look behind the scenes or a review of data used in the generation of the budget document. Thus, special studies, or analyses of alternatives, represent the key to the potential of this decision technology. It is also appropriate to present background data on objectives, programmatic formats, and fiscal dimensions to move into the most sophisticated, and perhaps the most difficult to implement, aspects of PPB, namely, analysis. Analysis is the subject of chapter 10.

Summary

Resources are consumed in the pursuit of outcomes. Program budgeting seeks to facilitate decision making on resource use. Program accounting is one of the distinguishing features of PPB. During the late 1960s a number of independent efforts were concerned with "program-oriented" accounting in budgeting. By definition program accounting is a system of identifying, collecting, and classifying fiscal resources consumed in the pursuit of program objectives.

PPBS can be viewed as a kind of an information system to illuminate policy decisions. It rests on an accounting base, that is, the manner in which fiscal transactions are classified. Financial accounting is a special type of record keeping based on classifying quantitative fiscal data. Ever since 1909 efforts have been exerted to stimulate the use of uniform financial records and reports in schools. Expenditure accounts headings have been recommended in Office of Education publications released in 1948, 1957, and 1972. The yet-to-be released 1972 USOE Handbook II, Revised continues the groupings by functional character headings but modifies previous efforts. Its recommendations are similar in many ways to those made by the Midwestern States Educational Information Project and by Lindman.

Neither the original 1957 Handbook II nor the unpublished 1972 revised version provide a way to group expenditures and their functions by programs. The revised handbook modified functional-character accounting classifications to make activities more relevant to what goes on in schools today. They add precision to definitions and details for objects of expenditures and funds and for the coding of these and other fiscal transaction. These are significant contributions that may help to move toward, but do not actually constitute, program accounting.

Accounting by purpose demands designation by programs; expenditures clustered around functions and, in turn, aggregated around organizational outcomes; and a multiyear time frame for recording fiscal data. Most current program accounting efforts in education fail to meet these tests.

Traditional accounting rationale is rooted in objects of expenditure. Clustering objects around functions represents a step forward from a management point of view. This is where schools are today. Adding the word *program* or the term *program-oriented* to budget or other fiscal documents does not automatically convert a functional-character classification system into PPBS. It requires a three-way organization of fiscal data: by object, by function, and then by objectives satisfied. Some use the term *by program* rather than *by objectives satisfied*. In education, most so-called subject matter programs do not implicitly or explicitly specify objectives. The coding of expenditures and the use of computer-based data processing may facilitate subsequent grouping of fiscal data into program accounting and budgeting.

Traditionally, most educational and charitable institutions have avoided costing of services performed. The trend to accountability is only one factor shattering this tradition. Measuring performances and outcomes against resources consumed may proceed without threatening the quality of services.

Cost accounting is an important dimension of PPBS. It is a branch of accounting that facilitates the identification of costs related to a specific function or end. Cost accounting is only as good as the fiscal accounting system on which it is based. It arose in manufacturing, but it serves nonprofit institutions by providing data on efficiency and cost control, planning and allocating resources of people and funds, and establishing a rationale for "pricing" for cost reimbursement. The latter is important to schools in determining tuition rates on federal program reimbursements.

Unit cost analysis is built on cost accounting. It carries the analysis the extra step to determine outputs per standard measurable unit. Its significance to performance budgeting has been indicated in previous chapters. The unit selected must be appropriate to the issue being raised in analysis. Prorating of costs common to several services is one of the important elements affecting the accuracy or quality of unit cost analysis. Neither cost accounting nor unit cost analysis are equivalent to cost-effectiveness analysis. There is nothing novel about unit cost analysis in education. It has been a procedure practiced in education for most of this century. As an end in itself, unit cost analysis is of limited value in decision making, but it may be an important step in pursuing further analytic studies.

Cost accounting contributes to but does not constitute program budgeting. Novick and others believe that many have fallen into the trap of equating cost accounting systems with program budgeting. This is a common error in education. Most school systems and universities that purport to be operating in the PPBS mode are in fact engaged merely in cost accounting. Determination whether PPBS is being implemented requires a look at how data are organized in budget exhibits to ascertain whether outcomes are the prime focus, whether alternatives are being generated, and whether there is quantitative and cost-effectiveness analysis.

Notes

1. L. Merewitz and S. H. Sosnick, *The Budget's New Clothes* (Chicago: Markham Publishing Co., 1971), chaps. 2, 3.

2. E. L. Lindman, *A Three-Dimensional Program Account Classification System for Public Schools*, working paper no. 6 (Los Angeles, Calif.: UCLA, Center for the Study of Evaluation of Instructional Programs, 1968), p. 1; J. E. Mitchell et al., *MSEIP Documentation of Project Development and General Systems Design*, Midwestern States Educational Information Project (Des Moines, Iowa: State of Iowa Department of Public Instruction, 1969), p. 115; U.S. Office of Education, *Financial Accounting, Handbook II*, rev'd, State Educational Record and Report series (Washington, D.C.: Office of Education, 1972). Not yet published.

3. E. L. Enke, "The Accounting Pre-conditions of PPB," *Management Accounting*, January 1972, pp. 33-37.

4. Ibid.

5. Ibid.

6. Ibid.

7. E. M. Foster and H. E. Akerly, *Financial Accounting for Schools*, circular 204, rev'd 1948 (Washington, D.C.: Government Printing Office, 1952), p. 16.

8. P. L. Reason and A. L. White, *Financial Accounting for Local and State School Systems, Standard Receipt and Expenditure Accounts*, Bulletin 1957, USOE, Handbook II (Washington, D.C.: Government Printing Office, 1957).

9. S. J. Knezevich and J. G. Fowlkes, *Business Management of Local School Systems* (New York: Harper & Row, 1960), pp. 116-22.

10. Office of Education, *op. cit.*

11. Ibid.

12. J. E. Mitchell et al., *op. cit.*, pp. 129-31.

13. Lindman, *op. cit.*

14. Office of Education, *op. cit.*

15. Merewitz and Sosnick, *op. cit.*, p. 15.

16. Ibid.

17. J. E. Mitchell et al., *op. cit.*

18. Merewitz and Sosnick, *op. cit.*, pp. 27-31.

19. Ibid., p. 31.

20. Knezevich and Fowlkes, *op. cit.*, p. 152.

21. Ibid., p. 155.

22. R. K. Macleod, "Program Budgeting Works in Non-profit Institutions," *Harvard Business Review* (September-October 1971): 49.

23. Ibid.

24. Ibid.

25. Ibid.

26. Knezevich and Fowlkes, *op. cit.*, p. 153.

27. R. E. Callahan, *Education and the Cult of Efficiency* (Chicago: University of Chicago Press, 1962), chap. 4.

28. Ibid., pp. 74-75.

29. Research Corporation of the Association of School Business Officials, *Report of the First National Conference on PPBES in Education* (Chicago: The association, 1969), p. 22.

30. Ibid.

Selected References

Enke, E. L. "The Accounting Pre-conditions of PPB," *Management Accounting*, January 1972, pp. 33-37.

Lindman, E. L. *A Three-Dimensional Program Account Classification System for Public Schools.* Working paper no. 6. Los Angeles, Calif.: UCLA, Center for the Study of Evaluation of Instructional Programs, 1968.

Macleod, R. K. "Program Budgeting Works in Non-profit Institutions." *Harvard Business Review* (September-October 1971): 46-56.

Merewitz, L., and Sosnick, S. H. *The Budget's New Clothes.* Chicago: Markham Publishing Co., 1971, chap. 2.

Mitchell, J. E. et al. *MSEIP Documentation of Project Development and General Systems Design.* Midwestern States Educational Information Project. Des Moines, Iowa: State of Iowa Department of Public Instruction, 1969.

U.S. Office of Education. *Financial Accounting, Handbook II*, rev'd, State Educational Record and Report Series. Washington, D.C.: Office of Education, 1972. Not yet published.

10. Analysis dimension in program budgeting: generating alternatives and preliminary thought on systems analysis

PPB is a decision system. Planning, programming, and budgeting are processes aimed at improving decision making. The end product of the processes is information structured to facilitate another dimension of program budgeting, that of generating alternatives and the analysis to appraise each. The identification and appraisal of available alternatives enables the decision maker to render more prudent resource allocation decisions. Analysis is a means of sharpening the planning dimension. One output of the planning process is a set of objectives. Another is better decision making based on analysis of alternatives.

Fisher summarizes the major characteristics of PPBS under three headings: "structural (or format) aspects, analytical process considerations, and data or information system considerations to support the first two items."[1] The structural aspects of PPBS include the design of program formats, that is, the preparation of statements of designed outcomes and specification of the related activities. The analytical dimension incorporates systematic efforts to review alternative uses of resources to achieve end products. This is done in terms of costs of inputs and utility of outputs. The information needed to support program budgeting would, of course, include progress reports and controls as well as the data required to fulfill the demands of the analytical dimension.

The author would add a fourth major characteristic of program budgeting, namely, the decision rendering dimension. This is the dimension that acts on the analysis and selects the optimum choice. Evaluation of the choices are then reviewed in the light of experiences and subsequent recycling. The decision dimension is the subject of chapter 12. A description of the concern for alternatives and a general introduction to systems analysis is the focus of this chapter. The next chapter shall focus on the quantitative analysis techniques and other systems analysis approaches.

Merewitz and Sosnick consider "quantitative evaluation of alternatives or benefit cost analysis" to be one of the distinguishing features of PPBS.[2] This assumes that alternatives exist and there are satisfactory means for assessing each alternative. The means for evaluating alternatives is the subject of the next chapter, which describes in greater detail cost effectiveness, cost utility, and cost benefit analyses.

PPBS and Alternatives

PPBS is recognized as one of a set of approaches that are consistent with the systems approach to administration. It calls for rational problem-solving behavior. As an approach, it is as old as civilized man's grappling with difficult situations with all the reason and experience at his command. John Dewey deserves to be recognized as the modern philosophical precursor to systems analysis. His steps in thinking stressed the scientific method and influenced, knowingly or otherwise, much of twentieth-century scientific thought and writing. Dewey's steps in thinking are:

1. Stimulation to thinking through experiencing a "felt need";
2. Location and clarification of the problem;
3. Involvement in activities or thought processes which would suggest possible solutions to problems being experienced;
4. Hypothesizing, that is, initiating designs to guide the search for the gathering of pertinent facts and ideas;
5. Mental elaboration using reason to determine consequences of the suggested hypotheses of solutions;
6. Experimentally corroborating hypotheses selected by overt or imaginative actions.

Science calls for all solutions born of human thinking to be tested and corroborated in the real world.[3] For some time Dewey's analysis of thinking was considered to be the most comprehensive and innovative dealing with human thought processes.

The systems approach to problem solving follows steps very

similar to those identified by Dewey. The first calls for identification of or recognition that there is a problem, the second depends on analysis and clarification of the various dimensions of the problem, the third phase begins the search for alternatives and is followed by selection of a solution from among alternatives. Implementing the solution is the next step. Finally, the solution must be tested or evaluated in the real world. Different terms or words may be used, but in substance, the various recommendations on problems are similar.

All systems techniques are mission oriented and first of all demand a precise statement of what is to be accomplished. This is related to what Dewey referred to as "problem clarification." Although Dewey did not use the term *recycling,* namely, redoing the entire process as often as is necessary to arrive at an effective solution, he implied the substance of recycling. This testing and reworking of solutions in the real world until an issue is really resolved may be perceived as the built-in self-correcting mechanism within science.

One writer declares, "wisdom is the ability to discover alternatives."[4] In referring to program budgeting, David Novick puts it even stronger by declaring, "the name of the game is alternatives."[5] Another set of writers concurs and declares, "evaluating alternatives is both the why and the how of program budgeting for educational planning."[6] Hatry and Cotton add, "The cornerstone of PPBS is the systematic identification and analysis of alternative ways to achieve government objectives."[7] The overwhelming weight of opinion makes it very clear that a search for alternatives, that is, making the administrator aware of the full spectrum of options available to him, is a significant dimension of PPBS. Again, it is emphasized that a "program budget" limited to displays of costs and output implications of approved programs fails to reach the full potential of the system. Alternatives must be known. Program analysis is usually described in supporting documents to the program budget. At the federal government level these activities are referred to as Special Studies.

Alternatives Defined

What are alternatives? According to Enthoven and Smith, "by alternative, we mean a balanced, feasible solution to the problem, not a straw man chosen to make an alternative preferred by the originating staff look better by comparison."[8] In short, the options identified must be realistic, or the analysis that seeks to appraise each loses much of its significance. The explicit consideration of alternatives "by top level managers in DOD, is a vital part of the defense decision making process."[9] PPBS in the Department of Defense sought "to insure that the Secretary can judge several alternatives in which strategies, focus, and costs have been considered together."[10]

What are the practical implications of these approaches for educational institutions? One is that a school does not operate in all dimensions of the PPBS mode unless the chief executive insists that staff members engage in the search for or generation of meaningful alternatives to problems or desired outcomes. To illustrate, the chief executive should reject advisory committee or consultant recommendations limited to the implementation of only one method of teaching reading to disadvantaged pupils. The PPB system calls for identification and description of the full range of reading options available at this point in time with the likely impact of each on reading outcomes for given target populations.

Quade views alternatives as "the means by which it is hoped the objectives can be obtained."[11] In other words, the administrator searches for the specific instrumentalities presently available, in view of the resources and technology, for pursuing an objective. To illustrate, a school's objective may be to reduce the incidence of vandalism in secondary schools by a given percentage within a definite period of time. The chief school executive has the right to expect staff with stated competencies to present alternatives to be pursued to attain the desired reduction. These could include employment of a school security force, requests for increased local police patrols, and a system of rewards for information leading to the arrest and conviction of vandals. This is by no means an exhaustive listing of options available. The point being made is that the attitude of searching for feasible alternatives must replace the propensity to present the one and only way to accomplish an objective.

Systems Analysis

The discovery or invention of alternatives is a precondition for analysis. The analytic process is operative only if two or more options are available. The purpose of analytic study must be kept in mind. It is not an end in itself. It is justified when it helps decision makers select prudent courses of action. It is a formal approach to resolving complex problems of choice. It attacks problems rationally by comparing alternatives for reaching an objective in terms of the costs and effectiveness of each option. Systems analysis "permits the judgment and intuition of the experts in relevant fields to be combined systematically and efficiently."[12]

As one authority puts it, the essential elements of analysis are:[13]

1. *The objective (or objectives).* Systems analysis is undertaken primarily to help chose a policy or course of action.

2. *The alternatives* are the means by which it is hoped the objectives can be attained.

3. *The costs.* The choice of a particular alternative for accomplishing the objectives implies that certain specific resources can no longer be used for other purposes.

4. *A model* is a simplified, stylized representation of the real world that abstracts the cause and effect relationships essential to the question studied.

5. *A criterion* is a rule or standard by which to rank the alternatives in order of desirability.

The same writer identifies the following as "principles of good analysis":[14]

1. Tackle the right problem: "an accurate answer to the wrong question is likely to be far less helpful than an incomplete answer to the right question."

2. Use systems oriented analysis: recognize the interaction and interdependencies of elements within a complex system.

3. Recognize the presence of uncertainty: "most important decisions are fraught with uncertainty."

4. Attempt to discover new alternatives as well as to improve obvious ones.

5. "Strive to attain the standards traditional to science even though confronted with the vagaries of public policy."

Enthoven includes the following observations about the nature and substance of systems analysis:[15]

1. It may be considered to be "quantitative common sense" for it "is the application of methods of quantitative economic analysis and scientific method."

2. It should not be confused or considered synonymous with the application of computers to problem solving. Enthoven admits to a "preference for the slide rule" and the "back of an envelope."

3. It is "not arcane, mysterious or occult" for "a good systems analyst should be able to give a clear non-technical explanation of his methods and results to the responsible decision-makers."

4. It is a "systematic attempt to bring to bear on the problem of planning the defense program many relevant disciplines and to do so in an integrating way."

5. It can be perceived as applied economic analysis, for economics is "the science of the allocation of limited resources," and "like it or not, we have only a limited amount of goods and services available at any one time."

6. One of the important tools is "marginal comparisons" that is, the determination of the impact of an additional increment of resources to yield or produce a given increment of a desired output or capability. The economist focuses on such concepts as "marginal product" and "marginal costs" and the relationships between them. He seeks to know when the "eventually diminishing marginal returns" will set in, that is, when an additional unit or increment of resources begins to yield a proportionately smaller unit or increment of output. The point is reached when, for example, doubling the resources for a given program will produce less than double the desired outcomes.

7. "The method of science is open, explicit, verifiable, and self correcting." It is assumed that any problem is subject to testing and verification, particularly through the use of quantitative analysis techniques.

8. Quantitative analysis is possible *"even when uncertainties are present."*

Mottley confirms that systems analysis is promoted by economists by declaring "the more ardent proponents of the systems analysis technique today are economists."[16] Enthoven differentiates between systems analysis and operations research but does not imply that one or the other is intellectually or otherwise superior.[17] He argues that operations research (OR) accepts "specified objectives and assumptions" and "then attempts to compute an optimum solution" from a predetermined range of alternatives. In contrast, systems analysis (SA) is broader in orientation for it begins by assessing the objectives and redefines them if necessary. Furthermore, SA is less concerned ordinarily, "with computing an optimum solution." It presents the decision maker with a range of choices rather than the one best. Operations researchers accept empirical data as being accurate enough to make precise computations. Systems analysis questions data, and its practitioners recognize that it represents an inexact rather than precise science. In general operations research focuses on statistics and applied mathematics. In contrast, systems analysis focuses on basic economic concepts, "mostly the simple concepts of marginal product and marginal cost." Operations research techniques are applicable to a relatively limited range of problems. As Enthoven puts it, "systems analysis, on the other hand, is an approach to broader problems, such as, determining the preferred characteristics for a new attack aircraft, the design of the Polaris systems, a determination of how many Polaris submarines are required, or the study of anti-submarine ships, or the number of attack carriers that should be included in the navy task force."[18]

Mottley describes a concept of "strategic analysis," which is "primarily concerned with a phenomenon or unit called the 'course of action'."[19] He has designed a selection process for deriving a preferred course of action, which is diagrammed in figure 10-1.

A "course of action" in this approach is analyzed in terms of its "suitability," "feasibility," and "acceptability." The judgment of the decision maker is brought into play to determine the final or preferred course of action. By suitability Mottley meant determining whether the activity is "too broad in scope," "too long range to be justified," "too large for a single company to finance," the benefits

Figure 10-1. Selection process for deriving a preferred course of action[20]

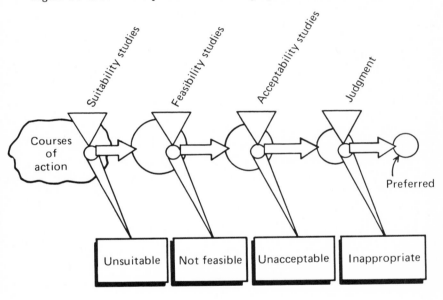

Legend

⟹ Retained courses of action

▽ Data and evidence derived from studies

◯ Sorting gate controlled by selection criteria

of an activity could not "be realized by those who invest in it," etc. By feasibility he implied meeting "required standards," "conditions of an operational environment," "restrictions imposed by the state of the art," and "limitations on the resources required." The criterion of acceptability deals with such concepts as timing and assumptions regarding contingent events and timing costs in performance.[21]

Implementation of Analysis in Educational PPBS

The analysis of programs based on objectives in the light of resource demands and alternatives for such programs represents an important but perhaps the most frequently overlooked dimension in the application of PPBS in education. It has been the author's experience that many educational administrators avoid the subject of analysis because of its rigorous discipline and its emphasis on quantitative analysis techniques. However, if PPBS is to be used as a systematic means for resolving major resource allocation decisions, educational institutions must develop the capability to engage in the identification of alternatives for programs and the analysis of each in terms of costs and benefits.

The next chapter will focus on the variety of analytic techniques that are available, the various degrees of depths in analysis, and illustrations of program identification description, alternative judgments, and analyses in education. It may be a chapter that those concerned primarily with a superficial understanding of PPBS seek to avoid. This in no way denies its importance, however, if the full potential of PPBS is to be fulfilled.

Summary

Planning, programming, and budgeting are processes aimed at improving decision making. They also are essential to facilitate another dimension of PPBS: analysis. The structural aspect of PPBS includes designing program formats. The analytical dimension seeks to systematically review alternative uses of resources to achieve end products. The structural and analytical elements need the support of an information base. Decision making could be considered a fourth dimension of PPBS.

PPB is one of the many techniques within the systems approach to administration. It calls for rational problem-solving behavior. Early in this century John Dewey established steps in thinking, which defined the scientific method and continue to influence writers in the field.

It calls for problem identification, clarification of major dimensions, searching for alternatives, selection of one alternative, implementing the solution, and finally testing the solution in the real world. Recycling is one of the self-correcting mechanisms of science. The sequence of problem-solving activities is reviewed periodically until the issue is indeed resolved.

According to Novick, the name of the "game" in PPBS is alternatives. Searching for alternatives to achieve objectives is one of the cornerstones of PPBS. Alternatives should be balanced and feasible solutions to a problem, not artificially contrived and superficial. To operate in the PPBS mode, the chief school executive should insist on a presentation of options rather than what one person may feel is the single best solution.

Alternatives are instrumentalities, available at a given point in time, to pursue an objective. Their discovery or invention is a precondition for analysis. The analytic process is operative only when two or more options are available. Systems analysis is a formal approach to resolving complex problems of choice.

The essential elements of systems analysis are objectives, alternatives, costs, model, and criteria. Principles of good analysis call for tackling the right problem, using systems-oriented analysis, recognizing the fact of uncertainty, searching for new alternatives, and striving to attain the standards traditional to science. Systems analysis is sometimes called "quantitative common sense." It should not be mysterious. It draws its rationale from economic analysis, which stresses marginal product, marginal cost, and an eventually diminishing marginal utility. The more ardent proponents of systems analysis are economists.

Systems analysis is different from operations research. In general, operations research tends to emphasize statistics and applied mathematics. It does not question objectives or the accuracy of empirical data. Its techniques are applicable to a more limited range of problems than systems analysis.

Educational administrators tend to avoid analysis, particularly quantitative analysis. Analysis is imperative if meaningful appraisal of alternatives is to be part of PPBS. Without it the full potential of PPBS cannot be fulfilled.

Notes

1. G. H. Fisher, "The Role of Cost Utility Analysis in Program Budgeting," in *Program Budgeting*, ed. David Novick (Washington, D.C.: Government Printing Office, 1964), p. 33.

2. L. Merewitz and S. H. Sosnick, *The Budget's New Clothes* (Chicago: Markham Publishing Co., 1971), p. 73.

3. John Dewey, *How We Think* (Boston: D. C. Heath & Co., 1933), pp. 106-116.

4. P. Eldridge, *Maxims for a Modern Man* (Cranberry, N.J.: A. S. Barnes & Co., 1965), p. 4.

5. D. Novick, "Program Budgeting: Its Origin, Present Status and Future," in *Report of the First National Conference on PPBES in Education* (Chicago: Research Corporation of the Association of School Business Officials, 1969), p. 26.

6. M. B. Carpenter and S. A. Haggert, *Analysis of Educational Programs within a Programming Budgeting System*, P-4195 (Santa Monica, Calif.: RAND Corporation, 1969), p. 1.

7. H. P. Hatry and J. F. Cotton, *Program Planning for State, County, and City*, State-Local Finances Project (Washington, D.C.: George Washington University, 1967), p. 25.

8. A. C. Enthoven and K. W. Smith, "The Planning, Programming, and Budgeting System of the Department of Defense: An Overview from Experience," in *Public Expenditures on Policy Analysis*, ed. R. H. Haveman and J. Margolis (Chicago: Markham Publishing Co., 1970), p. 486.

9. Ibid.

10. Ibid.

11. E. S. Quade, "Systems Analysis Techniques for Planning—Programming—Budgeting," in *Planning-Programming-Budgeting*, ed. F. J. Lyden and E. G. Miller (Chicago: Markham Publishing Co., 1971), p. 296.

12. Ibid., p. 295.

13. Ibid., pp. 295-96.

14. Ibid., pp. 299-300.

15. A. C. Enthoven, "Systems Analysis and the Navy," in *Planning-Programming-Budgeting*, pp. 265-80.

16. C. M. Mottley, "Strategic Planning," in *Planning-Programming-Budgeting*, 2d ed., ed. F. J. Lyden and E. G. Miller (Chicago: Markham Publishing Co., 1972), p. 127.

17. Enthoven, *op. cit.*, pp. 284-85.

18. Ibid., p. 285.

19. Mottley, *op. cit.*, p. 134.

20. Ibid., p. 135.

21. Ibid., pp. 136-37.

Selected References

Enthoven, A. C. "Systems Analysis and the Navy." In *Planning-Programming-Budgeting*. Edited by F. J. Lyden and E. G. Miller. Chicago: Markham Publishing Co., 1971, pp. 265-91.

_____ and Smith, K. W. "The Planning, Programming, and Budgeting System of the Department of Defense: An Overview from Experience." In *Public Expenditures on Policy Analysis*. Edited by R. H. Haveman and J. Margolis. Chicago: Markham Publishing Co., 1970, pp. 485-501.

Fisher, G. H. "The Role of Cost Utility Analysis in Program Budgeting." In

Program Budgeting. Edited by David Novick. Washington, D.C.: Government Printing Office, 1964, pp. 33-48.

Hatry, H. P., and Cotton, J. F. *Program Planning for State County City.* State-Local Finances Project. Washington, D.C.: George Washington University, 1967.

Mottley, C. M. "Strategic Planning." In *Planning-Programming-Budgeting.* 2d ed. Edited by F.J. Lyden and E. G. Miller. Chicago: Markham Publishing Co., 1972, pp. 123-40.

Novick, D. "Program Budgeting: Its Origin, Present Status and Future." In *Report of the First National Conference on PPBES in Education.* Chicago: Research Corporation of the Association of School Business Officials, 1969, pp. 3-27.

Quade, E. S. "Systems Analysis Techniques for Planning—Programming—Budgeting." In *Planning-Programming-Budgeting.* Edited by F. J. Lyden and E. G. Miller. Chicago: Markham Publishing Co., 1971, pp. 292-312.

11.   Analytic procedures and procedures in program budgeting

Item seven of Bulletin 66-3 issued by the Office of the President, Bureau of the Budget, in October 1965, specifically called for analysis in the following terms:

> An analytic effort will be undertaken to examine deeply program objectives and criteria of accomplishments. Whenever applicable this effort will utilize system analysis, operations research, and other pertinent techniques. The analysis should raise important questions, compare the benefits and costs of alternative programs and explore future needs in relationship to planned programs.[1]

In the followup Bulletin 68-2 on PPB, dated July 1967, a continuing emphasis on the importance of analysis was evidenced in item eight indicating the need for execution of "special studies," as follows:

> Special studies are a vital element of PPB. By providing the analytic basis for decisions on program issues in the PM (program memoranda), they determine the quality of the PPB system's contribution to the decision-making process. Special Studies will, in general, formulate and review program objectives in terms useful for making program comparisons; they will review in terms of cost and benefits the effectiveness of prior efforts, compare alternative mixes of programs, balance increments in costs against increments in effectiveness at various program levels with attention to diminishing returns and limitation of physical resources, and assess the incidence of benefits and costs as well as their totals.[2]

In spite of the importance attached to analysis by the originators of PPB and the popularizers of this system in the federal government, the analysis dimension is limited, with few exceptions, in much of the literature in education dealing with program budgeting. This is an unfortunate slight for there can be no meaningful operational PPB system without analysis or special studies.

As Hatry and Cotton put it, "the cornerstone of PPBS is the systematic identification and analysis of alternative ways to achieve government objectives."[3] Analysis produces a key output for the PPB system. It is not enough to provide verbal justifications for programs included in the programmatic budget formats. Such verbal justifications are made more meaningful when accompanied by analysis data. Again Hatry and Cotton declare, "the [verbal] justifications provide no objective basis for evaluating the cost-benefit relationship of the proposed activities, and they seldom explore the costs and benefits of varying the size of the proposed activity or of other major ways of performing the objectives."[4]

Types of Analysis

Analysis can be defined in simplistic terms as being the process of systematically posing incisive and relevant questions about program alternatives, specifically the full costs of each and the magnitude of benefits that can reasonably be anticipated from each option seeking to satisfy one or more objectives. At its heart is the quantitative evaluation of alternatives. The tool for assessing each alternative is labeled "cost-benefit," "cost-effectiveness," or "cost-utility" analysis. Once again a semantic problem enters the picture. Many writers consider cost-benefit, cost-effectiveness, and cost-utility analysis to be synonymous and therefore use the terms interchangeably. Others argue that cost-benefit—or as some prefer, benefit-cost—analysis may be used only when the cost dimension and the benefit dimension are measured in the same unit, usually dollars. As suggested earlier in this volume, cost-benefit analysis is not unique to PPB. It has been known for more than a century. It was used rather frequently in water resource planning at least a generation before program budgeting was conceived. To illustrate, the cost of constructing a dam was computed in dollar amounts for such factors as labor, material, and land procurement. Costs are measures of resources consumed. The benefits derived from a public investment in a dam may be measured in dollar amounts as well. This is accomplished by estimating the dollar value of electricity produced at the dam, savings from property destruction prevented by flood control and the recreational opportunities created by impounded waters. Note that a ratio or index is the resulting figure when the benefits in dollars are divided by the costs in dollars.

Effectiveness is most often used when the advantages that accrue to a public investment cannot be measured in units similar to those for determining costs. In such cases a given level of effectiveness is assumed, and the alternative methods for achieving it are costed to determine the lowest level of resource inputs for the same degree of effectiveness. Thus, the indicator of effectiveness of an elementary school program may be of the units of gain (usually specified as grade levels) in pupil comprehension or skills during a single year as measured by a valid and reliable standardized test. Reading instructional strategy A may call for an expenditure level equivalent to $100 per pupil enrolled; strategy B, $150 per pupil enrolled; and strategy C, $95 per pupil enrolled. Each strategy may be estimated to produce the same gain or effectiveness in reading per pupil enrolled during the school year. Obviously, strategy C would have the most impressive cost-effectiveness ratio. Measures of effectiveness, as determined by a test or other instrument, are of little help to decision making unless related to resources consumed.

Others refer to analyses governing situations where it is impossible to measure disadvantages (costs) and advantages (benefits or effectiveness) in comparable units, and the advantages cannot be expressed in precise terms, that is, measured by an instrument such as a reliable and valid standardized test. In such cases a utility value is estimated by a jury qualified to do so or by other acceptable means, and the costs of various strategies for achieving the same degree of utility are computed. This gives rise to the term cost-utility analysis.

Many of the early writers, such as Fisher, declared, "numerous terms in current use convey the same general meaning but have important different meanings to different people: 'cost-benefit analysis,' 'cost-effectiveness analysis,' 'systems analysis,' 'operations research,' 'operations analysis,' etc."[5] Because of the terminological confusion Fisher rejected all the above and accepted cost-utility analysis instead.

Unless specified to the contrary, in this volume cost-benefit, cost-effectiveness, and cost-utility analysis will be considered synonymous and used interchangeably. Likewise, in view of the fact that the strict interpretations of the term *cost-benefit analysis* is least likely to be appropriate to education, the author will use cost-effectiveness analysis in preference to others. In general, such analyses are concerned with generating an index that reveals in a meaningful and systematic way the advantages (effectiveness) as compared with disadvantages (costs) of an alternative to one or more desired outcomes. It begins with clarifying purposes and continues by organizing cost data related to outcomes. Analysis is the culminating step that applies such data in the appraisal of options.

General Nature of Cost-Effectiveness Analysis

Various writers have outlined the essential steps in the analytic process. They may be summarized as follows:

1. Specification of objectives;
2. Identification of alternative means to reach objectives;
3. Generation of a model of the problem under study;
4. Computation of costs (disadvantages) for each alternative means to an objective;
5. Determination of effectiveness (advantages) for each alternative;
6. Computing the degree of relationship between cost and effectiveness for alternatives (usually expressed as a ratio);
7. Agreeing on a criterion, that is, a rule or standard, to be used for ranking and selecting alternative means to an objective;
8. Recognizing the importance of the iterative process for continuing refinement of the analysis.

Cost-effectiveness analysis is not applicable to all problems. It is not likely to make a decision, and is even less likely to serve as an adequate substitute for the judgment of an educational executive. Fisher pointed out that "most major long-range-planning decision problems must ultimately be resolved on the basis of intuition and judgment," and, therefore, "the main role of analysis should be to try and *sharpen* this intuition and judgment."[6] The use of such techniques may bring the extreme response of assuming that analysis can take everything into account. This is an unfortunate and inaccurate interpretation of this mode of operation.

Fisher, one of the very early writers on cost-utility analysis, noted its limitations: "the really interesting problems are just too difficult and there are too many intangibles (e.g., political, psychological, and sociological) that cannot be taken into account in the analytical process especially in a quantitative sense." He went on to contrast the extreme positions of those believing "that all problems should be tackled in a purely quantitative fashion" (100 percent analysis position), to those at the opposite extreme believing that "decisions must be made purely on the basis of intuition, judgment, and experience" (the zero analysis position).[7] The truth is somewhere in between. Again, the objective is not to replace the decision maker and his judgment, but to sharpen intuition and judgment through meaningfully organized and analyzed information.

Carpenter viewed "analysis of the resource requirements, cost, and effectiveness of on-going programs" as "the base upon which the Program Budgeting System must be built." She concurred with the position indicated by Fisher in the previous paragraph, however, by indicating that although analysis may support resource allocation shifts among programs, "the decision makers' subjective value, judgments concerning the desirable emphasis among programs" will be reflected as well. The analysis "is to provide information to which the planner can apply his judgment in order to choose the alternative that best meets his needs within his constraints, such as budget level or community pressures." She identified the two steps "crucial to good analysis directed toward assisting in the choice among alternatives" as "problem definition" and "definetion of alternative means for solution." In her way of thinking "a key aspect of the analysis required to describe on-going programs is a description of what the program actually is—what people, facilities, equipment, and materials are really used and *how* they are used to attain the objectives."[8] Following the conceptualization of good analysis came the characteristics of the "good analyzer" as the person with "a thorough knowledge of the educational system and an appreciation for the complex interactions among the various parts of the system" and "a rational, objective, intellectual approach with a large measure of uncommon 'common' sense."[9]

Levels of Analysis

Hatry and Cotton contrast the various levels of analysis as "less vigorous" versus "in-depth" analysis.[10] The most common type during the early years of implementing PPB in an educational system is the less vigorous or at best superficial analysis. The primary benefit is skill in asking the right questions and seeking the best-informed guesses on the problem. Following identification of the feasible objectives and major alternatives, the best available estimates are made of the effectiveness and costs for each alternative. This would also include estimates of major assumptions and uncertainties associated with them. Obviously, this outline of an attitude in problem solving does not include the use of sophisticated analytical tools. It can be likened to a dialogue with questioning and responses in a rational problem-solving style. It does represent a beginning in illuminating key factors that may enhance the quality of decision making. By the same token, the staff demands of the so-called less vigorous analysis are not very great and the time consumed in the completion of such tasks is not very large.

In contrast, "a fully implemented PPB should provide for the preparation of in-depth studies" that "draw heavily upon the analytical tools of the professional disciplines including mathematics, economics, operations research, engineering and the computer sciences." It takes time to reach this point for it may be "difficult to find and fund staff with the appropriate backgrounds to perform the in-depth analysis."[11] More sophisticated and in-depth attacks consume large blocks of time. Lead time is an issue, that is, a decision must be of the variety that could be delayed for a month or longer to permit in-depth analysis of pertinent issues. Therefore, the more sophisticated analytic studies must be of necessity confined to the truly significant and priority decision likely to have the broadest impact on operations and directions for the institution. It should be apparent that staff requirements are also different, because personnel with special quantitative analysis capabilities are required.

There is a danger of making an implicit assumption that cost-effectiveness analysis will yield clear-cut solutions to all types of problems. The best that can be hoped for is that significant information will be generated that will be considered relevant by the decision maker. There are severe limitations to in-depth studies, particularly in social institutions where objectives are difficult to clarify, pertinent data are hard to come by, and benefits are multiple or difficult to measure.

One impact of Bulletin 66-3 was the large increase in the number of staff members in key federal bureaus engaged in analysis to fulfill the requirements of PPB. Those who assume that PPB can be implemented in its fullest without additional cost might well reflect on Carlson's data: "as of the fiscal 1969 budget year, the total of new positions for PPBS in the federal government was about 825 professionals."[12] About one-third were net additions to federal agency staffs; the rest were previously employed personnel retrained to assume PPB roles. Annual expenditures in the federal government for personnel connected with PPB was roughly $40,000,000 for fiscal year 1969. Training demands for analysts and analytically oriented program managers in the federal government alone called for the involvement of a number of universities, such as Harvard, MIT,

Stanford, the University of California at Irvine, and the University of Maryland. Using 1969 as the base year, Carlson observed that, "useful analysis in the domestic agencies has increased about 200 percent during the last four years, and in the Defense Department by a higher percent during the last eight years."[13]

There is some confusion about the total number of employees in the federal government dedicated to PPB. Carlson estimated that the total professional and support personnel required for implementation of PPB in fiscal 1969 was 1,145. Another source examining the status of PPB in the federal government declared, "the staff size is difficult to ascertain," but after indicating the special problems and warnings attendant to such estimates the source concluded that, "there are about 1600 full-time PPB employees in 21 agencies surveyed by the GAO (Government Accounting Office)."[14] Moreover, "another 2100 employees spent part-time on PPB for an additional full-time equivalent of about 900 full-time PPB employees," which produced a grand total of, "2500 full-time equivalent employees allocated to planning, programming, and budgeting functions." These are the 1969 figures as well.

Carlson concluded that special analytic studies were "a successful part of the PPB innovation" even though some federal agencies concentrated "their limited analytical people upon fairly minor issues."[15] Some major policy issues were made with the assistance of analysis. One of the contributions of PPB in the federal government was to increase the demand for relevant analytic work.[16]

Philosophical Criteria

Man has wrestled for a long time with the problem of evaluating alternative conditions and seeking to understand when change is beneficial and when it is not. Pareto submits the following criterion to assess the desirability of change: change is good "if it would make some persons better off (in their own judgment) and make no one worse off (in their own judgment)."[17] In general, then, a change is desirable if at least some are better off and no one is worse off. By the same token it is undesirable if no one benefits or feels better off, and there are some who declare that they are worse off. This is sometimes referred to as the "Pareto criterion" and has been "widely accepted by economists since the early 1930's." Although the economists argue that the Pareto criterion, "is ethically appropriate," and answers from it are "potentially verifiable," the situations in which the standard can be applied, "are likely to be rare."[18]

In short, it sounds great but has very limited application in making important judgments.

Another standard for assessing change was suggested by two other economists and is identified as the "Kaldor-Hicks criterion." Its importance stems from the fact that "it is almost the same as the criterion used in benefit-cost analysis." It declares: (a) "change is desirable if it is desirable according to the Pareto criterion, (b) a position that is Pareto-better than the initial position could be attained by making the change and then having the persons who gained give or trade something to the persons who lost."[19] This criterion states that change is desirable if the gainer's gain is greater than the loser's loss. Or as Hicks put it, "if A is made so much better off by a change that he could compensate B for his loss and still have something left over, then the change is an unequivocal improvement."[20]

There are other philosophical criteria for judging change, such as the "Little criterion," which declares that a change is good "if it causes a good redistribution of wealth, and if the potential losers could not profit or bribe the potential gainers to oppose it."[21]

Programmatic Structures and Analysis

Haggart defined programming or "program structuring" as "categorizing the activities of education into programs based on their contribution toward meeting the objectives of education." She viewed it as an "iterative process" which was continued "with the goal of achieving a workable program structure." This structure provides a format for a program budget that in turn was viewed as "a display of the expenditure consequences, over time, of activities resulting from current policies and decisions." The end product was an "informational base" or "informational framework" useful in "assisting current programs and in evaluating the alternatives in terms of their impact on the cost and effectiveness of all the programs."[22]

Haggart argued further that "both the nature and the role of the program structure have changed since PPB was first introduced" in the federal government. A program structure was first a "series of output-oriented categories" in Bulletin 66-3 issued by the Bureau of Budget in 1965, and then became grouping of "the activities of an agency into a set of program categories that facilitates analytic comparisons of the costs and effectiveness of alternative programs" in Bulletin 68-2 in 1967. In 1968 another federal bulletin, according to Haggart, "added the idea of the program structure in support of the decision making process." Haggart concluded that "today there is an emphasis on developing a program structure that is *closely tied to the decisions to be made* at different levels of decision making."[23]

The author concurs with Haggart and others who view the development of a programmatic structure in education as an important mechanism for organizing an information base to facilitate the pursuit of analysis, which in turn facilitates decision making. Haggart summarized the characteristics of a program structure under the following two broad headings:[24]

1. Relates objectives and activities
   A. Identifies objectives
   B. Provides measurable objectives
   C. Includes all activities
   D. Allows for growth
2. Supports decision making
   A. Illuminates priorities
   B. Highlights trade-off areas
   C. Promotes realistic analysis
   D. Provides for imaginative change
   E. Is manageable

This chapter is concerned primarily with analysis, and therefore focuses on how the programs identified and described help to illuminate the problems of choice at higher and lower decisional levels. PPB, or program budgeting, is a system—that is, the inadequacies in one part of the system's operation will be reflected in another. Specifically, if the manner in which the programs are described and structured fails to provide sufficient data on how resources are being utilized and what results are being received, it will be difficult, if not impossible, to execute the appropriate analysis; the system, therefore, may fail in its mission of improving resource allocation decisions. In the field of education, some so-called "program structures" that simply reflect subjects taught at various levels without revealing their contributions to the achievement of education objectives and with inadequate data on costs and/or benefits greatly exacerbate the problems of analysis. Perhaps this is one reason why analysis is ignored or neglected in so much writing on the application of PPB to education.

Figure 11-1 helps to illustrate Haggart's thesis on the relationship between the development of the structural and analytical dimensions in a program budgeting system. The first column or "inventory" can be seen as the base case data or a description of what exists in an educational system.

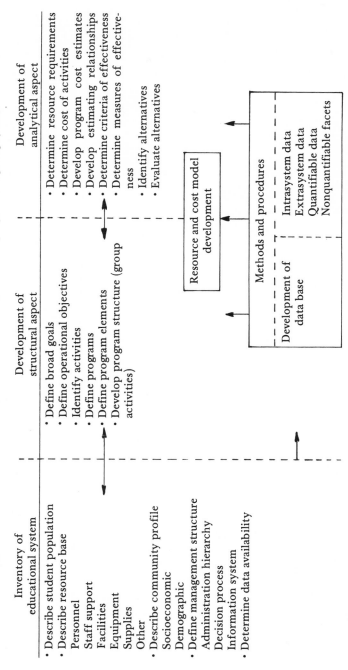

Figure 11-1. Schematic of activity areas in the development of a program budgeting system[25]

Inventory of educational system

· Describe student population
· Describe resource base
  Personnel
  Staff support
  Facilities
  Equipment
  Supplies
  Other
· Describe community profile
  Socioeconomic
  Demographic
· Define management structure
  Administration hierarchy
  Decision process
  Information system
· Determine data availability

Development of structural aspect

· Define broad goals
· Define operational objectives
· Identify activities
· Define programs
· Define program elements
· Develop program structure (group activities)

Development of analytical aspect

· Determine resource requirements
· Determine cost of activities
· Develop program cost estimates
· Develop estimating relationships
· Determine criteria of effectiveness
· Determine measures of effectiveness
· Identify alternatives
· Evaluate alternatives

Resource and cost model development

Development of data base

Methods and procedures

Intrasystem data
Extrasystem data
Quantifiable data
Nonquantifiable facets

Table 11-1. Program budget example[26]

Learning fundamental intellectual skills program
    Language and communication skills (subprogram)
    Quantitative and reasoning skills (subprogram)
    Study skills (subprogram)

Learning about the world
    Learning about U.S. and other societies
    Learning about the physical world and living things
    Learning about literature and the arts
    Learning knowledge and skills for everyday application

Development of the individual physically, socially, and emotionally
    Physical development
    Development of means of self-expression
    Development of interpersonal relationships

Learning knowledge and skills in preparation for future employment or occupa-
    tional training (classified by occupation)

Learning academic subjects to prepare for higher education (classified by aca-
    demic subject)

Assessment, guidance, and counseling services

Program development and evaluation

Instructional resources and media services

Auxiliary services to students
    Health services
    Transportation
    Food service

Community services

Haggart offered a list of "programs organized by what is to be learned by other student-oriented objectives (traditional subjects are program elements)," as shown in table 11-1. A hypothetical program budget example based on this program structure is shown in table 11-2.

To reinforce the previous arguments, the eloquent summary statement by Haggart deserves careful review:

> The program structure should be designed to support analysis for educational planning. In turn, the needs of analysis should be considered in developing a program structure for education. The goal of

Table 11-2. Program budget example[27]

Program number	Program description	Budget (in thousands)				
		Year: 1	2	3	4	5
1	Learning intellectual skills	$ 4,655	$ 4,905	$ 5,265	$ 5,630	$ 6,025
2	Learning about the world	4,445	4,785	5,130	5,484	5,875
3	Developing the individual	2,700	2,920	3,135	3,350	3,590
4	Preparation for employment	805	865	930	995	1,070
5	Preparation for higher education	665	720	765	820	880
	Direct instruction total	13,270	14,195	15,225	16,280	17,440
6	Assessment, guidance and counseling	990	1,035	1,105	1,185	1,275
7	Development and evaluation	425	455	490	525	560
8	Instructional resource and media services	250	240	260	275	295
	Instructional support total	1,665	1,730	1,855	1,985	2,130
9	Auxiliary services	1,085	1,185	1,310	1,445	1,595
10	Community services	700	110	110	115	120
11	Operations and maintenance	2,840	3,050	3,190	3,480	3,750
12	Capital outlay	450	725	1,325	1,695	2,195
13	Administration	2,560	2,805	3,010	3,215	3,445
	Total	$22,570	$23,800	$26,025	$28,215	$30,675

Physical data

		Numbers				
Students						
	Elementary	20,000	20,510	21,510	22,180	23,070
	Junior high	7,500	7,780	8,090	8,415	8,750
	Senior high	6,500	7,070	7,355	7,650	8,155
	Total	34,000	35,360	36,775	38,245	39,775
Teachers		1,260	1,310	1,365	1,416	1,473
Total personnel		1,900	1,975	2,055	2,135	2,220
Schools		45	46	47	49	51
Square feet, in thousands		3,250	3,285	3,320	3,450	3,570

the program structuring aspect of PPB for education is to develop a workable program structure that provides the information necessary for all levels of planning. This goal can be realized if the program structuring effort is done concurrently with the analysis of educational alternatives and with the development of an analytical capability.[28]

Deferred Benefits

Cost-effectiveness analysis seeks to rank the alternatives used in such a way that decision makers are in a better position to make more prudent resource allocations. Problems sometimes arise where investments in building school plants or a large dam call for construction expenditures to be made over two, three, or more years rather than in a single fiscal period. In such cases there are sizable planning, land procurement, and construction costs. Furthermore, the benefits or effectiveness may not be enjoyed until several years after all costs have been incurred. In short, there is a problem of timing, because costs and benefits occur in widely separated years, complicating what appears to be a simple problem of computing costs and relating them to measures of benefit or effectiveness. To overcome this situation, economists speak in terms of present values and discount rates to equate the best measures of costs incurred in the near term with benefits enjoyed in the long term. "Calculating a present value involves multiplying each cost and benefit that occurs in the future by a *discount factor*."[29] High discounts mean that enjoying a benefit in the present is awarded higher value than one to be enjoyed in the future. There are formulas for computing discount factors to reflect a time preference. They deal with interest rates paid for money borrowed. The reader is referred to other sources for formulas to compute present values of net benefits, for this refinement in cost-benefit analysis will not be reviewed here.[30]

Quantitative Analysis Techniques: C/E Curves

Thus far the discussion has revolved around the general concepts and steps in proceeding with cost-effectiveness analysis. Those not quantitatively oriented may find it difficult and therefore may hesitate to invest the effort and time to understand the mathematics of such analysis. The objective is not to make mathematicians of all administrators but to present the basic operational elements needed to understand the limitations and contributions of cost-effectiveness.

By way of introduction, figure 11-2 presents a typical and often used cost-effectiveness curve.

Figure 11-2.

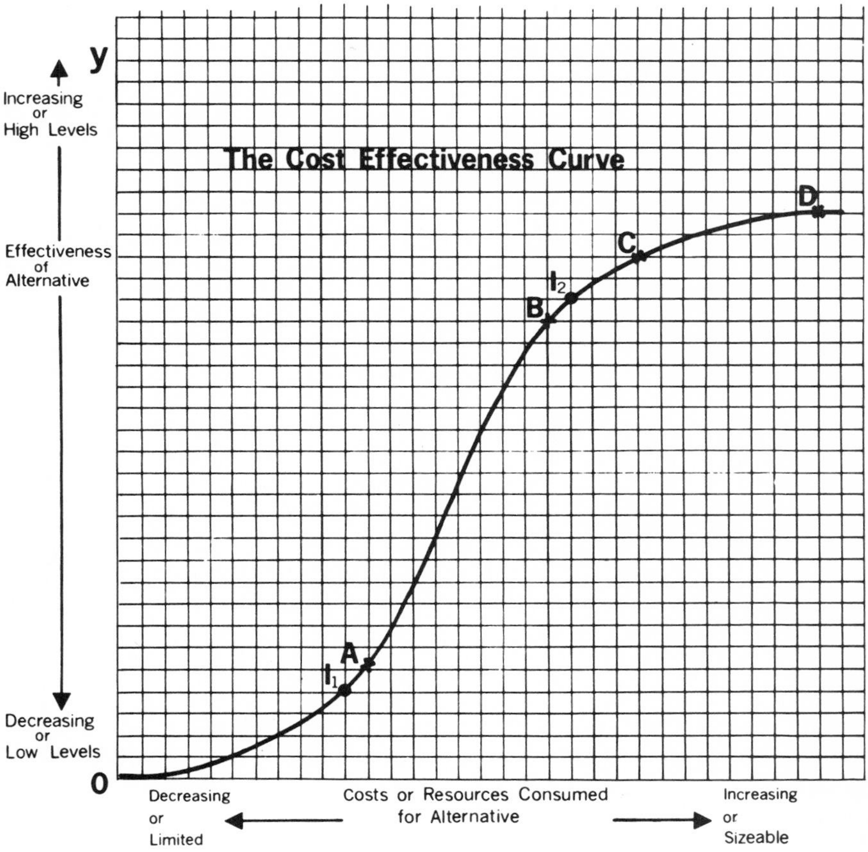

The cost-effectiveness curve shown is an idealized version of the relationships indicated. The costs or resources consumed for an alternative are scaled along the horizontal (x) axis. The effectiveness of an alternative is measured along the vertical (y) axis. "Poor" levels of effectiveness are at the lower portions of the vertical axis or just above the zero point. Increasing levels of resource use are found to the right of the zero point along the horizontal, or x, axis.

Assume that effectiveness is measured in terms of a unit of gain in instructional effectiveness. This may be expressed as the amount of gain registered on an achievement test or percent of pupils showing increases in learning of varying degrees. The horizontal axis represents costs, such as the unit cost per pupil enrolled to follow a given instructional strategy or actual dollar outlays.

A review of certain designated points on curve OABCD, or the cost-effectiveness curve, may help to explain major or significant dimensions of the curve. I_1, just below A, on the curve OABCD represents an inflection point, i.e., where the curve begins to change direction significantly. Moving from point O to I_1 on the curve defines a region where unit costs (or resources consumed) are increasing far more rapidly than unit gains in effectiveness. This is typical of the so-called start-up costs for most operations. The "tooling up" process demands a fixed investment cost before any significant degree of effectiveness may be hoped for. Obviously the area underneath the partial curve OI_1 is the zone where the least effective solutions are found. The most inefficient relationship between costs and effectiveness are found beneath OI_1, meaning that sizable increases in cost produce significantly smaller increases in effectiveness.

Higher on the curve, just above B, is I_2, another inflection point. The partial curve between inflection points I and I_2 stands in sharp contrast to partial curve OI_1. From point I_1 upward unit gains in effectiveness are significantly greater than unit costs. This may be illustrated by drawing triangle AKB of figure 11-3 for points A and B are between I_1 and I_2. For an approximate increase of eight additional units of cost (going to right from point A to point K, line AK), there is a gain of sixteen additional units of effectiveness (going up from point K to point B, line KB). Line AK is parallel to the cost (horizontal) axis, and BK is parallel to the effectiveness (vertical) axis. As long as the strategy being used in instruction falls somewhere along the AB portion of the curve, or above and to the left of it, there is likely to be a significantly higher payoff in effectiveness for additional investments in resources.

Point C, along the upper edge of the cost-effectiveness curve, is beyond inflection point I_2 and begins to define a zone with a significantly different set of relationships between costs and effectiveness than that noted between A and B. This may be illustrated by a further study of partial curve CD. In contrast, triangle CLD shows that for an expenditure of approximately *eight units of additional cost* (line CL) only *two additional units of effectiveness* will be gained. From about point B (actually from second inflection point, I_2) on the curve, entry is made into what the economist calls the region of strongly diminishing returns for resources consumed. As

Figure 11-3

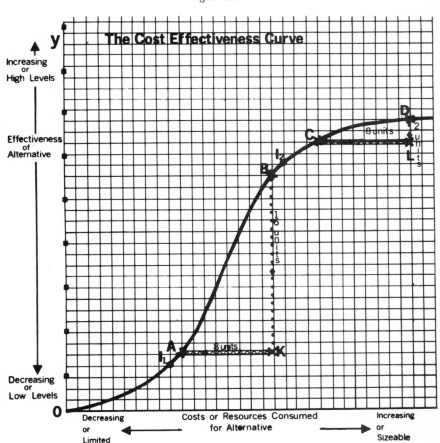

Where: $\dfrac{BK}{AK} > \dfrac{DL}{CL}$ or $\dfrac{16}{8} > \dfrac{2}{8}$ or $2.0 > 0.25$

can be noted, within this region sizable additional unit costs increases result in relatively small gains in additional effectiveness. Eventually a point will be reached (perhaps it is point D) where no matter what magnitude of additional resources are expended, there will be either no additional unit gains in effectiveness or perhaps even a decline.

This kind of information will help the chief executive to determine where to invest or reduce additional resources. Assume that point A is program A and point C is program C. Investing eight additional cost units in program A moves it to point B and increases effectiveness by sixteen units. Adding eight additional cost units to C yields only two additional units of effectiveness. Using the relationships in figure 11-3, the administrator will invest additional resources in program A rather than program D.

Figure 11-4 shows more information about the curve. The locus of the least efficient solutions are found in the region below curve OABCD. In contrast, the locus of the most efficient solutions, or programs with the highest likely payoffs, is found in the region above curve OABCD.

This is an illustration of incremental or marginal analysis used by economists. Along partial curve AB the marginal product (effectiveness) exceeds the marginal cost (unit cost per pupil enrolled). Educational administrators need data on where along the curve a given instructional strategy or program will fall. There are taxpayers who assert that "more money may not be the answer to educational improvements." This would be particularly true if the strategy or program being pursued has reached or gone beyond point B (actually I_2) on the cost-effectiveness curve, or is below and to the right of the curve, that is, entered the region of strongly diminishing returns in effectiveness for additional resources consumed.

Other points *not* on the cost-effectiveness curve are plotted to probe further into the meaning of the curve and are presented in figure 11-5. Note point R below the curve in figure 11-5 and point S above it. Although program R consumes more resources, program S is many times more effective. Program S is in the region with the more efficient solutions; in contrast, program R falls in the region of subefficient solutions.

Likewise, program or strategy W is more efficient than strategy S although both are in the region of most efficient solutions, even though W has a lower effectiveness because program W requires fewer resources than S. Likewise, R and Q are in the same region below the curve. Q may have a higher effectiveness rating but it demands significantly greater resources than does program R. The ratio

Figure 11-4

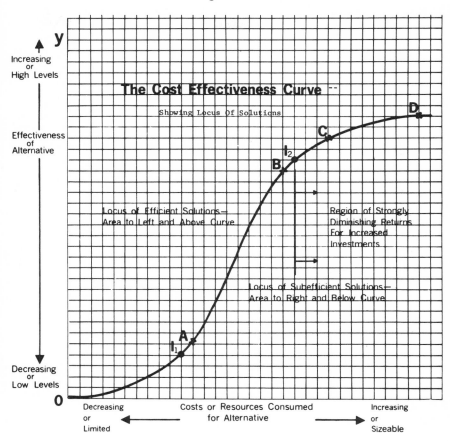

The Cost Effectiveness Curve --
Showing Locus Of Solutions

Locus of Efficient Solutions—
Area to Left and Above Curve

Region of Strongly
Diminishing Returns
For Increased
Investments

Locus of Subefficient Solutions—
Area to Right and Below Curve

I_1 = First Inflection Point; I_2 = Second Inflection Point

Figure 11-5

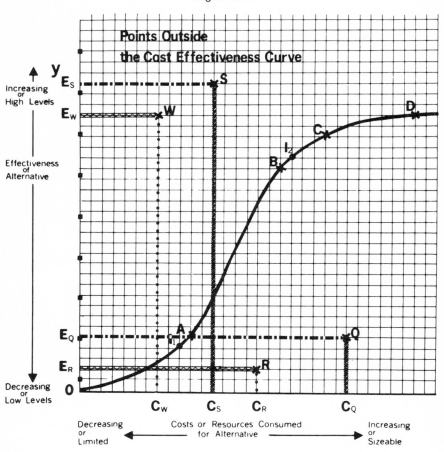

Where: $\dfrac{E_W}{C_W} > \dfrac{E_S}{C_S} > \dfrac{E_Q}{C_Q} > \dfrac{E_R}{C_R}$

of cost to effectiveness (computed by dividing effectiveness by cost) for program W is

$$\frac{E_w}{C_w} \quad \text{or} \quad \frac{\text{amount of effectiveness for W } (E_w)}{\text{cost of W } (C_w)}$$

For program S the cost-effectiveness ratio is

$$\frac{E_s}{C_s}$$

For program Q it is

$$\frac{E_q}{C_q}$$

And for program R it is

$$\frac{E_r}{C_r}$$

As can be seen in figure 11-5:

$$\frac{E_w}{C_w} > \frac{E_s}{C_s} > \frac{E_q}{C_q} > \frac{E_r}{C_r}$$

This can be read as the cost-effectiveness ratio for W is greater than that for S, Q, and R. Likewise, the cost-effectiveness ratio for S is greater than that for Q and R, and, finally, the cost-effectiveness ratio for Q is greater than that for R.

Of what value are cost-effectiveness relationships in administrative decision making? Figure 11-6 is very similar to figures 11-2 and 11-3. Assume that the educational budget must be cut (the reverse of what was posed in figure 11-3). For purposes of illustration, assume further that point B is school program B and point D is school program D. Should there be across-the-board cuts, that is, should program B and program D be reduced by the same amount or percent? Or should one be reduced more than the other? The positions of the programs on the curve can help the decision maker. Cutting program B by eight units of cost puts it at point B_1, where its effectiveness has been reduced by sixteen units. But cutting program D by eight units of cost puts it at point D_1, where its effectiveness has been decreased by only two units. If the decision

Figure 11-6

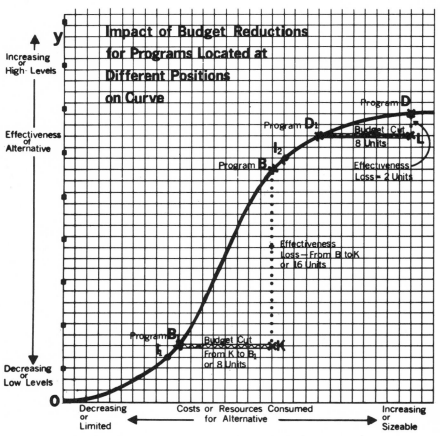

I. Options: Cut both programs B and D by equal amounts (shown above)
              Cut program B only
              Cut program D only

II. Where: Program D with no budget cut; program D_1—program D after cut
            Program B with no budget cut; program B_1—program B after cut

III. Note: BK (effectiveness loss after cut) > DL (effectiveness loss after cut) maker seeks to reduce the budget with the least loss in effectiveness, the best alternative is to cut program D but not program B. This assumes that intangibles such as political or other pressures will not outweigh losses in program effectiveness. In general, however, prudent resource allocation or reduction decisions demand knowledge of the relationship between resources and effectiveness for each program. This is the real and practical power of PPB. To engage in planning, programming, and budgeting without conducting the necessary analysis is to lose much of the great potential of program budgeting.

Much that is useful can be gained from a cost-effectiveness curve. It assumes that data are available on the costs and degrees of effectiveness for educational programs or strategies, and further assumes that the program's sensitivity to changes (increases or decreases) in resources dedicated are known. Unfortunately, there are no precise data on what would happen to a given program in terms of its effectiveness if resources for it are increased or decreased. All that is known is the emotional reaction that things are bound to get better if we spend more or that the program will go to pot if sizable reductions in resources are perpetrated. Such emotional outbursts are not readily quantifiable. PPB demands precise data, that is, an information base. Little of such data are available in education. PPB will fall far below its potential in education unless and until such important data are available. This demands analysis as well as research.

Quantitative Analysis: C/E Computations

Cost-effectiveness may be described by mathematical formulas as well as a curve. In reality, curves are plotted from mathematical formulas and related variables data. The usual formula for cost-effectiveness is

$$C/E = \frac{\sum\limits_{t=1}^{n} \dfrac{Q_t}{(1+r)^t}}{\sum\limits_{t=1}^{n} \dfrac{C_t}{(1+r)^t}}$$

where

Q_t = annual output quantity

t = number of years

r = interest rate

C_t = annual output cost

Σ = the Greek letter S (in capital form) or Sigma, and means *sum of the terms.*

Perhaps one of the more confusing aspects of such formulas to nonmathematicians is the propensity of mathematicians to use Σ or S, Sigma, as a shorthand way of saying "sum of all the terms." In the formula the sum of the quantity of output produced or yielded in each year (it may be one, three, or any number of years) is computed to obtain a value for the numerator. Likewise, the sum of the costs incurred to obtain the outputs for each year is computed to derive the value of the denominator. A simple formula would be

$$C/E = \frac{\text{output}}{\text{costs}}$$

Bear in mind that in complex projects there may be no output produced or evident for several years, whereas start-up costs may be incurred during that period of zero output. The complex cost-effectiveness formula is designed to cover more situations (e.g., those where the output is deferred) than the simple one. Nonetheless, you end by simply dividing the measure of effectiveness (output) by the cost (input).

To return to the symbol Σ, meaning "sum of," certain notations of limits are stated above and below the symbol. Thus, n is placed above the symbol Σ and t = 1 is below it. Lower case n above Σ indicates the terminal point in a range that starts with 1. It is the number of years over which the computation is made. In this case, n suggests any number. "Number of years" is represented by t; thus, t = 1 means that the beginning value of t is a positive, whole number of 1. It means you start the summation process for year 1, for t is neither zero nor a negative number. Zero and negative numbers do not make sense when talking about years.

Putting it all together, the numerator for the complex formula may be described: the sum of all values for Q_t (annual output quantity), divided by the quantity 1 plus r, and this total quantity raised to the t power, where t is the number of years for the project. For example, if r—the interest rate—is 8 percent and t is three years, the numerator would be Q_t divided by $(1 + .08)^3$.

The denominator reads similarly: C_t or annual costs incurred divided by the quantity 1 plus r raised to the t power. What the formula states is that effectiveness and costs are computed for each year of the project. If the project lasts three years, the effectiveness or output is computed for each of three years and then added together. If the project continues for ten years, effectiveness is computed for each of ten years and the totals combined. A similar procedure is followed for costs for a three- or ten-year project. The combined effectiveness figure for all years for the project placed in the numerator are then divided by the combined cost figures found in the denominator.

Cost-Effectiveness Computation

Nowrasteh offered the following example for a project that covered three years (t) and where the interest rate (r) was 10 percent.[31] The quantity of output was the lowest in the first year (0) and the highest in the third year (120). In this illustration, t = 1 and n = 3, so Sigma would be shown as

$$\sum_{t=1}^{n=3} \text{ or } \sum_{1}^{3}$$

The data needed to compute cost-effectiveness are shown in tabular form:

Year (t)	Output quantity (Q_t)	Output costs (C_t)	Interest rate (r)
1	0	$8,000	10%
2	60	6,000	10%
3	120	6,000	10%

The complex formula is

$$C/E = \frac{\displaystyle\sum_{t=1}^{n} \frac{Q_t}{(1+r)^t}}{\displaystyle\sum_{t-1}^{n} \frac{C_t}{(1+r)^t}}$$

which in this illustration of a three-year project becomes

$$\dfrac{\dfrac{Q_{t_1}}{(1+r)^1} + \dfrac{Q_{t_2}}{(1+r)^2} + \dfrac{Q_{t_3}}{(1+r)^3}}{\dfrac{C_{t_1}}{(1+r)^1} + \dfrac{C_{t_2}}{(1+r)^2} + \dfrac{C_{t_3}}{(1+r)^3}}$$

Substituting the values shown in the table:

$$C/E = \dfrac{\dfrac{0}{(1+.10)^1} + \dfrac{60}{(1+.10)^2} + \dfrac{120}{(1+.10)^3}}{\dfrac{8,000}{(1+.10)^1} + \dfrac{6,000}{(1+.10)^2} + \dfrac{6,000}{(1+.10)^3}}$$

$$= \dfrac{\dfrac{0}{(1.10)^1} + \dfrac{60}{(1.10)^2} + \dfrac{120}{(1.10)^3}}{\dfrac{8,000}{(1.10)^1} + \dfrac{6,000}{(1.10)^2} + \dfrac{6,000}{(1.10)^3}}$$

Therefore,

$$C/E = \dfrac{139.80}{16,742.70} = 0.008$$

The cost-effectiveness ratio is a low figure, and it is difficult to interpret its significance as shown alone. The formula does not attach a value figure to the output; it indicates only an absolute quantity. It is assumed that, in comparing costs in relationship to output for alternative strategies, the outputs for each alternative are of identical type and quality. The interpretation applied to this cost-effectiveness figure is important.

Standing alone, the C/E index computed may be puzzling. A series of cost-effectiveness ratios, one computed for each alternative, enables ranking for comparison of one with the other. Obviously, the higher the value of the ratio, the more attractive it becomes to the decision maker.

Cost-Benefit Computation

The cost-benefit, or benefit-cost, index or ratio assumes that both costs and benefits are stated in monetary equivalents. This formula has the now-familiar Σ, meaning "sum of," necessary in multiyear projects. The simple formula would be

$$B/C = \frac{R(\text{output value})}{C(\text{output costs})}$$

The more complex and general benefit-cost formula covering periods of more than one year is

$$B/C = \frac{\sum\limits_{t=1}^{n} \dfrac{R_t}{(1+r)^t}}{\sum\limits_{t=1}^{n} \dfrac{C_t}{(1+r)^t}}$$

Note that the denominator expressing costs is exactly like that in the complex version of the cost-effectiveness formula. The numerator is also a fraction, with the new symbol R_t, which is a value figure obtained by multiplying P_t by Q_{t_1}, where P_t is the unit price in monetary terms and Q_t is the output quantity in any one year. The math shorthand would be $R_t = P_t \cdot Q_t$. Again,

t   = number of years

r   = interest rate

C_t = annual output cost

P_t = unit price for an output in any one year

Q_t = output quantity in one year.

Again we turn to Nowrasteh for a practical example of a three-year project with the data presented in tabular form.[32]

Year (t)	Output units (Q_t)	Price per unit of output (P_t)	Output costs (C_t)	Interest rate (r)	Value of output (R_t)
1	0	$150	$8,000	10%	0
2	60	$150	$6,000	10%	$ 9,000
3	120	$150	$6,000	10%	$18,000

Substituting these values in the general formula:

$$B/C = \frac{\dfrac{(150)(0)}{(1+.10)^1} + \dfrac{(150)(60)}{(1+.10)^2} + \dfrac{(150)(120)}{(1+.10)^3}}{\dfrac{8000}{(1+.10)^1} + \dfrac{6000}{(1+.10)^2} + \dfrac{6000}{(1+.10)^3}}$$

$$= \frac{0 + \dfrac{9,000}{(1.10)^2} + \dfrac{18,000}{(1.10)^3}}{16742.70}$$

Therefore,

$$B/C = 1.252$$

The B/C index or ratio computed is greater than 1.0, showing that the total benefits are greater than the total cost over the period of time indicated, and therefore it may be a feasible investment. More definitive judgments are possible with benefit-cost ratios computed for other alternatives to allow ranking and selection on the basis of the project with the highest B/C index.

A publication by the Center for Vocational and Technical Education represents perhaps the most comprehensive and sophisticated description to date in the field of education on the techniques of quantitative analysis in PPBS.[33] The reader is referred to this source for a more detailed review of mathematical and statistical analysis techniques of value in PPB. It stands in stark contrast to the typical article or periodical in education, which avoids the analysis phase.

Various types of budgets and costs will be incurred at various times during the implementation of a project. This is shown by a set of curves in figure 11-6.[34] Curve A represents the research and development costs that, of course, precede operations by several years. A project may "begin" with such activities. Sooner or later a peak in research and development costs will be reached followed by a decline for such expenditures. These declines are offset by the start of sharply rising initial capital investment costs, shown in curve B. Operating costs come into the picture after research and development expenditures have come to an end and initial capital investments are in a decline. Operating costs are shown as curve C. Benefits depend on operations and are therefore the very last to be enjoyed. Operating costs exceed benefits (curve D) for some time. It is rather late in the time sequence that curve D intersects curve C and then rises above it. Keep in mind that curves are for specific costs

Figure 11-7. Various types of benefits and costs incurred over time[35]

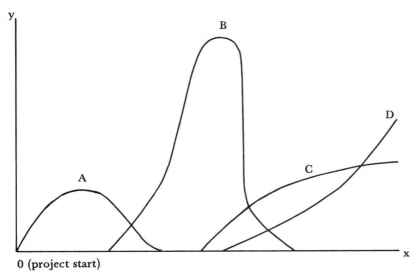

0 (project start)

Time dimension

Curve A = Research and development costs
Curve B = Initial capital investment costs
Curve C = Operating costs
Curve D = Benefits

indicated. The *total* cost curve would be the sum of curves A, B, and C. Curve D for benefits would not intersect the total curve until some time in the more distant future, depending in part on how total costs are computed.

This volume is addressed to top-echelon administrators; it introduces the topic of analysis to such professionals and does not seek to make skilled mathematicians, statisticians, or quantitative analysts of them. It is beyond the scope of this book to present all the quantitative analysis techniques. Such skill development is reserved for more highly specialized and mathematically-oriented texts. There are a number of volumes that delve into quantitative analysis techniques, for example linear programming, regression equations, marginal analysis, game theory, and queuing theory. The administrator seeking to implement PPB needs access to personnel with quantitative analysis skills. In large institutions they may be employed on a full-time basis. In smaller institutions specialists in mathematical techniques may have to be employed on a part-time or consulting basis.

Quantitative Analysis and Graphic Analysis Used in Decision Making

Hatry and Cotton described a situation in which quantitative and graphic analyses facilitated making a difficult choice. The illustration is outside the field of education and comes to grips with the problem of reducing unemployment. Two alternatives for reducing unemployment in community A were generated.[36] One option was to pay the moving expenses of the unemployed to migrate to city B where job opportunities were available, i.e., to relieve unemployment in the community by offering a mobility grant to the unemployed. The second alternative was to organize an occupational skill development school and to pay a training grant to help the unskilled qualify for skilled positions available in communities A and B. In the latter case, the data showed that there were more job opportunities for the skilled worker than for the unskilled.

The percent likely to move was related to the portion of moving costs paid for by the grant. Likewise, it was assumed that the percent of workers qualifying for skilled jobs was related to the length of the training period. In this illustration the impact of the mobility grant alone and the training approach alone was computed to ascertain the possible unemployment reduction. Finally, the effectiveness and the costs for some combination of mobility and training was computed. The analysis was presented in a series of curves derived from data presented in tables 11-3, 11-4, 11-5, and 11-6.[37]

Thus, in table 11-3 the first line reads: if the training program were four weeks long, .8 of the unemployed would enroll, .2 of these would qualify as skilled workers at the end of the four-week period, and the cost per enrollee would be $200. Table 11-4, using the second line, may be interpreted as follows: if .3 of the moving expenses were offered, .5 of the unemployed would be willing to move from community A where unemployment was high to city B where job opportunities were available.

Table 11-5 is more complicated, for it represents the combined cost of both the mobility and training grant options under various conditions. It may be interpreted by following line 3 across: if .7 of the moving expenses were offered alone (no training), the total project cost would be $1,270,000. With .7 of the expenses paid to

Table 11-3. Training program data

Length of train-ing program in weeks (t)	Fraction of un-employed willing to enroll (f_t)	Fraction of un-employed success-fully qualified (Q_t)	Cost per enrollee in dollars (T_t)
4	.8	.2	200
8	.7	.4	500
12	.6	.5	900

Table 11-4. Mobility grant program data

Fraction of moving expenses offered (m)	Fraction willing to move (P_m)
0	.3
.3	.5
.7	.9
1.0	.95

Table 11-5. Costs of combined programs (thousands of dollars, rounded to nearest $10,000)

Percent moving	Combined costs			
	Length of training in weeks (t)			
	0	4	8	12
0	0	330	710	1,090
.3	310	610	990	1,370
.7	1,270	1,470	1,850	2,230
1.0	1,910	2,050	2,430	2,810

Table 11-6. Effectiveness of combined program (reduction in number of unemployed)

Percent moving	Combined effectiveness			
	Length of training in weeks (t)			
	0	4	8	12
0	400	660	740	740
.3	400	700	900	1,000
.7	400	780	1,140	1,200
1.0	400	790	1,170	1,200

those willing to move plus four weeks of training for those who
stayed, the combined costs would be $1,470,000; with eight weeks'
training it would total $1,850,000; and with twelve weeks' training
the combined costs would be $2,230,000. In table 11-6 the com-
bined program (mobility and training) effectiveness data are presented. Effectiveness is measured by a reduction in the number of
unemployed. Thus, reading line three, if .7 of the moving expenses
were offered and there was no training, the "combined" reduction in
unemployment would be 400 (because 400 would move with the
inducement of a mobility grant). If the same mobility grant was
combined with four weeks of training, the reduction in unemployment would be 780; with eight weeks of training, the reduction
would be 1,140, and with twelve weeks of training, the reduction
would be 1,200.

After reviewing data in tables 11-5 and 11-6 in particular, it
appears that the maximum unemployment reduction would be
1,200, but the costs for this would be $2,230,000 or $2,810,000
depending on the percent of moving expenses offered. In short,
spending more may not always yield greater effectiveness.

PPB calls for data to be presented in a manner likely to help the
decision maker. Tables 11-3, 11-4, 11-5, and 11-6 provide a wealth of
information, but the data could be presented to the decision maker
in other ways to facilitate the determination of the range of possible
desirable choices. Hatry and Cotton accomplished this by translating
the quantitative data in tables 11-3 to 11-6 into a set of curves shown
as figures 11-8 and 11-9, to further describe the impact of two
programs to reduce unemployment in a more dramatic way.[38]

In figure 11-9 four different effectiveness levels are shown as
curves, E_1 the lowest and E_4 the highest. Thus, any combination of
m (mobility grant level) and t (training program length) that intersect
on curve E_4 have the same level of effectiveness. The "higher" the
effectiveness curve (E_4 is the "highest"), the greater the costs. Let us
analyze curve E_4 further by noting points a and b located on it.
These points represent different program mixes which have the same
degree of effectiveness. Thus, point a shows a mobility grant level of
m_a and training period of t_a. Point b represents a lesser mobility
grant offer than m_a, shown as m_b, but a longer training period,
shown as t_b. Nonetheless, both mixes of m_a and t_a as well as m_b and
t_b result in the same level of effectiveness. Point c represents another
mix with a mobility grant level, shown as m_c (between m_a and m_b),
and a training period of t_c (between t_a and t_b). The program mix

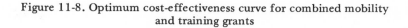

Figure 11-8. Optimum cost-effectiveness curve for combined mobility and training grants

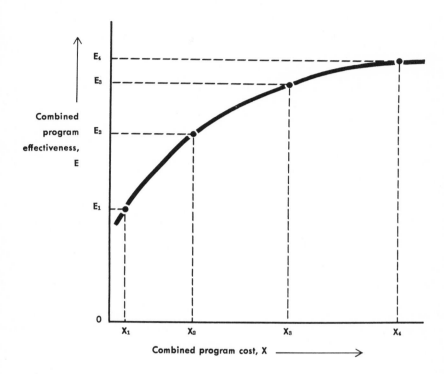

that ends up at point c has a lower level of effectiveness because it is located on curve E_3.

Figure 11-10 is derived from the data summarized in tables 11-5 and 11-6. The optimum cost-effectiveness curve, shown as a dotted line, was derived from a mathematical formula which will not be discussed herein. The solid black line, or broken curve, was generated from points that are the closest, that is, have the best fit, to the optimum cost-effectiveness curve, shown as a dotted line above it. It includes such program combinations as: (0,0), (0,4), (.3,4), (0,8), (.3,8), (.3,12), (.7,8), and (.7,12). For these pairs of numbers the combined program costs are taken from tables 11-5. The first

Figure 11-9. Contour map of effectiveness for two types of grants

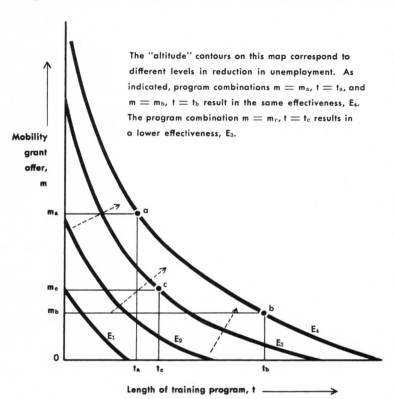

The "altitude" contours on this map correspond to different levels in reduction in unemployment. As indicated, program combinations $m = m_a$, $t = t_a$, and $m = m_b$, $t = t_b$ result in the same effectiveness, E_4. The program combination $m = m_c$, $t = t_c$ results in a lower effectiveness, E_3.

Mobility grant offer, m

m_a

m_c

m_b

E_1 E_2 E_3 E_4

0

t_a t_c t_b

Length of training program, t ⟶

number is the percent of moving expenses offered, and the second the length in weeks of the training period. The combined program costs are then related to combined program effectiveness for these pairs which can be taken from table 11-6.

Further explanation makes it necessary to refer the reader to tables 11-5 and 11-6 as well as the curve in figure 11-10. (0,0) means no mobility grant and no training grant. In table 11-5, no grants means no cost, \$0, as the total cost of the combined programs. Hatry and Cotton assumed that 400 people were so anxious to work that they moved to where the jobs were even though no mobility grants

Figure 11-10. Combined program cost-effectiveness

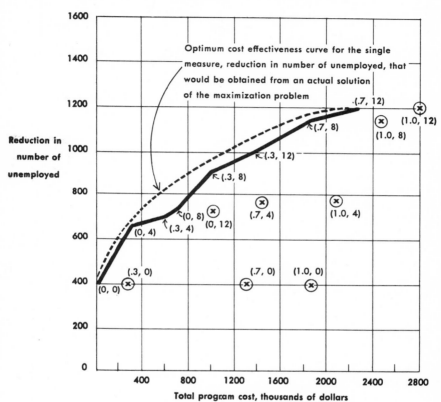

*Circled points represent inferior solutions: *i.e.,* greater cost and less
effectiveness than other solutions; m and t values are shown in parentheses: (m, t)

were available. In short, the mere announcement of jobs, which costs "nothing," produces an effectiveness level shown in table 11-6 as 400. (0,4) means no mobility grant and four weeks of training. The cost of this combination is evident in table 11-5 as $330,000 and the effectiveness in table 11-6 as 660. This gives us two points to plot on the curve, namely, $330,000 along the horizontal or "total program cost" axis, and then up to 660 on the "reduction in number of

unemployed" axis. One more combined program effect such as
(.7,12), near the top point on the solid broken curve may help
promote understanding of figure 11-10. The total cost of a mobility
grant of .7 and a training grant for twelve weeks is $2,230,000 (from
table 11-5) and the total effectiveness for the same combination is
1200 (from table 11-6). To plot this, move along the cost axis to
$2,230,000, then go up to 1200 paralleling the effectiveness axis.

Other combinations may be derived from tables 11-5 and 11-6,
such as (1.0,0) and (1.0,4). The points *not on* the black broken curve
line represent program combinations with greater costs and less
effectiveness than those on the black line. Notice that total program
costs are placed along the horizontal axis. To repeat, the vertical axis
in figure 11-10 shows the effectiveness as measured by reduction in
unemployment.

What does figure 11-10 do for a decision maker—specifically, how
does it help him allocate resources among different program combinations? To begin with, it should be noted that a range of desirable
options are separated from the less efficient solutions. Immediately
apparent is that mobility grants alone don't help much to reduce
unemployment for a limited number of unskilled jobs are available in
city B. Of even greater importance is whether the decision maker
should strive for a combined program that will cost the least or that
will reduce unemployment the most. This is where his judgment
comes into play, for a range of choices that approximate the optimum in cost-effectiveness are presented to him through analysis.
For example, if keeping costs below $1,000,000 is judged to be
crucial to impress taxpayers, he may select (.3,8), or a combination
of .3 mobility grant and eight weeks of training. On the other hand,
if he wishes to reduce unemployment by more than 1,000 without
regard to cost, then (.7,12) would be the wiser choice. Again, note
that the analyst presents data in a meaningful way and does not
attempt to substitute his judgment for that of the decision maker.

The illustration taken from Hatry and Cotton could be restated in
educational terms. Assume that a special vocational-technical center
is operated by an intermediate school district and is located fifty
miles from your city school district. The pupils from the city schools
could attend the vocational-technical school on a tuition-free basis.
Paying a portion or the total cost of transportation of your pupils to
the vo-tech center (similar to the mobility grant in the above problem) would be one alternative. Another option would be to institute
a job training program of varying length in the city schools, since not
all would be accepted because enrollment quotas are assigned to each

district by the intermediate unit. The analyst could produce an array of data to help the city school administrator arrive at the most prudent use of limited resources for job training.

It has not been the purpose of this chapter to present the full range of quantitative analysis techniques that could be used in PPB. Rather, a taste of what is needed was presented. Administrators operating in the PPB mode need not attain a high degree of capability in mathematical analysis. We do imply that employing staff members or consultant help for various periods of time is needed to complete in-depth analysis of various alternatives to program objectives. The sooner K-12 school systems and universities acquire such analytical capability for the range of significant objectives, the sooner they will reach the full potential that lies within this decision technology.

Analysis requires resources and special capabilities. It would be difficult to conduct meaningful analysis without resources, i.e., time and money. It is unrealistic to assume that school systems have such capabilities now in their staffs, although perhaps a few do. PPB is not necessarily a money-saving device. It is better viewed as a way to get more "pedagogy for the penny"; therefore, additional investments in analytical staff members, the purchase of consultant help, or the training or retraining of existing staff members is imperative. It was pointed out that in the fiscal year 1969, the federal government had a full-time equivalent staff of 2,500 persons in twenty-one departments concerned with PPB. Most of these focused on the analysis dimension.

There is a danger of promising more than can be delivered by PPB if the educational organization lacks the staff capability to perform the important analysis dimension. It is well known that a credibility gap is created when promises are not fulfilled, that is, more is promised than can be delivered.

Dangers and Constraints in Analysis

It has been repeated many times that analysis should sharpen, not be considered a substitute for, administrative judgment. The reasons for this vary from recognition that not all factors involved in decision making can be quantified and included within a mathematical formula to situations where a full range of desired solutions are possible rather than only one. Intangible effects such as the politics of a situation may intervene in rendering the final judgment. Some writers argue that all resource allocation decisions in government are constrained by political factors. The administrator may recognize that investing an extra $100,000 in a program for children with learning disabilities may reach only 100 students, while if the same funds were dedicated to the improvement of reading within the school by one-half the grade level, approximately 1,000 pupils could be benefited. These data make it obvious that ten times as many could be served by investing additional resources in reading improvement than in programs for children with learning disabilities. Similarly, the administrator may sense that parents of children with behavior disabilities are very dedicated, vocal, and aggressive. The political clout of a small dedicated group may be far greater than that of larger but less organized groups. Other pressures within an institution may dictate investments of resources in programs for those with learning disabilities even though data from analysis indicate that a larger number could benefit from other types of programs.

Another danger in analysis may be seen in data compiled in an excellent study by Weisbrod on the economic impact of various cancer control projects. The data shown in table 11-7 indicate grant costs and other data for types of cancer control projects.[40] The size of possible grants could vary from a low of $13,250,000 for a head and neck cancer examination program, to $97,750,000 in a uterine-

Table 11-7. Costs and benefits of cancer control programs: 1968-72

	Uterine-cervix	Breast	Head and neck	Colon-rectum
1. Grant costs (in thousands)	$97,750	$17,750	$13,250	$13,300
2. Number of examinations (in thousands)	9,363	2,280	609	662
3. Cost per examination	10.44	7.79	21.76	20.10
4. Examinations per case found	87.50	167.30	620.20	496.00
5. Cancer cases found	107,045	13,628	982	1,334
6. Cost per case found	913	1,302	13,493	9,970
7. Cancer deaths averted	44,084	2,936	303	288
8. Cost per death averted	2,217	6,046	43,729	46,181

cervix cancer detection program. Data are shown for cost per examination (line 3), examinations per cancer case detected (line 4), total number of cancer cases detected (line 5), cost for identifying each cancer case (line 6), cancer deaths averted (line 7), and the cost per death averted (line 8). Effectiveness may be measured in deaths averted. Cost-benefit may be indicated by costs per death averted. It is apparent from this table that the smallest number of cancer cases found were those of head and neck cancer. The highest incidence of cancer cases found per examination, however, were in the uterine-cervix program. The largest number of cases were identified in this control program.

It should be apparent from the bottom line that the best investment appears to be in a continued cancer control program for detection of uterine-cervix cancer. The cost per death averted index was only $2,217 per uterine-cervix cancer as compared with a high of $46,181 for colon-rectum cancer detection. One fact is not immediately evident from the data presented in the table. The value of detecting and arresting cancer in the "male breadwinner" is not evident. Obviously, if the investment of the cancer control program were confined to uterine-cervix cases it would contribute nothing to the early detection and possible prevention of death from cancer among males. Likewise, there are other types of cancer not shown in the programs specified in table 11-7. This is what is meant by the importance of inserting the element of judgment. Analysis merely sharpens intuition and judgment, it does not eliminate the need for it.

Mushkin called for making analysis and evaluation simple, and then declared:

> Program analysis is an exercise in common sense, not in elaboration, not in instrumentation. Hard questions are being asked; answers are being sought to these questions; and that's about it. . . .
>
> A shortage of experienced analysts exists. We have found that people with good common sense and a knowledge of their programs can learn to ask questions, can be given occasion to ask questions, and can learn how to carry out minianalysis. . . .
>
> Implementation of program analysis and evaluation in education begins to make concrete a reason for experimentation—experimentation that can help uncover the facts that we know altogether too little about, but that have important bearing on the effectiveness of public expenditures. . . . . If one moves in the direction of an integrated program planning system, the real need for research and demonstration comes to be underscored in a mere significant way because there is immediate application of the research and demonstration findings.[41]

Summary

From at least October 1965, when Bulletin 66-3 was released, analysts through "special studies" were considered to be a "vital element of PPB." The special studies include reviewing program objectives, cost-benefits of prior efforts, alternative program mixes, and the balance between cost and effectiveness increments. By contrast, in education only superficial attention is given to analysis in all but a few references. There can be no meaningful operational PPB system in educational institutions without analysis and special studies.

Analysis is a systematic way of raising relevant questions about program alternatives, particularly full costs and anticipated benefits. At its heart is quantitative appraisal of alternatives. A basic tool is cost-effectiveness analysis; cost-benefit and cost-utility analysis are synonymous with it, by and large. Some argue that cost-benefit or benefit-cost analysis is used when both costs and benefit can be expressed in monetary terms. A ratio or index is the resulting figure when the benefits, translated into dollar amounts, are divided by costs, also expressed in dollars. Effectiveness indicators are used when public benefits cannot be translated easily into dollar units. The writer's preferences for cost-effectiveness analysis is based on the belief that most educational outcomes are not likely to be computed with facility into dollar values.

Analysis helps but is not a substitute for the judgment of an executive. What it does is sharpen intuition and judgment. There are various levels ranging from less rigorous to in-depth analysis. In the former, the scientific attitude or frame of mind is used to attack a problem. In in-depth analysis, considerable reliance is placed on the analytical tools of the professional disciplines, including math, economics, operations research, and the computer sciences. Cost-effectiveness analysis presents a range of options rather than clear-cut solutions to all problems. In-depth analysis requires large staffs with special analytical capabilities. The status of analysis leaves much to be desired, even in the federal government, although PPB does stimulate a demand for relevant analytical work. Good analysts are scarce and known by their knowledge of the system under study and a lot of intellectual ability joined with common sense. There is a relationship between the design of program structures and the ability to perform needed analysis. Analysis needs should be reflected in the program structure to be created. Programming helps to provide the information base necessary for all levels of planning and analysis.

Appraisal of alternatives is an old effort. The Pareto criterion defines a change as good if it makes some persons better off and no one worse off. It has limited applications. The Kaldor-Hicks criterion is similar to benefit-cost analysis and incorporates the Pareto criterion. In addition, there is a Pareto-better position where the persons gaining give or trade something to compensate those who lost. In short, change is desirable if the gainer's gain is greater than the loser's loss. The Little criterion declares change good if it brings about a redistribution of wealth, and the potential losers could not profitably bribe the potential gainers to oppose it.

Often a complex project requires expenditures covering several years, and the benefits will be not enjoyed until later. Computation of costs and benefits are made more complicated when benefits and costs do not occur during the same periods. Calculation of "present values" with discount rates are necessary to overcome this problem of timing.

The common cost-effectiveness curve reveals the relationships between measures of effectiveness and of costs of one or more programs. The curve has two inflection points, that is, points where the curve changes directions. Programs on the steeply rising portions demonstrate a more efficient relationship between costs and effectiveness, that is, small increases in resources dedicated to a project yield larger increases in project effectiveness. The reverse is true on the relatively flat parts of the curve. Such curves may help the decision maker determine whether to cut programs across the board or selectively. Programs on the flat part of the curve can have their funds cut more than those on the rising portion without the same relative loss in efficiency. The problem in education is the lack of information about where a program fits on such a curve. The curve helps to explain why more money does not always result in significant improvements.

Cost-effectiveness may be described by a mathematical formula as well as by a curve. In simple terms, the formula calls for the measure of effectiveness to be divided by the measure of costs. What complicates the matter is that effectiveness and costs may not occur during the same periods and may be extended over several time periods. To meet these conditions, complex mathematical relations are set up to indicate years over which the program will operate and interest rates.

The combined effectiveness and costs of two programs operating in concert to satisfy goals may be demonstrated through the use of contour maps of effectiveness, sometimes called indifference curves. The point in all this is that PPB calls for data to be presented in a manner likely to facilitate decision making. The purpose of this chapter has been to present some, although not the full range, of the quantitative analysis techniques. The reader may search out specialized volumes in this area should more detailed data or a higher level of skill be desired.

Analysis has its limitations as well as advantages. Data not included, particularly those that are hard to quantify, may have a significant impact on a decision. When and where to use analysis or how to modify its results are matters of judgment.

Notes

1. See Appendix A.
2. See Appendix C.
3. H. P. Hatry and J. F. Cotton, *Program Planning for State, County, and City* (Washington, D.C.: State-Local Finances Project, George Washington University, 1967), p. 24.
4. Ibid., p. 25.
5. G. H. Fisher, "The Role of Cost Utility Analysis in Program Budgeting," in *Program Budgeting*, ed. D. Novick (Washington, D.C.: Government Printing Office, 1964), p. 37.
6. Ibid., p. 39.
7. Ibid., pp. 39-40.
8. P. Carpenter, "Analysis of Educational Programs," *A Symposium on Educational Planning and Program Budgeting*, papers presented at the 1971 annual meeting of the American Educational Research Association, P4675, mimeographed (Santa Monica, Calif.: RAND Corp., 1971), p. 17.
9. Ibid., p. 30.
10. Hatry and Cotton, *op. cit.*, pp. 25-26.
11. Ibid., pp. 26-27.
12. J. W. Carlson, "The Status and Next Steps for Planning, Programming, and Budgeting," in *Public Expenditures and Policy Analysis*, ed. R. H. Haveman and J. Margolis (Chicago: Markham Publishing Co., 1970), p. 378.
13. Ibid., p. 379.
14. K. E. Marvin and A. M. Rouse, "The Status of PPB in Federal Agencies: A Comparative Perspective," in *Public Expenditures and Policy Analysis*, p. 455.
15. Carlson, *op. cit.*, p. 376.
16. Ibid., p. 384.
17. L. Merewitz and S. H. Sosnick, *The Budget's New Clothes* (Chicago: Markham Publishing Co., 1971), p. 78.
18. Ibid., pp. 79-80.
19. Ibid., p. 81.
20. J. R. Hicks, "The Rehabilitation of Consumer's Surplus," *Review of Economic Studies* 8 (1940-41): 108.
21. As quoted in Merewitz and Sosnick, *op. cit.*, p. 82.
22. S. A. Haggart, "The Program Structuring of PPB for Education," *A Symposium on Educational Planning and Program Budgeting*, p. 1.
23. Ibid., pp. 2-3.
24. Ibid., p. 4.

25. Ibid., p. 2.
26. Ibid., p. 11.
27. Ibid.
28. Ibid., p. 13.
29. Ibid., p. 87.
30. See Merewitz and Sosnick, *op. cit.*, pp. 86-132.
31. D. M. Nowrasteh, *Planning and Management Systems for State Program of Vocational and Technical Education: An Application of Research*, Information Series no. 48 (Columbus, Ohio: Center for Vocational and Technical Education, 1971), pp. 16-17.
32. Ibid., pp. 17-18.
33. J. H. McGivney and W. C. Nelson, *Program Planning Budgeting Systems for Educators*, vol. 1, *An Instructional Outline*, Leadership Series no. 18 (Columbus, Ohio: Center for Vocational and Technical Education, 1969), pp. 122-24 in particular.
34. Ibid., p. 110.
35. Ibid.
36. Hatry and Cotton, *op. cit.*, pp. 45-69.
37. Ibid., p. 57.
38. Ibid., pp. 55 and 52.
39. Ibid., p. 56.
40. B. A. Weisbrod, *Economics of Public Health: Measuring the Economic Impact of Diseases* (Philadelphia: University of Pennsylvania Press, 1961), p. 10.
41. Selma J. Mushkin, "Educational Planning and Program Budgeting: A Commentary," *A Symposium on Educational Planning and Program Budgeting*, pp. 65-67, 68.

Selected References

Fisher, G. H. "The Role of Cost Utility Analysis in Program Budgeting." In *Program Budgeting.* Edited by D. Novick. Washington, D.C.: Government Printing Office, 1964.

Haggart, Sue A. "The Program Structuring of PPB for Education." *A Symposium on Educational Planning and Program Budgeting: An Analysis of Implementation Strategy*, P4675. Mimeographed. Santa Monica, Calif.: RAND Corp., 1971, pp. 1-14.

Hatry, H. P., and Cotton, J. F. *Program Planning for State, County, and City.* Washington, D.C.: State-Local Finances Project, George Washington University, 1967.

Haveman, R. H., and Margolis, J., eds. *Public Expenditures and Policy Analysis.* Chicago: Markham Publishing Co., 1970, chaps. 6-14.

McGivney, J. H., and Nelson, W. C. *Program Planning Budgeting Systems for Educators.* Vol. 1, *An Instructional Outline.* Leadership Series no. 18. Columbus, Ohio: Center for Vocational and Technical Education, 1969, chaps. 6-11.

Merewitz, L., and Sosnick, S. H. *The Budget's New Clothes.* Chicago: Markham Publishing Co., 1971.

Nowrasteh, D. M. *Planning and Management Systems for State Program of Vocational and Technical Education: An Application of Research.* Information Series no. 48. Columbus, Ohio: Center for Vocational and Technical Education, 1971.

12. PPBS as decision technology and its impact on the political process

Some efforts to reveal the essence of PPBS are similar to the efforts of the proverbial blind men describing an elephant. Programming budgeting is a complex system. Distortion can result if the focus is on the fiscal dimension, operation in MBO mode, analysis, or any other single aspect without regard to the others. This warning does not appear to stop the longing to identify one element as revealing the fundamental substance of PPBS. It is the author's position that decision making comes closer to being the "name of the game" than any other single factor. PPBS was born of efforts to enhance the administrator's decision-making capability, particularly in regard to the problem of allocating scarce resources among competing purposes.

This position can be documented by the number of writers who have suggested that PPBS is the technology for improving government decision making and resource allocation. Carlson declares that "the Planning, Programming, Budgeting System (PPBS) is an approach to decision making designed to make as explicit as possible the costs and consequences of major choices and to encourage the use of this information systematically in making of public policy."[1] In an effort to identify the intent of PPBS, Marvin and Rouse state, "there seems to be little doubt that it was the intention of both President Johnson and the supporters of PPB to develop a systematized approach to decision-making and not merely to introduce analytic tools."[2] The above sources were members of the so-called federal bureaucracy, specifically in the Bureau of the Budget and the Government Accounting Office, when the statements attributed to them were made. In Congress, Senator Proxmire went on record saying, "as a U.S. Senator, I also have a strong interest in the potential of PPB for improving decision making in the legislative branch as well as in the executive."[3] To these can be added sources from outside the federal government such as Hoffman, who concludes that "the system (PPB) was intended to improve federal decision-making about resource allocation in several important ways."[4] Hatry and Cotton concur with this line of thought, stating that "PPB is a system aimed at helping management make better decisions on the allocation of resources among alternative ways to attain government objectives."[5]

Additional documentation is available but would simply belabor the point. Clearly, there is a consensus among many writers that decision making deserves recognition as one of the significant dimensions of PPB.

Program budgeting in government must be seen as decision making in a political context. Public schools and universities are not only social institutions, they are also an integral part of government and influenced by its processes. Decision making in public education in particular must be executed in the political context as well. Politics is used in its broadest and best sense rather than in its narrowest and partisan sense. Among the severest critics of program budgeting are the political scientists, who argue that oversimplification of PPBS or failure to see the situation in which it must operate will severely constrain the impact of the decisions based on the system. But first let us look at the nature and substance of decision making as a process.

Nature of Decision Making

Man is a decision-making animal. He has the power to make choices. Instinctive behavior is less characteristic of higher animals than of lower animals. Stated simply, decision making is a process of making a choice among two or more options. The process of decision making has captured the interest of experts in a variety of disciplines. It is the concern of psychologists or behavioral scientists, as well as economists, political scientists, and administrators or managers of institutions. The quantitative basis of the decision making associated with systems analysis has brought in others, such as statisticians, operations researchers, and systems analysts. The dimension of decision making stressing the use of scientific technologies in the various processes is of particular interest to a breed known as the management scientist. PPBS is identified with the decision technology school. Historically, most of the quantitative approaches to decision making appeared during and after World War II.

This interest in decision making coming from professionals in various disciplines has resulted in some significant contributions to the understanding and improvement of the process. Concern for decision making, however, cannot be construed as being of recent origin. The modern roots of a more formal, orderly, and rational analysis of decision making can be traced to John Dewey and his "steps in thinking," which he defined early in this century. To John Dewey, thinking was a rational process that could be broken down into a specific sequence.[6]

Writers who have focused on decision making seem to have adapted the sequence of rational thought developed by Dewey. The following is a typical set of factors or steps in decision making:

> 1. There must be a situation that calls for a decision before there can be decision making (felt need).
> 2. It is imperative to define or diagnose the nature of the problem (location and clarification).
> 3. The problem can be analyzed by gathering data pertinent to it (further clarification).
> 4. Alternative courses of actions must be generated or preferred solutions formulated (suggestion of possible solutions).
> 5. Each alternative course of action should be appraised, preferably through the use of a model that portrays the essential properties of the phenomena under study (hypothesizing).
> 6. Consequences, such as cost-benefit analysis, of each possible choice must be examined (mental elaboration).
> 7. Selecting a choice, that is, making the decision.
> 8. After the choice is rendered and the decision put into effect, the decision should be evaluated (experimental corroboration).[7]

Other writers refer to "phases" in the process. For example, Simon refers to intelligence activity as the initial phase of decision making.[8] This calls for reviewing environmental conditions to discover decision-making situations, and is similar to the first two of the eight general steps cited above. His next phase is "design activity" and the last is "choice activity." In effect, the actual decision or choice determination is preceded by important processes that lay the groundwork for the selection. Simon professes belief that training could help persons become more effective decision makers.

Taylor considers "creative thinking" and "problem solving" as related to decision making.[9] In creativity, the emphasis is placed on generating or identifying new and useful alternatives. In decision making, the end product is a choice from among options. It is hoped that problem solving will produce a resolution of a difficulty. All three are types of thinking and use similar processes.

Newman and Sumner identify the various stages in the creative act, which is recognized as involving activities similar to the decision-making process. These stages are:[10]

1. *Saturation.* Immersing oneself in the situation so as to know the problem and setting from all angles.

2. *Deliberation.* Serious study of all sides of the problem by analyzing, reviewing, rearranging, and rethinking all points of view and noting previously obscure relations.

3. *Incubation.* Allowing ample time for ideas to gel.

4. *Illumination.* The coming of the sudden great idea or solution, the closing of the "insight gap," the emergence of the most promising notion.

5. *Accommodation.* Further development of the bright idea by reframing and modifying it on the basis of other peoples' reaction to it.

Various writers have referred to types of decisions and approaches to them. To illustrate, Simon speaks of "programmed" and "nonprogrammed" decisions.[11] Programmed decisions cover activities that are repetitive and occur frequently enough so that specific procedures may be defined beforehand. Nonprogrammed decisions include situations where no previous experience can serve as a guide to action, and therefore intelligent and creative behavior is necessary to cope with them. Others write about "brainstorming" as a kind of group decision making or group thinking on difficult problems.

The more recent emphasis on improving decision making has been related to the use of sophisticated analysis procedures, particularly those calling for quantitative analysis techniques. PPBS is related to those techniques since it seeks to improve the decision-making capabilities of the executive by focusing on objectives, developing a programmatic format, identifying alternative courses of action, and using sophisticated analytic techniques. In other words, PPBS can be grouped as one of the rational approaches to resource allocation decision making.

Decisions must be made in a variety of situations where conditions range from "certainty" to "risk" to "uncertainty." These are the decision situations that economists speak and write of. It must be emphasized that economics is largely a nonexperimental science. In the first case, "certainty," it is assumed that decision makers know all alternatives as well as the consequences that stem from each alternative. In other words, a given course of action will lead invariably to an outcome already known. This assumption embraces the ideal situation.

Decision making under "risk" is similar in some respects to certainty situations in that it is again assumed that all possible alternatives are known to the person responsible for making the choice. The difference is that it is not known whether pursuing a given alternative will always lead to a specified outcome. A given course of action is only *likely* to produce a specific outcome on a probabilistic basis. The probability of an outcome's occurring following the exercise of an option can be computed. Thus, it could be stated that if the decision maker selects course of action A, the probabilities are eight in ten (or some other ratio) that specified result S will occur.

Lastly, decision making under "uncertainty" also assumes that knowledge of all alternatives is available. The basic differences in such situations are that achieving specified outcomes by pursuing a course of action cannot be computed. There is no way of knowing whether option B will lead to outcome Y with any degree of regularity such as seven times out of ten. PPBS is useful in decisions where the outcomes are uncertain. Thus, as Quade states, "systems analysis represents an approach to or way of looking at complex problems of choice under uncertainty that should have utility in the Planning-Programming-Budgeting (PPB) process."[12] The problems are compounded in education where it is difficult to identify *all* alternatives. The probabilities of outcomes from pursuing an alternative appear to defy computation as well. PPBS cannot be said to be operative if all feasible alternatives are not generated.

PPB and Decision Making

It is hoped that program budgeting is a technology that can stimulate decision makers to ask the right questions about resource allocations among the competing objectives within multipurpose institutions. Obviously, this capability to select the optimum answer through the use of PPBS may be confounded by many things, such as insufficient data, lack of instruments for precise measurement, and inability to interpret results accurately. Decision making in the real world, whether with PPBS or without it, is confounded by emotional and political factors, which tend to put constraints on the application of rational approaches to decision making. Once again, it places emphasis on the importance of judgment in rendering decisions with reference to resources allocation in social institutions.

Bach and Holstein identify a number of distinct steps in applying "the mathematical approach to any decision-making problem":[13]

>   1. Managers must agree on the objective of maximizing or minimizing a specific criterion.
>   2. All costs must be described quantitatively in comparable units including intangible costs and those not regularly identified by financial and cost-accounting systems.
>   3. A reporting and planning period must be selected for the accumulation of analysis of information relevant to scheduling decisions.

They stress that "mathematics can be an effective decision-making tool even in circumstances in which the values assigned to costs represent no more than approximations."[14]

It was pointed out in chapter 11 that indifference curves can be used as part of decision making under certainty. These are the curves of constant utility. Of course, this assumes that data is available to indicate utilities attached to various approaches.

Other techniques related to decision making under risk are known as the "theory of games" and "decision trees." In game theory, the decision maker has an opponent. His actions become roughly "contingent upon what one or more other decision-makers do."[15] Again Taylor points to its limitations, saying "although game theory is relevant to many kinds of situations involving conflict of interest, it can by no means be applied to all such situations."[16] There are two-person games, with a "person" being defined if necessary as one group. There are "zero-sum" games where whatever one loses, the other gains. The algebraic sum of losses and wins equals zero. If it does not it is called a "non-zero-sum" game.

The decision tree is in reality a diagram of key decision points and the flow of the process. It helps to pinpoint risks and attitudes of decision makers toward it. Hammond points out the basic principle in this technique as "if the decision-maker wishes to make the best decision consistent with his attitude toward risk, he must choose that course of action which has the highest preference."[18] He combines preference curves with decision trees. He outlined the procedure as:

>   1. Convert all of the end positions of the decision diagram into preferences.
>   2. To find the decision maker's preference for an event fork, take the mathematical expectation of the preference values at the end position of the fork.

3. At each fork, choose the act with the highest preference.
4. Continue backwards through the tree, repeating steps two and three until the base of the tree is reached.[19]

Using an oil exploration illustration, he presents the "decision tree" shown in figure 12-1. The facts are that taking a seismic test costs $30,000. The probabilities of locating oil are higher with such a test, particularly if it is favorable. If oil is discovered, there is a gain of $400,000 but $100,000 must be invested in drilling.

It has been argued that the decision maker's capability can be enhanced if data are presented to him in a meaningful way. This is an assumption that has not been proved by empirical evidence but appears to have gained acceptance because of its inherent rationality. Thus, it is assumed that if an organization adopts a programmatic format and the resources required to pursue a given program are known, the decision maker will be in a better position to evaluate the prudent use of resources in the organization.

There is yet another assumption, namely, that analysis will be the basis for rational decision making. To repeat, the scientific method has a built-in corrective mechanism, that of recycling activities until the best solution is obtained.

PPB in a Political Context

The more exciting, if not dramatic, recent developments in decision making seek to enhance its rationality by emphasizing systems analysis or operations research, with particular focus on quantitative analysis techniques. These approaches have broad appeal to the devotees of management science but much less to others more interested in the political realm.

Thompson argues that the sophisticated decision technologies, and PPB is lumped into this category, have severe limitations, for "science cannot solve social problems."[21] According to Thompson, the political decision-making process is based on such techniques as "compromise," "consensus," "majority," "negotiation," "bargaining," and "coercion."[22] The assumption is that these generalized and seemingly human interrelationships supersede, if not obviate, the necessity for sophisticated quantitative analysis.

McGivney and Bowles recognize that "PPBS is designed as a decision-making mechanism for the optimal allocation of scarce resources," but add that "since resources are in fact allocated by political systems, PPBS inevitably gets caught up in politics and the political processes."[23] They argue further that PPBS assumes "goal

Figure 12-1. Decision tree showing analysis using preferences[30]

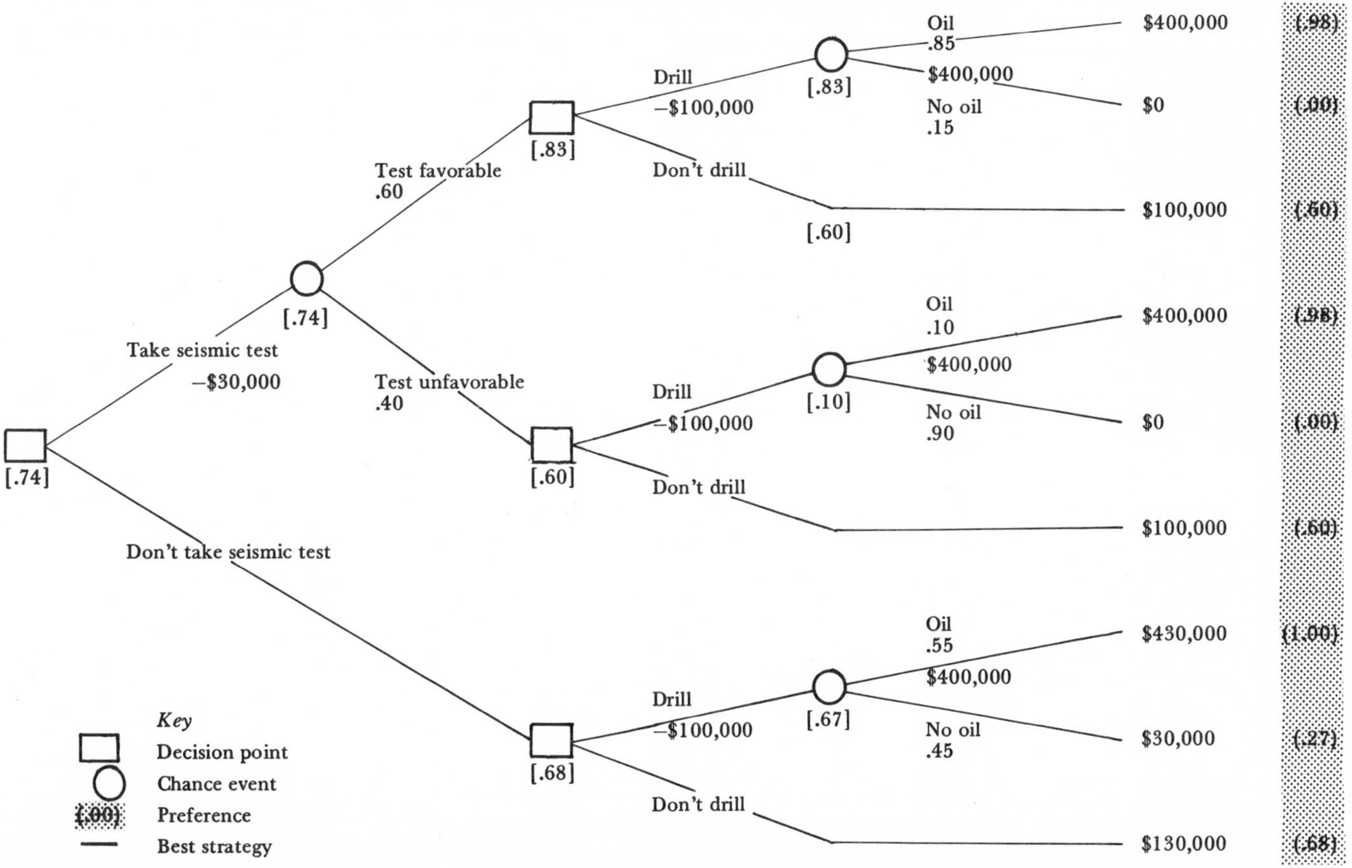

Key

Decision point

Chance event

Preference

Best strategy

congruence." This may not always be true, and when there is disagreement on policy goals or objectives other types of decision-making mechanisms are needed, such as "persuasion," "bargaining," and "power play politics."[24] They did not mean to imply, however, that PPBS was not a useful tool in decision making, but rather sought to stress the political context in which rational decision tools must operate.

Rather early in the implementation of PPB in the federal government, Wildavsky pointed to the limitations of this system in public decision making, or "policy analysis," as he called it. "PPBS does not help in making choices between vast national goals such as health and defense, nor is PPBS useful in making trade-offs between more closely related areas of policy such as health, education, and welfare."[25]

In general, the inadequacies of PPBS as a decision technology in the political arena are subjects of a variety of critical articles by political scientists. More will be said of this in the final chapter. The general theme of critics of PPBS in public decision making is that it is too complex and confusing, it lacks political and social realism, tends to denigrate human judgment and experience, and fails to recognize political decision-making processes such as compromise, bargaining, and power politics.

In all fairness, the developers of PPBS never said that it would actually "make a decision" or eliminate the need for human judgment, or that it should ignore intangibles that cannot be quantified, such as political or other factors. Unfortunately, some of the more enthusiastic followers may have left such an impression by implication. The position of the early PPBS developers such as Fisher has been that such processes as cost-utility analysis would play "a somewhat modest, though very significant role in the over-all decision-making process"; that "the main role of analysis should be to *sharpen*" intuition and judgment; and that "in practically no case should it be assumed that the results of analysis will *make* the decision."[26]

To repeat, PPBS in public education must be interpreted within the political context. Decision making in this perspective is fraught with emotions and pressures of the moment as well as rationality and long term consequences. Knowing the limitations and constraints of a technique is important if it is to make a significant contribution. PPBS as a decision technology is not a panacea for resolving all the ills of society or of education. Nonetheless, PPBS has a contribution to make toward sustaining the trend toward greater rationality in decision making. As Simon puts it, "two persons given the same possible alternatives, the same values, the same knowledge, can rationally reach only the same decision."[27] The many conditions necessary to reach the "same decision" should be duly noted.

Summary

PPBS is bigger than any of its elements viewed in isolation. The decision-making dimension comes closer to being the "name of the game" than any other single factor. PPBS was born of efforts to enhance the decision-making capability of the administrator. This is documented by writers in the federal bureaucracy, Congress, and the private sector. As applied to government, PPBS is concerned with decisions rendered in a political context. This is true for public education as well.

To make a decision is to choose among two or more options (alternatives). The process is a subject of study in several disciplines such as psychology, economics, political science, and administration. More recently fields such as statistics, operations research, and systems analysis have entered study of decision making.

Most steps in the decision process trace their origins to the classic work of John Dewey, *How We Think*. In general there must be a situation calling for a decision, diagnosis and further problem definition, gathering of data on the problem, determination of alternative courses of action, hypothesizing to portray essential properties, appraising the consequences of each option, making the choice, and experimental corroboration of the decision in the real world.

Creative thinking and problem solving are related to decision making. The end products are new alternatives in the first case, resolutions of difficulties in the second, and a course of action or choice in the third. All three are types of thinking and make use of similar processes.

The most recent emphasis on improving decision making is based on sophisticated analysis techniques. PPBS is grouped with such rational approaches applied to resource allocation choices. Economists refer to conditions under which decisions must be made, such as those under certainty, risk, and uncertainty. All alternatives are assumed to be known in each case. But a given course of action leads invariably to a specific outcome in the first instance, leads to an outcome only a probabilistic basis rather than invariably in the second, and not even the probabilities of achieving an outcome can be computed in the last case.

PPBS is a decision technology that may stimulate the search for the right kinds of questions to be raised about resource allocations. Its results may be confounded by insufficient data, imprecise measuring instruments, and inability to interpret results correctly. Steps in the quantitative approach to decision making can help the system. Other techniques such as game theory and decision trees may be used with it. Game theory is concerned with situations where an opponent is present and his actions influence your decisions. Key decision points and preferences are important in the decision tree diagram.

Thus far the emphasis has been on rationality in improving the decision process. Public schools and universities must be placed in the perspective of politics and public decision making as well. Political scientists argue that such political decision techniques as compromise, bargaining, and power politics are ignored in PPBS. They criticize its inadequacies as a decision technology, saying that it is too complex and confusing, lacks political realism, and tends to denigrate human judgments.

On the other side of the ledger, the developers of PPBS never claimed that the system would "make" a decision, only facilitate. They did recognize the impact of political and other intangibles that could not be quantified. Program budgeting seeks to sharpen human judgment, not eliminate it.

Decision making is fraught with emotions and pressures of the moment as well as rationality and long-term consequences. PPBS is part of the long-term trend toward greater rationality in the process.

Notes

1. J. W. Carlson, "The Status and Next Steps for Planning, Programming and Budgeting," in *Public Expenditures and Policy Analysis*, ed. R. H. Haveman and J. Margolis (Chicago: Markham Publishing Co., 1970), p. 367.

2. K. E. Marvin and A. M. Rouse, "The Status of PPB in Federal Agencies: A Comparative Perspective," in *Public Expenditures and Policy Analysis*, p. 445.

3. W. Proxmire, "PPB, the Agencies in the Congress," in *Public Expenditures and Policy Analysis*, p. 414.

4. F. S. Hoffman, "Public Expenditure Analysis and the Institutions of the Executive Branch," in *Public Expenditures and Policy Analysis*, p. 424.

5. H. P. Hatry and J. Cotton, *Program Planning for State, County, and City* (Washington, D.C.: State-Local Finances Project, George Washington University, 1967), p. 14.

6. John Dewey, *How We Think* (Boston: D. C. Heath & Co., 1910). See chapter 10 for a list of the steps.

7. S. J. Knezevich, *Administration of Public Education*, 2d ed. (New York: Harper & Row, 1969), p. 60.

8. H. J. Simon, *The New Science of Management Decision* (New York: Harper & Row, 1960), pp. 2-4.

9. D. W. Taylor, "Decision Making and Problem Solving," in *Handbook of Organizations,* ed. J. G. March (Chicago: Rand McNally, 1965), pp. 48-82.

10. W. H. Newmann and C. E. Sumner, Jr., *The Process of Management* (Englewood Cliffs, N.J.: Prentice-Hall, 1961), pp. 78-87.

11. Simon, *op. cit.,* pp. 9-14.

12. E. S. Quade, "Systems Analysis Techniques for Planning-Programming-Budgeting," in *Planning-Programming-Budgeting,* ed. F. J. Lyden and E. G. Miller (Chicago: Markham Publishing Co., 1967), p. 292.

13. R. H. Bach and W. K. Holstein, *Production Planning and Control* (Columbus, Ohio: Charles E. Merrill Publishing Co., 1963), pp. 109-110.

14. Ibid., p. 110.

15. Taylor, *op. cit.,* p. 54.

16. Ibid.

17. J. S. Hammond III, "Better Decisions with Preference Theory," *Harvard Business Review* (November-December 1967), pp. 123-37.

19. Ibid.

20. Hammond, *op. cit.*

21. V. Thompson, *Bureaucracy and Innovation* (Tuscaloosa, Ala.; University of Alabama Press, 1969), p. 57.

22. Ibid.

23. J. H. McGivney and B. D. Bowles, "The Political Aspects of PPBS," *Journal of Planning and Changing* 3, no. 1 (April 1972): 5.

24. Ibid., p. 10.

25. A. Wildavsky, "Rescuing Policy Analysis from PPBS," in *Public Expenditures and Policy Analysis,* p. 470.

26. G. H. Fisher, "The Role of Cost-Utility Analysis," in *Planning-Programming-Budgeting,* p. 186.

27. Simon, *op. cit.*

Selected References

Fisher, G. H. "The Role of Cost-Utility Analysis in Program Budgeting." In *Planning-Programming-Budgeting.* Edited by F. J. Lyden and E. G. Miller. Chicago: Markham Publishing Co., 1967, pp. 181-98.

Hammond, J. S., III. "Better Decisions with Preference Theory." *Harvard Business Review,* November-December 1967, pp. 123-37.

Newmann, W. H., and Sumner, C. E., Jr. *The Process of Management.* Englewood Cliffs, N.J: Prentice-Hall, 1961.

Simon, H. J. *The New Science of Management Decision.* New York: Harper & Row, 1960.

Taylor, D. W. "Decision Making and Problem Solving." In *Handbook of Organizations.* Edited by J. G. March. Chicago: Rand McNally, 1965, pp. 48-82.

Thompson, V. *Bureaucracy and Innovation.* Tuscaloosa, Ala.: University of Alabama Press, 1969.

13. The total system: appraisal and state of the art

As stated in the previous chapter, the fable of the blind men describing the elephant carries a message for those who would limit the definition of a system in terms of only one or a few of its dimensions. Each of the major dimensions of PPBS were described in previous chapters. The word *system* deserves reemphasis as we approach the end of the volume. PPBS is a unified system. No part can be understood completely if divorced from the others. Nor can it be said that the system is operative if some of its dimensions are absent. In this case the whole is greater than the sum of its parts, because it is an interrelated system. Failure to implement one or more dimensions may well have an impact on the effectiveness of the others.

This chapter seeks to put it all together. A rational sequencing for an operational PPB system is presented. Illustrations are offered which it is hoped may illuminate its nature. This is followed by a paradigm for the appraisal of program budgeting operations. Lastly, the state of the PPB art in elementary, secondary, and higher education is reviewed.

In its totality, program budgeting may be seen as a scientific attitude translated into a set of processes and related to a set of objectives. It may be considered a rational problem-solving approach, particularly if the problems are defined as those related to how best to allocate limited resources among many and competing purposes. It was stated in the first chapter that PPBS is a decision technology.

Mastery of its concepts and skills in initiating and maintaining its operations should enable the decision maker to sharpen the quality of his choices in dividing resources among various programs. The phases within an operational PPB system must be considered in the light of these attitudes and purposes in contributions of the system.

The overriding concern is what PPBS looks like when you put it all together. A review of the major phases that must be integrated is a step toward that view.

Rational Sequencing of Phases

The nine major and interrelated phases of an operational PPB system can be put together in sequence. This is a synchronized attack on a complex problem of operating in the PPBS mode.

Phase 1. Identifying and clarifying in operational terms, the missions and objectives of the organization as a whole and for each of its major subdivisions.

Phase 2. Developing a programmatic format for the entire organization and its major subdivisions.

Phase 3. Searching for alternatives to the objectives of each major program.

Phase 4. Identifying the type and magnitude of resources (human, fiscal, spatial, and material) demanded for the pursuit of each feasible alternative for a major objective.

Phase 5. Systems analysis of each alternative to a major objective.

Phase 6. Deciding on the alternative and related strategies to be pursued for each major program.

Phase 7. Preparing a budget for resources required in a programmatic format and multiyear time frame based on decisions rendered on alternatives. This program budget is organized and written in terms that are meaningful for presentation to legislative and public bodies.

Phase 8. Appraising decisions rendered and program budgets prepared at the end of one or more fiscal periods.

Phase 9. Recycling to refine the PPB system.

Each phase requires further clarification.

PPB is a mission-oriented approach. The general outcomes statements must be further refined so that a related set of written objectives may be developed from them. Mission definition and objectives clarification are considered together. The completion of this activity is the essential first step. No organization can be said to be operating in the PPB mode without completion of these tasks. Objectives issued must meet the test of serving as effective guides to action. As stated earlier, they must be written in behavioral and measurable terms that are appropriate to a given managerial or operational level. The objectives should focus on the anticipated outcomes rather than on the activities to be pursued without regard to outcomes. Thus, it is almost meaningless to state that the objective is to administer the school system or university as efficiently as possible. Administration is an activity, not an outcome. Even the explicit statement that it will be done "as efficiently as possible" is suspect. Its vagueness makes it impossible to measure. In short, PPBS demands initially that outcome statements be prepared in a manner to facilitate operations and other phases. This must be available for the organization as a whole as well as for its major subdivisions.

Phase 2 is closely related to phase 1. By definition, a program is a set of activities clustered around objectives. There can be no program specification without a set of objectives to begin with. The generation of the programmatic format implies a reorganization with all activities reclustered around measurable and meaningful objectives rather than larger functional categories per se. Even if the subject matter format is continued as a way of describing educational experiences (curriculum) within the institution, it is no longer enough simply to identify the name of the discipline, a specific course, or the activities to be pursued. It should be made explicit that the objective is to bring student competency in manipulating a set of concepts or demonstrating a group of operational behaviors or skills to a predetermined level for a fixed percentage of students. In short, the traditional English or science program may or may not be a program in the PPBS sense. It becomes a program when the objectives to be satisfied are made known. It was also pointed out earlier that relatively new educational responsibilities tend to lend themselves more readily to the development of a programmatic format, that is, a format that clusters related activities around a given objective. Programs are defined and the entire organization and its subdivisions recast in a programmatic format before proceeding to the next level of PPBS development.

Phase 3 calls for a search for alternative strategies for pursuing each objective. The objectives and alternatives must be realistic in terms of resources and capabilities. This search and the products generated may serve as indicators of the creativeness of the executive and his staff. Alternatives identification need not be confined to one person. All with special expertise or interest in an area may contribute to the search for plausible alternatives. Obviously, the larger the organization, the more necessary the sharing of this responsibility becomes.

Assuming a list of alternatives has been identified, the next step is to translate the related activities into costs. Phase 4 is not the program budget but only a single element that many confuse with a program budget. There is an accounting of the resources demanded for the achievement of each alternative within a given program. It is an important interim step facilitating selection of the most appropriate alternative. Cost accounting and unit cost analysis are completed so the fiscal consequences of pursuing a given option are known in depth. It is not necessary that all these interim cost data be made available to the public. Such a wealth of data could overwhelm rather than explain to those with limited time to comprehend its purposes. Such data are gathered to frame the consequences of pursuing a given alternative. The expenditures demanded for salaries of personnel employed, materials purchased, equipment procured, or space rented or constructed may be viewed as an "expenditures budget" for each alternative. Cost accounting and unit cost data are revealed in these minibudgets. These are placed in the multiyear time frame characteristic of PPBS.

There can be no systems analysis without identified alternatives and specific resource requirements. Phase 5 clearly rests on prior conditions, namely, stipulation that more than one strategy can be pursued for realizing an objective and that resource consumption patterns are known. The farther one moves in the PPB system, the more evident it becomes that the various parts are interrelated. Complete and accurate costing of activities for pursuing a given alternative is only one element. The benefits, or levels of effectiveness or utility, that could be anticipated from each alternative must also be calculated. Time constraints may limit the depth of analysis. If sufficient lead time is available and staff capabilities allow it, in-depth analysis is preferred. The outcome of the analysis phase is a ranking of the cost-benefit, cost-effectiveness, or cost-utility index for each option. Analysis is not an end in itself. It is what follows that counts.

Phase 6 focuses on the decision dimension executed in a particular way. It represents a commitment to rationality, that is, decisions are based on quantitative analysis of the alternatives identified in phase 3 and analyzed in phase 5. Time is an important element, and the future consequences of a present decision must be known. Most complex problems demand several years of resource expenditure before benefits may be realized. More is involved than mathematical computations and interpretations of quantitative analysis data. The act of decision making requires the use of judgment and experience to plug in the intangible political and other factors or to go beyond the constraints of computations.

It is only after significant resource allocation decisions based on programs are identified that a program budget document can be generated. In reality the program budget is the tip of the iceberg. Much of what is involved in PPBS may not be readily apparent to the reader of the budget document. It represents the kind of backup data an administrator keeps on record to support resource allocation decisions. It may be brought out on request for those who desire further justification, or reviewed to ascertain what went wrong following a decision to pursue a seemingly prudent course of action. Within this budget, objectives are made explicit, and expenditure data are organized around objectives to portray a programmatic format and extended time range.

To repeat, the actual development of the program budget document is preceded by many and important phases. It was pointed out in previous chapters that one of the significant features of PPBS is the emphasis placed on the preparation and pre-preparation phases of the budgeting cycle. In the traditional or control budget, the preparation stage is of limited duration: only as long as necessary to compile the figures on anticipated expenditures. The emphasis in traditional budget documents was placed in the execution stage.

In reality the program budget document itself is a summary of formal decisions. Its final preparation stage is perhaps the simplest. What happens is that decisions on resource allocations are pulled together for purposes of presentation. The difficult and time-consuming chores have already been done. One does not appreciate the massiveness or complexity of operating in the PPBS mode from the 10 percent that may be visible to those who read the budget document. It is the unseen 90 percent that determines the quality and effectiveness of the budget document. Thus, if the alternatives are puerile or the analysis shoddy, however impressive the appearance of the final document, it has a relatively low probability of fulfilling its potential.

Phase 8 is concerned with the appraisal of the decisions recorded in the program budget document. It is the very nature of science to install a self-correcting mechanism in any set of procedures that makes claim to being rational. It is how well the end product—that is, the budget document—works in the real world that counts. Therefore, program budgeting demands an evaluation of these decisions even though this may make the executive uncomfortable. Initially the Research Corporation of the Association of School Business Officials inserted "evaluating" in the PPBS acronym, making it

PPBES. Formal plans for the appraisal of budget preparation activities—the presentation, approval and appropriations, and execution—are all reviewed in the final part of the budgetary cycle, i.e., appraisal. It involves both the legislative and executive arms of the organization.

Phase 9 is recyling and is closely related to appraisal. It represents the action that follows the accumulation of data concerned with appraisal. In a sense, appraisal and recyling can be looked at as two stages of what is essentially the same function. One accumulates the relevant data and the other stimulates action bringing forth a redesign of one or more dimensions of the system. Recyling, like appraisal, assumes that a perfect document is not generated the first time around. Through patient appraisal and recyling of the processes a better one may be produced for each subsequent period of operation.

Evaluation of PPBS Operations

The PPB model, with the various dimensions outlined previously, provides the basis for generating an evaluation instrument to determine where an educational institution is in the implementation continuum and to what degree it is satisfying the various precepts of PPB. It is easy for an organization to claim to be operating in the PPB mode. It is more difficult to document such claims. Separating achievement in actual operations from sheer rhetoric may be accomplished by use of a standard instrument. The design of such an instrument starts with specification of criteria statements related to various dimensions of PPB. In addition, indicators for each criterion must be spelled out. Lastly, a scoring scale must be constructed to determine the degree to which the criterion's statement is satisfied.

The author developed the systems approach to staff evaluation. This approach is adapted to evaluation of progress toward PPB. Its purpose is not to label or pass judgment on an organization's operations, but to focus on how to assess where the organization is implementing PPB as a system. Stress is placed on identifying strengths, weaknesses, and possible omissions rather than on acquiring a particular score within.

For the purposes of the evaluation systems model, the major subsystems of PPBS are similar to sequential phases reviewed in the initial section of this chapter. They are phrased in terms of outputs expected from each of the phases.

Subsystem 1. Production of meaningful and measurable outcome statements.
Subsystem 2. Design of a programmatic format for the organization and its major subdivisions.
Subsystem 3. Identification of high-quality alternatives.
Subsystem 4. Development of resource accounting subsystem to facilitate cost accounting, unit-cost analysis and program accounting data for each alternative.
Subsystem 5. Analysis of alternatives.
Subsystem 6. Development and use of rational decision-making approaches.
Subsystem 7. Preparation and presentation of the program budget document.
Subsystem 8. Plans for program budget appraisal.
Subsystem 9. Readiness and execution of recycling functions.

The following scoring scale is offered to facilitate the rendering of judgments of the degree to which each criterion statement is satisfied.

PPB implementation evaluation system scoring scale

Scoring	Interpretation
DNA	DNA means, literally, "data not available." Figuratively speaking, it may be used to signify that the criterion item does not apply and/or it is not possible to determine with certainty if the criterion exists and to what degree.
0	Element or criterion ignored, omitted, or so inadequate as to be of little or no value.
1	Element or criterion present or indicated, but poorly developed and/or of extremely limited value.
2	Element or criterion present but inadequately developed and/or of limited value.
3	Element or criterion present and fairly adequately developed for the purposes indicated.
4	Element or criterion present, in highly developed form, and of considerable value in facilitating.
5	Outstanding and worthy of special commendation for its excellence.

A DNA category is included. DNAs are eliminated from consideration in computation of an "effectiveness percentage" and hence are not treated as zeros. This category should be used sparingly and only when confusion is very evident. The score deserved is attached to each criterion in the instrument. Subtotals are entered for each of the nine subsystems. The sum of the subtotal yields a total raw score. This score is divided by a perfect score and then multiplied by 100 to obtain the "effectiveness percentage." This should be followed by identification for the "strengths" (those items receiving a score of three, four, or five), "weaknesses" (those items scoring one or two), and finally, "serious problems" or "omissions" (those items scoring zero or where a DNA had to be inserted). The judgments and decisions on the implementation of PPBS are based on these factors.

The following is a summary form for analysis in scoring the components of the PPB system.

The SJK PPBS Implementation Evaluation Instrument

I. Identification data

    A. Name of organization being evaluated _____
    B. Date of evaluation _____
    C. Name of appraiser(s) _____

II. Subsystem criterion statements and scoring

Criterion statements	Score
A. Subsystem 1. Production of meaningful and measurable objectives	
1. Performance objectives are identified in terms of *instructional outcomes* for the clientele served by the institution.	_____
2. Performance objectives are identified in terms of *instruction support outcomes* for all dimensions of the institution.	_____
3. Performance objectives are identified to sustain operations for the educational institution at the present level.	_____
4. Performance objectives are identified for introducing meaningful change within the institution.	_____
5. Both long- and short-range ramifications of objectives are evident.	_____
6. Objectives for all dimensions of the institution are defined with the clarity needed to direct action.	_____
7. Outcome statements are evident in the formal program budget document.	_____
Subtotals for 1-7 (subsystem 1 score)	_____
B. Subsystem 2. Design for a programmatic format	
8. Activities and resources related to each instructional outcome are organized into programs.	_____
9. Activities and resources consumed for instructional support services are organized into programs with objectives written in clear and measurable terms.	_____
10. Activities and resources necessary to keep the system operating at present levels are organized around programs related to clearly written and measurable terms.	_____
11. Activities and resources needed to move to new and higher levels of effectiveness are clustered around outcomes to form programs.	_____

Criterion statements	Score
12. Long- as well as short-range programs are identified.	————
Subtotals for 8-12 (subsystem 2 score)	————

C. Subsystem 3. Identification of alternatives
    13. There is evidence that two or more alternatives have been identified for each program. ————
    14. There is evidence that the alternatives identified are realistic and feasible options or strategies for attaining the objectives. ————
    15. There is evidence that the procedures for identifying or generating alternatives involve widespread participation of those with expertise in or who are affected by program decisions. ————
    16. There is evidence that ample resources in terms of staff and money are available to search for and clarify alternatives for each program area. ————
    Subtotals for 13-16 (Subsystem 3 score) ————

D. Subsystem 4. Development of resource-accounting subsystem
    17. Major expenditure accounting headings are based on functional-character classification. ————
    18. There is coding of all expenditure objects subaccount and major account headings to facilitate electronic data processing of expenditure data. ————
    19. Prorating procedures have been identified and are relevant and uniform with nationally recommended standards. ————
    20. There is evidence that the accounting system facilitates cost accounting by programs. ————
    21. There is evidence that unit cost analysis is used with appropriate units for analysis. ————
    22. There is evidence that resource utilization patterns for each alternative have been carefully and accurately identified. ————
    23. There is evidence that resource utilization patterns for each alternative are organized in terms of long- as well as short-range implications. ————
    Subtotals for 17-23 (subsystem 4 score) ————

E. Subsystem 5. Use of analysis
    24. An adequate permanent professional staff with analytic capabilities or qualified consultants are available to pursue analytic activities. ————
    25. There is evidence that at least initial analysis is preceding high-priority programs. ————
    26. There is evidence that in-depth analysis is conducted for at least two major program areas. ————
    27. There is evidence that quantitative analysis techniques are being used for ranking the cost effectiveness of alternatives in major program areas. ————
    Subtotals for 24-27 (subsystem 5 score) ————

F. Subsystem 6. Development and utilization of rational decision-making approaches

Criterion statements	Score
28. There is evidence that cost-effectiveness analysis of program alternatives are considered in resource allocation decisions.	_____
29. There is evidence that nonquantifiable factors are considered in resource allocations decisions.	_____
30. There is evidence that long-range consequences of present decisions are recognized.	_____
Subtotals for 28-30 (subsystem 6 score)	_____
G. Subsystem 7. Preparation and presentation of program budget document	
31. Program memoranda for at least all new or modified programs are required in the preparation of the program budget document.	_____
32. A programmatic classification system based on measurable outcomes is used to present data in the program budget document.	_____
33. Data used to justify resource allocation decisions are included in at least an appendix to the program budget document for all new or expanded budget areas.	_____
34. Budget increments are justified in terms of the level of program effectiveness to be influenced by such decisions.	_____
Subtotals for 31-34 (subsystem 7 score)	_____
H. Subsystem 8. Plans for program budget appraisal	
35. There is evidence that relevant plans have been developed for the appraisal of budget document preparation and execution.	_____
36. Resources are allocated in terms of staff and money for the appraisal of program budget preparation and execution.	_____
Subtotals for 35-36 (subsystem 8 score)	_____
I. Subsystem 9. Readiness and execution of recycling function	
37. A calendar has been developed for the implementation of recommendations resulting from program budget appraisal.	_____
38. Resources are allocated in terms of time, staff, and money for the improvement of the program budgeting process.	_____
Subtotals for 37-38 (subsystem 9 score)	_____
Grand total	_____

III. Scoring analysis

A. Effectiveness percentage $= \dfrac{\text{total score}}{190} \times 100 =$

$$= \dfrac{\text{total score}}{(38 - \text{DNAs}) \times 5} \times 100 =$$

B. Strengths (items scoring 3, 4, or 5) _____

C. Weaknesses (items scoring 1 or 2) _____

D. Serious problems or omissions _____

The grand total may be translated into an "effectiveness percent-age." If each of the 38 items received a perfect score of 5, the maximum score would be 190. Certain refinements may be possible. Thus, a lesser perfect score could be computed by subtracting the number of DNAs from 38. This quantity in turn could be multiplied by 5. In this manner the DNAs would be treated differently from a zero.

This instrument has not been validated. Research is in progress to test it further. But even without data on the reliability and validity of the instrument shown, it can be argued that some type of instrument is needed to assess where an organization is in implement-ing PPBS. Present reports on the state of the art are not meaningful for lack of comparable data.

State of the Art in the Early 1970s

Many different lists of local or K-12 school districts and univer-sities that are alleged to be operating in the PPBS mode have been published in the past five years. There appears to be a discrepancy between what is claimed and what is in fact being accomplished. Much that is written about who in education is operating, or at least developing, PPBS must be classed as wishful thinking or at best honest intent. Until rather recently there were outright and unquali-fied statements to the effect that a district or a university was implementing program budgeting. A far more cautious attitude now prevails. One hears that districts or universities are "developing PPBS" or have "program-oriented budgeting." Where an educational institution may be in the development is not specified, and there is no standard definition of what constitutes a "program-oriented" budget or accounting system.

What is known and can be documented is that interest in imple-menting PPBS is increasing. The zero point for K-12 as well as university institutions was in the late 1960s: 1967 would be a commonly recognized starting date. Interest is being stimulated by state legislative mandates or recommendations by state departments of education on the desirability of installing program budgeting systems. State laws exist in California, Colorado, and Indiana, to mention a few. Some call for immediate implementation. Others, such as the Indiana law, demand that the program be installed no later than July 1, 1977.

In 1971 the Association of School Business Officials (ASBO) conducted a survey of over 2,830 member local school districts. Only

387 of the 1,377 responding districts claimed to be installing PPBS or actively considering implementation. That figure, however, represents a sizable increase from the thirty-five that started with the ASBO research project in 1967. Again, it is difficult to assess how far along each of the 387 were in 1971. With the exception of California, where interest among educational institutions in PPBS appears to be greatest, there are fewer than ten school districts seriously considering implementing PPBS. As Hartley declares, "it appears that between 800 and 1,000 schools are in the process of developing program budgets in 1971-72, but one should keep in mind that a program budget is simply one component."[1] Eight hundred to one thousand is a wide range, and the fuzzy statement "developing program budgets" is difficult to interpret with precision. Data on where we are in education is very difficult to come by and even more difficult to interpret.

Hoye conducted an informal survey among institutions of higher learning, most of which were located in the western United States, and most of these in California.[2] In this informal study only one in four returned the simple questionnaire. About twenty-one claimed to be interested in or working on some version of PPBS. If the universities alleged by other writers to be operating in a program budgeting mode were added to this figure, the total would be less than forty. In general, the very limited data available on the status of PPBS in universities indicate that the introduction of the concepts is very recent, the definitions of PPBS are not the same, and operations are rudimentary.

The state of the PPBS art in education in the early 1970s depends to a considerable extent on the conceptualization of program budgeting accepted. Many school systems and universities have written statements of goals and objectives. An analysis of these, however, indicates that they are very general, they emphasize activities rather than outcomes, are difficult to measure, and thus fail to achieve the high quality necessary to the operation of PPBS.

The typical claim to the installation of a "programmatic" structure shows a listing of subjects taught, aggregated into broad disciplines. At the university level it revolves around types of degrees pursued. In speaking of public systems of higher education, Dyer claims that "unfortunately, most public systems are classified by systems analysts as 'ill-structured,' and they do not possess the clear input-output relationships required for complete mathematical modeling."[3] Very few, if any, identify alternatives to program objectives. Even fewer attempt analytic studies based on quantitative analysis, particularly cost-effectiveness or cost-benefit analysis. If analysis is conducted, it is generally superficial. At this time analysis is not likely to be a keystone in resource allocation decisions in educational institutions.

More often than not, the typical school system and university claiming to be operating in the PPB mode in the early 1970s documents its case by cost-accounting and unit cost analysis studies made for instruction in various subject matter areas. As stipulated earlier, this is closer to performance budgeting than to program budgeting. The organization of cost data or resource use patterns for a program represents the beginning, not the end, of cost-effectiveness analysis. It is significant that an ERIC abstract, with many sources listed focusing on cost studies or cost-benefit studies, was entitled *Program Budgeting and Cost Analysis.*[4]

Under the leadership of Dr. W. R. Duke of the Alberta Department of Education, the province of Alberta, Canada, organized a PPBES project. It was emphasized that "the PPBE System approach to research allocation differs from traditional forms of budgeting in that ultimately the emphasis is on the outcomes or benefits of education rather than the inputs or resource requirements."[5] This project recognized that the first of "the initial steps in establishing a PPBE System" was the development of a standardized accounting system and also a program format for budgeting. What was called Program Accounting and Budget (PAB) was viewed as an important subset of PPBES. Ten pilot school systems in Alberta were selected to field test a manual for PAB. No claim was made that the ten pilot schools, the province, or others in Canada had successfully implemented PPBES. The program accounting classification or structure selected was based on "functions," for example, instruction, pupil personnel services, and administration. A function like instruction was broken down into "programs," basically following the subject matter curriculum classification, such as mathematics, science, and business education. The program was divided further into "subprograms" that amounted, in the case of instruction, to a listing of specific course offerings. Recommendations were made for developing the Multiyear Plan, which covered a period of three years. Alberta gives evidence of a dynamic interest in PPBES and has taken an important first step in implementing a system in publishing a detailed, field-tested manual for what they call Program Accounting and Budgeting. Near the conclusion of that manual it is declared that "in order to reap the full benefits of a PPBE System, program accounting data should be used as an input to the more important processes of planning, budgeting, evaluation and analysis."[6] It can be said that educational systems in Canada as well as in the United States demonstrate movement toward PPBS although no fully implemented practices can be documented as yet.

Based on a continuing search during the past five years in the United States and Canada, it is the author's opinion that there was no K-12 school district, university, or junior college that implemented or operated a comprehensive PPB system in 1972. In follow-up efforts on published lists of program budgeting schools, a sample of districts reported to have installed the program budget revealed that often local school officials questioned the accuracy of writers who considered their school system to be an implementer or, in some cases, a developer of PPBS. It was very difficult to substantiate alleged claims reported in magazine articles.

The best that can be said about the state of the art in education in the early 1970s is that interest continues to climb and to be stimulated by legislation. To repeat, no fully implemented PPB system can be identified among schools or universities. Few, if any, educational administrators make resources allocation decisions based on PPBS. A number are organizing what they define as "program-oriented budgets," but these are rudimentary at best. At this writing (mid-1972) it is easier to talk about PPBS in education than to implement it fully.

Perhaps by the end of the decade more promising results in the use of PPBS in universities and K-12 school systems will be evident. For the present, however, more rhetoric than reality exists. It should be noted that no attempt will be made here to identify K-12 or university systems operating PPBS or "developing program budgets." Too many have already prepared such lists, with the usual inaccuracies. Their value is questionable, for they may contribute more to the confusion and rhetoric surrounding the term than to understanding or more skillful implementation. All too often on-site visits to publicized institutions end in disappointment as incompletely conceptualized PPBS and oversimplified budget documents are noted. The haste to gain recognition as a PPBS innovator may end in discontinuation in a relatively short period of time.

To move in the direction of PPBS in education remains a pioneering effort based on creativity and dedication to resolve perplexing problems.

Summary

PPB is a unified system. No single dimension stands alone. Failure to implement one part of the system will have an impact on all others.

There is an important and rational sequencing of the various phases of PPB. They can be summarized as:

Phase 1. Identifying and clarifying measurable and significant outcomes.
Phase 2. Generation of a programmatic format based on such outcomes.
Phase 3. Searching for and acceptance of meaningful program alternatives.
Phase 4. Identifying the type and magnitude of relevant resources demanded for the pursuit of each program alternative.
Phase 5. Systems analysis of each alternative.
Phase 6. Deciding on resource allocation using analysis results.
Phase 7. Preparation of the program budget document.
Phase 8. Appraisal of the preparation and execution of the program budget.
Phase 9. Recycling.

It should be noted that the actual development of a program budget document is preceded by many important phases. This document is like the tip of an iceberg. Ninety percent of what is important in PPB may not be readily apparent in such a document.

An instrument for the evaluation of PPB operations has been developed. The major subsystems are similar to the above nine phases. It includes thirty-eight criterion statements and a scoring scale. The objective of such an instrument is to identify strengths, weaknesses, and omissions in implementing or operating PPB. It can be used to create more definitive data on the state of the PPB art in education. At this writing the instrument is yet to be validated.

The state of the art of PPBS in educational institutions in the early 1970s is related to one's perception of the nature and substance of program budgeting. One source identifies 387 schools "developing PPB." Another states that 800 to 1,000 districts were developing "program budgets," but this is only one part of the total system. Fewer than forty universities are said to be in the PPB mode. The data are fuzzy and incomplete. There often is a great disparity between claims and actual practices.

In mid-1972 no school or university implemented a sophisticated and comprehensive PPB system. A tremendous amount of interest does exist. State laws continue to be enacted to stimulate movement of educational institutions toward program budgeting. To do so remains a pioneering effort calling for creativity and dedication.

Notes

1. H. J. Hartley, "PPBS: A Status Report with Operational Suggestions," *Educational Technology*, April 1972, pp. 19-22.

2. R. E. Hoye, "PPBS and Other Current Budgeting Systems for the Improvement of Instruction in Higher Education. A Survey of the Users," *College and University Business*, February 1973.

3. J. S. Dyer, "The Use of PPBS in Public System of Higher Education: 'Is It Cost Effective?' " *Academy of Management Journal*, September 1971, pp. 285-99.

4. ERIC Clearinghouse on Educational Administration, *Program Budgeting and Cost Analysis*, ERIC Abstract Series, no. 5 (Washington, D.C.: American Association of School Administrators, 1970).

5. W. R. Duke et al., *Program Accounting and Budgeting Manual*, interim ed. (Edmonton, Alberta, Canada: Alberta Department of Education, 1972), p. 2.

6. Ibid., p. 210.

Selected References

Hartley, H. J. "PPBS: A Status Report with Operational Suggestions." *Educational Technology*, April 1972, pp. 19-22.

Hoye, R. E. "PPBS and Other Current Budgeting Systems for the Improvement of Instruction in Higher Education. A Survey of the Users." *College and University Business*, February 1973.

14. Strategies for implementation and operation of PPBS

During most of the 1960s PPB received mountains of praise. There was a continuing stream of exhortations for all units of government, as well as education, to implement this decision system. The enthusiasm diminished a bit during the early 1970s, but by no stretch of the imagination could it be said that the pressures for the establishment of program budgeting subsided completely. There remain pressures from federal, state, and local levels for the installation of PPB in education. Thus federally funded projects in K-12 districts, as well as in universities, often include a proviso that program budgeting govern operations. References have been made elsewhere to state mandates, and the demand from local taxpayers for greater accountability adds to the continuing promotion of PPB systems in education.

In general it can be said that although the pleas for the establishment of PPB may appear to be less dramatic now and criticism of the practices appears to be mounting, this is a temporary lull rather than the beginning of a contrary trend. Pressures for PPBS are more likely to intensify than decrease during the 1970s. The present period affords an opportunity to pursue the development of PPB in a relatively rational environment with less rhetoric to confound the issues. Of course, all this assumes that program budgeting has a significant contribution to make. It is argued here that PPB is a decision technology of considerable potential. It does give an administrator new capabilities. It enhances the probabilities of more rational and prudent decisions with reference to resource allocation at a time when the pressures to reduce school budgets without severely curtailing programs are more intense and long lasting.

Innovation in Education

PPB is an invention. An invention should not be construed narrowly as being confined to a physical gadget or a machine. There are social inventions, as well—for example, a unique teaching method, a new way of deploying staff members, or a new approach to resolving problems. PPB is a social invention. It is intellectual technology useful in resource allocation decisions.

Innovation, in the more precise meaning of the term, is concerned with the process of disseminating a significant invention. In popular terminology, innovation implies a new thing or invention as well as its diffusion in society. Innovation is better conceived as a process based on an invention. The goal is improvement. To summarize, innovation is a process of diffusing an invention with the hope of producing an improvement.

The diffusion of PPB in an educational system may follow general change models. In other words, innovating with PPB is not dissimilar from the strategies employed in disseminating other social inventions in educational institutions. Defensible change strategies call for the sequencing of related activities.

A number of general educational change models are in existence. A model of the innovation process was produced by this author in another publication.[1] It follows Dewey's model of the thinking process, as most others do. The components of the model are (1) disequilibrium, (2) conceptualization, (3) identification or design for invention, (4) experimentation, (5) evaluation (return to step 2 if necessary), (6) pilot programs, (7) diffusion, (8) successful installations, and (9) new balance or equilibrium.

Briefly, the search for a new invention is triggered by a "felt need" or a condition of disequilibrium within a system. Conceptualization of the problem facilitates the search for a new invention. If existing approaches fail to satisfy needs, the design, research, development, and evaluation of a new invention are set in motion. Assuming evaluation shows the invention has merit, pilot programs are organized to allow further "debugging." If the large-scale field tests are successful, they are followed by diffusion of the invention. It is hoped that this will result in successful installation and establishment of a new equilibrium.

Another educational change model, known as the Guba-Clark Model, has four stages—research, development, diffusion, and adoption—with a total of eight subcomponents:[2]

1. Research
2. Development
    a. Invention: formulating new solutions
    b. Design: engineering and packaging of the invention
3. Diffusion
    c. Dissemination: informing or creating widespread awareness of the invention
    d. Demonstration: presenting the invention in an operational mode to enhance its image
4. Adoption
    e. Trial: tryout or test of the invention in a particular context
    f. Installation: operationalizing the invention within an institution
    g. Institutionalization: complete assimilation into the system as an ongoing program to reduce it to the status of a "non-innovation"

The PPB change model to be used here is based on five major steps: (1) the *awareness stage,* (2) the *commitment stage,* (3) the *readiness stage,* (4) the *professional staff development stage,* and (5) the *operations stage.* Each will be reviewed in greater detail.

Stage One: Awareness

Before an institution can consider a change, there must be something to change to. This establishes the need for an invention. The invention in this case is PPB. In short, awareness must await the invention. The process begins by creating an awareness among various target groups that PPB has great potential. Within this stage are activities whose purposes are to stimulate, excite, create interest in, or communicate basic information about PPB. This has been done for PPB in large part during the 1960s by the various forces and agencies identified in previous chapters. Some argue that perhaps we have gone too far and that PPB is oversold. One would have to ignore professional educational conferences and cease reading, that is, live a comparatively isolated life, to remain unaware of PPB.

Rhetoric has its value in generating awareness. Hopefully the awareness will result in creating interest to move to the next stage, that is, from superficial understanding toward a search for greater depth and, eventually, commitment. In short, the goal is not simply to create awareness, but to generate interest in giving serious and favorable consideration. This stage is not likely to prove simple and short in the present environment.

Stage Two: Commitment

The commitment stage in the adoption of an invention comes when a decision has been reached to do something positive about it. The commitment may be forced on the executive by a legislative body. This has happened in a number of states where school administrators have little choice but to embrace the concept to satisfy legislative mandates. In other states, there is still room for individuals within the organization to seek approval and written commitment from boards of education to develop the PPB system in school organizations.

Although it sounds trite, there is vital importance in Wildavsky's statement that "the first requirement of the effective policy analysis is that top management wants it."[3] According to another group of writers, "the attitude of the agency head has been the single most important factor in the development of a PPB system and its integration with the agency decision-making system."[4] The commitment to install PPB in the Department of Defense came from Secretary McNamara, the top executive in that department, and it was President Johnson who issued a statement calling for the establishment of the system in all federal agencies. Strong support from the president did much to stimulate the installation of PPB in the federal government. Commitment is exemplified by formal written statements and related behaviors of the top executive levels. Commitment from those in lower echelons may supplement but can never replace a directive from the top. This should not imply, however, that commitments should remain at the top levels. Eventually acceptance must spread to all levels of the organization. This means acceptance from teachers and middle management personnel, as well as top executives, that PPB is a relevant invention and can contribute to the operation of the institution.

In educational institutions, written commitments from school boards or trustees, along with those from the superintendents and presidents, are imperative to the successful launching of PPB.

Stage Three: Readiness

The implementation of a complex invention like PPB cannot be successfully accomplished by one will alone, that is, a commitment from top executives. Strategies, or sets of action plans, are necessary to translate a commitment into reality. The organization must be made ready to embrace and operate in the PPB mode. This is a most difficult but crucial phase.

Realistic and feasible accomplishments in terms of available resources and capabilities must be assessed in both the short and the long range. How the dissemination shall proceed is yet another concern. The readiness stage is partially satisfied with an output of plans or short- and long-range strategies.

Another dimension of readiness is gathering the resources necessary to implement the strategy. Resources in the form of staff, space, money, and materials must be allocated for the purpose of disseminating PPB. Consultants may be needed and the authority to hire and funds to employ should be available by the end of the readiness stage.

In summary, the two outputs of the readiness stage are (1) the development of a set of implementation strategies and (2) the gathering of resources necessary to realize these strategies.

Stage Four: Professional Staff Development

Changes in organizations necessitate changes in the people concerned. Operations may be compromised if the staff fails to acquire new insights and operational skills. The discrepancy between promise and practice can be traced to human factors. People are the ultimate "users" or "appliers" of PPB in the real world. Very often resistance can be traced to fear that existing understandings and skills will become obsolete and that there will be little opportunity to gain important new ones. Distortion of a social invention when applied in the real world may be the result of inexpert execution among inadequately prepared staff members. A key stage in an overall change model is professional staff development aimed at helping people acquire needed skills and insights.

Skills and understanding of PPB among staff members may be gained through experiences in externally directed preparation programs, such as those offered by universities or other agencies. At the present time only a limited number of institutions and agencies offer opportunities to develop skills in PPB. The American Association of School Administrators National Academy for School Executives has been sponsoring PPBS clinics since 1969. Such experiences provide the entry level operational skills.

Internally developed programs help build greater insights and skills on the foundation of initial preparation. PPB skills are not gained in a single year. They must be sharpened over an extended period of time. More will be said about staff development later in this chapter.

The use of consultants may be part of staff development. A consultant is only as good as his experience and insights. This raises the issue of who is an expert in PPB. Some may claim more than they are able to deliver. It is imperative to know what a consultant can and cannot do.

Stage Five: Operations

Commitment, readiness, and staff capabilities increase the probabilities of successful operation. It is in the operation stage that the contributions of all other stages are tested. Thus, whether the magnitude of resources and the professional preparation program for staff members are adequate will be ascertained after operations begin.

Formal implementation begins with operations. This is where specific strategies become action programs. The two major operational strategies will be described in the sections that follow.

There are other implicit assumptions, namely, that PPB is a fairly simple system to install, that capabilities to operate in this mode can be acquired by all professional staff members with little difficulty, that a programmatic format for education either exists or can be imposed on the institution in a relatively short period of time, that the volume of research and other data needed on educational outcomes and the effectiveness of various strategies for obtaining such outcomes are available, and that unlimited resources will be on hand to translate the across-the-board implementation policy into reality.

Raising these issues leaves the impression that the author questions whether such conditions are likely to prevail in most organizations, and that impression is correct. PPB is a complex system to install. It is unrealistic to imply that institutions, which for years have been emphasizing activities and functions rather than outcomes, can in a short time be redesigned into a programmatic format. In the author's opinion, a meaningful programmatic format based on measurable performance objectives for all aspects of an organization may require many years.

Of no less concern is that most admonitions for schools and universities to adopt PPB have not been accompanied by grants of additional fiscal and other resources to get the job done. Innovations consume resources above and beyond regular operational demands. Special grants are needed to train the staff in new capabilities, to employ necessary consultants, to meet the initial costs demanded by all new systems, and to purchase necessary materials. Unfortunately, state legislatures have not seen fit to appropriate additional funds for PPB. The across-the-board policy for introducing PPB is more rhetoric than a feasible implementation alternative. It assumes that no experience is necessary to begin program budgeting. It should be recalled that the Department of Defense first experimented with this approach in the air force during the 1950s before introducing it in all subdivisions of the department in 1961. Likewise, President Johnson's Bulletin 66-3 came in 1965, some four years after experience had been acquired in one department of the federal government. As late as 1969 not all agencies and departments in the national government had implemented PPB, and those that had did not demonstrate equal progress and expertise.[5] There is nothing in the federal experience to support the across-the-board strategy, nor to suggest that implementation can take place within only one calendar year.

Alternative Operation Strategies

There are two basic strategies that can be pursued to actual operations. One will be called the "across-the-board effort" and the other the "partial-and-evolutionary" strategy. Each deserves further examination.

"Across the board," as the title suggests, means that all facets and programs of the educational institution will begin to operate in the PPB mode at the same point in time. It assumes that the complete installation of the system is feasible. Most state legislators make this assumption. Often laws mandating PPBS stipulate or at least imply that the entire educational institution will be operating in the PPB mode by a given target date, say next year or by 1977.

A more realistic operational strategy to pursue would be one based on a partial-and-evolutionary effort. Time lines would be established for the complete or partial installation of the system in departments of the institution. Program budgeting would start in the part of the organization or the specific educational program providing the best chances for smooth and rapid testing. It would be akin to pilot testing necessary for "debugging" of operations. Experiences gained during this "shakedown cruise" during one or more fiscal periods could be generalized, and the implementation extended to additional departments in subsequent years. Staff expansion, development of new capabilities, and resource consumptions would be far less than in the across-the-board strategy. It is significant that PPB is making the greatest progress in education, where federal or other funds are available to supplement local and state resources to implement the system.

The partial-and-evolutionary approach calls for the design of strategies to be used over a period of five to ten years. The initial challenge is to identify the program or the agency best qualified to serve as the pilot for the district. It has been suggested that PPB is more easily applied to relatively new program areas where objectives and target populations are more readily identified. In contrast, well-established operations have existed for a long time in nonprogrammatic formats, and a switch to programmatic structure may be a traumatic experience for many. As Marvin and Rouse put it, "new programs and old bureaucrats are often mentioned as major roadblocks to the development of PPB."[6]

In addition to the nature of the area selected, the willingness and the readiness of the professional staff deserve careful scrutiny. Attempting to implement PPB in agencies where professional staff resistance is high is to assume a gamble that could result in problems for years to come. The nature of the agency and the area itself are crucial to determining where PPB shall be piloted in the initial year and where its influence can spread to other agency and program areas.

The sequential steps in the implementation of PPB were identified in the previous chapter. It begins with identifying and clarifying the missions and objectives of the institution or given program and ends with recycling. This cycle may be used to enable any agency to identify where it is at a given point in time with reference to implementing the total system. A PERT chart may drawn with the milestones or significant events identified and the time of achieving each of these noted to help ascertain if a district is on target in implementing the system. Obviously, resources are demanded to get the job done, even though starting with one segment of the total institution requires fewer and more limited resources.

Whatever the operational strategy, there will be a period of time when parallel budget formats will have to be maintained. Laws may require the continuation of a line-item budget document or those based on functional character classifications as well as program budget documents. Some executives feel more comfortable if two parallel budgets are maintained for a short period of time. Many agencies in the federal government used a "two-track system," consisting of a traditional budget process in one track and the PPB system in the other.[7] This is a stopgap procedure and requires different kinds of documentation and budget exhibits for each track.

One signal of the acceptance of the program budgeting format is the discontinuance of a parallel set of documents using the more traditional and familiar nonprogram budget format.

Staff Capabilities for PPB

The importance of staffing in the implementation of PPB deserves further discussion. Having analyzed personnel in various agencies of the federal government, Marvin and Rouse conclude that the federal agencies most advanced in implementing PPB had "staffs which have had more formal education, more recently acquired training, have spent fewer years in the agency, and have had broader experience than the staffs in the less advanced agencies."[8] As stated before, change means modification of behavior in staff members.

PPB will call for new types of staff positions, that is, persons with unusual capabilities not required in existing operations. A central analytic staff is one illustration. To quote the study of federal experience by Marvin and Rouse, "the success of those agencies which have made progress toward the development of PPB has been attributed to the quality of leadership of the central analytic staff."[9]

PPB is an attitude as well as a rational approach to resolving the dilemma of allocating resources among competing services. It is imperative for the staff members in PPB leadership positions to learn new attitudes. It would be helpful if most would gain appreciation at least of what kinds of analysis may be necessary and the contributions of analysis to decision making.

Obviously, all key PPB staff members, and as many others as possible, must come to study PPB as a complete system and know it well enough to operationalize it. Teams of top-level managers, budget and fiscal specialists, and curriculum experts must study PPB together to make it an operative system. It was pointed out earlier that the federal government employs half a dozen or more institutions of higher learning to help prepare its staff for leadership and other operational modes in PPB. In 1969, one source estimated that there were in the federal government "2,500 full-time equivalent employees allocated to the planning, programming, and budgeting functions."[10] It would be unrealistic for educational institutions to assume that they are ready to implement PPB without first affording key staff members the opportunity to acquire the skills and insights necessary to operate in this mode. Keep in mind that staff members may negate, knowingly or otherwise, a new approach such as PPB by embracing the name but behaving as they have in the past.

Conferences on PPB confined to a single day merely whet a person's appetite and contribute little to skills in operationalizing the system. At least a week, and preferably two, of intensive training is necessary to understand PPB and all its dimensions.

The author had the privilege of organizing and staffing PPBS clinics during the early years of the AASA National Academy for School Executives. These proved to be very popular with large numbers enrolled from across the United States and Canada. The AASA National Academy also offers a second week in Advanced PPBS for those who want to probe further. Private consulting firms and agencies have entered the in-service development field for PPBS as well.

Staff growth in PPB understanding and skill involves visits to other institutions implementing the system. It was cautioned earlier that there is a great deal of disparity between what is claimed and what is actually practiced by those reputed to be operating in the PPB mode. Recognizing this will make the visit more profitable.

A general personnel competency development model was generated elsewhere and can, with modification, be applied to PPB.[11] Six stages of personnel growth in PPB competencies can be considered as extensions of stage 4 of the general change model described earlier in this chapter.

Phase 1 of the staff development model has three stages. Most of the activity takes place in the preoperational period. At least two different types of behavioral modifications are anticipated. The first is the stimulation of awareness and interest in the acquisition of PPB skills and undertakings. The second is the development of an entry competency level for PPB skills and concepts. This means that personnel know enough to begin contributing to operations.

Phase 2 in staff development also has three stages. It covers a rather long operational period spanning several years. During this phase staff growth through experience and planned development programs are continued. Full competency in PPB operations is assumed to be reached by stage 6. It can be recognized as attainment of truly professional competency level in PPB.

The general staff development model can be outlined as:

	Ground Zero	—	No PPB awareness, understanding, or skills
Phase 1	Stage 1	—	PPB awareness may be combined
Preoperational	Stage 2	—	PPB interest
	Stage 3	—	PPB entry level skills and concepts gained
Phase 2	Stage 4	—	PPB operational skills and concepts demonstrated
Operational	Stage 5	—	PPB skills and concepts refinement
	Stage 6	—	PPB professional competence achieved

The general model can be applied to specific target populations, that is, specialized talent groups within the organization.

Other Resources for PPB Implementation

Some argue that no additional resources are necessary for the implementation of PPB. Obviously this was not true, in one sense, in the federal government for the equivalent of 2,500 employees focused on PPB. The "no additional resources" position assumes that staff, money, space, and materials for PPB could come from transfers, that is, from other programs that are curtailed or discontinued. This is an argument for no net change in expenditures for the organization as a whole. It should not imply that no resources are required for PPB installation. The issue is whether the resources will come from new infusions of resources or from transfers.

Transfer possibilities are far more likely after the introduction of PPB than before it. If the wisdom to assess which programs could be abandoned without serious consequences already existed, there would be little need for implementation of a system seeking to produce more prudent resource allocation decisions. In the long run, the resources consumed while operating in the PPB mode could be offset by a reduction of expenditures in programs the system identified as failing to contribute to the organization's objectives.

There are a few in education who claim that PPB installation costs are insignificant or zero. This implies that no additional funds are necessary either from additions to the budget or from transfers within an existing budget. The experience in the federal government and other agencies supports the contention that this claim is illusory and based on faulty cost accounting or incomplete conceptualization of PPB. The author rejects it completely as an unsound way to proceed to implement a sophisticated PPB system. It is wishful thinking at best, and can prove most embarrassing to those who try it and are unable to add necessary staff or develop new capabilities as a result. It may generate a credibility gap, because more is promised than can be delivered. If one conceptualizes program budgeting simply as a sophisticated cost-accounting system, it could be argued that many schools and universities approximate this already. Then, the further extension of the concept would not call for significant increases in resources for the implementation of this version of "program budgeting." The fallacy in this is the inadequate and incomplete conceptualization of PPB. It is assumed that an operational PPB system is nothing more than cost accounting and unit cost analysis. Perhaps the largest consumption of resources in PPB operations occurs during the analysis phase. This dimension of PPB is omitted when it is viewed primarily as cost accounting.

It is stipulated that PPB cannot be implemented without the monetary resources to employ at least one individual, on a full- or part-time basis, dedicated to the development and implementation of the system. Additional funds will be required for consultants. This suggests that a minimum budget would be about $20,000 during the first year, a more realistic level being twice that amount for even relatively small districts. School districts with enrollments of 25,000 pupils or more and annual budgets of $100,000,000 or more should think in terms of three to five staff members dedicated to PPB and expenditures of about $75,000 annually. The issue of the minimum budget for implementation of PPB is pretty much a local situation. Variations are so great that no set figure can be ascertained at this time. There is considerable literature on the theoretical or conceptual side of PPB, but real experience is extremely limited, because of the very newness of the system.

Time is also a resource. An organization may move too fast in its attempt to implement the system across the board within as brief a period as one fiscal year. This is not an argument to do nothing because the implementation of PPB is too complex a task. It is possible to go too slow as well as too fast. The use of the systems approach in laying out realistic time frames is recommended for best use of the time element.

Information is also an important resource. Without a computer-based management information system the full potential of PPB may be hard to fulfill, if not impossible.

PPB is a means to an end. Obviously, if the effectiveness gain through the system is below the investments in resources made, it becomes difficult to justify operating on a cost-effectiveness basis. This is an argument that the very attitudes and precepts related to PPB can be applied to the procedures and strategies for its implementation. Costs incurred in the initial year should not be used to gauge future expenditure levels for PPB.

There is evidence of resistance among administrative staff members and even some within the ranks of teachers and instructors. PPB has been pictured by some as an inhuman system, similar to scientific management of another era. Some argue that it may introduce "a cult of cost effectiveness" and is therefore a step backward. Obviously, strategies for overcoming such arguments and demonstrating the advantages of the system are extremely important.

Implementation of PPB in the Federal Government: Case History

Bulletin 66-3 issued from the office of the president in October 1965 provides background data on how PPB was implemented in most agencies of the federal government (Bulletin 66-3 is reproduced in Appendix A). The bulletin begins with a statement of purpose and continues with a brief description of the range of "application of the instructions." The general "background and need" for a new planning and budget approved follow. The basic concepts and design of PPB, the "program structure," the "multiyear program and financial plan," and the "analysis" demands are then reviewed. The relation of the PPB system to the budget process with an illustrative annual cycle completes the detail for procedures employed.

Perhaps the most important sections of Bulletin 66-3 are the final two dealing with responsibilities and staffing procedures and the schedule for initial actions to be taken. The head of each agency was given personal responsibility for implementing PPB. There was a recognition of the need for specialized staff assistance as well. It is significant that a person responsible for development of PPB had to be designated within "10 days after the issuance" of the bulletin.

Administrators seeking to install the system in educational institutions might well consider a similar preliminary document. It could set the record straight for implementing PPB.

Several special kinds of documents were used in PPB operations in the federal government. These guidelines were described in Bulletin 68-2 of July 1967 (see Appendix C) and included three basic documents to be prepared by each agency for the Bureau of the Budget:

1. Program Memoranda (PM) in the beginning were prepared annually. These documents were supposed to contain succinct descriptions of output-oriented categories (programs) covering the total work of all agencies for the budget period. The objectives of each agency, alternatives considered, and support decisions taken were drafted each year for each program category and then incorporated in the PM. According to Merewitz and Sosnick, "The PM represent zero-base budgeting."[12] The PM were in effect a justification statement for the budget requests. They were to be limited to twenty pages plus a two- or three-page summary.

2. Multiyear Program and Financial Plan (PFP) tabulates data related to outputs, cost, and financing of agency programs placed in the framework of several and future years. The PFP, a comprehensive summary of agency programs, is done annually. It is similar to

what in education is sometimes called the "program budget." Emphasis is on the display of outputs, that is, a quantitative measure of end products or services produced by a program element. The present and future fiscal implications of decisions on agency programs contained in the PM are made in the PFP.

3. Special Studies (SS) represent further justification of decisions based on cost-effectiveness analysis of various programs. These are made normally whenever a new piece of legislation is contemplated.

In Bulletin 68-2 PPB was seen as a continuous process. Successive analyses were mentioned. However, program memoranda had to be drafted each year and submitted between February 15 and July 15. The program and financial plan was also prepared annually and followed the PM with the due date, in the Bureau of Budget, of September 30. Special studies are carried on continuously without regard to a target date.

The procedures in the federal government were modified somewhat in June 1971 and during the Nixon administration.[13] The early demands generated a tremendous amount of paper. According to Merewitz and Sosnick, "The U.S. Government quietly abandoned its compulsive version of PPB."[14] According to the director of the Office of Management and Budget, the PMs, PFPs, and Special Studies were no longer required on the previous schedule. The interpretation given by Merewitz and Sosnick to this recent federal action was that PPB was not being abandoned, but that the office "discarded program accounting, detailed description of activities, and zero-base budgeting, and it has restricted multi-year costing and benefit-cost analysis to expenditures that would represent new policy decisions."[15]

People bring meanings to terms. As a result a supplement had to be issued to Bulletin 66-3 to provide additional details on program memoranda and program and financial plans. The supplement to the bulletin appeared only four or five months following the initial one and was dated February 21, 1966. It is found in Appendix B. This was followed by Bulletin 68-3 dated July 18, 1967. It reviewed many of the same elements, documents, and procedures but defined each of these in greater detail, particularly the special studies. These bulletins came out of the Bureau of the Budget. One group of writers declared that officially the bureau supported PPB but in the "Bureau's examining units the attitude has been more ambivalent."[16]

It is evident that the federal government implemented the system through a series of top management decisions. It could not have been implemented across the board in federal departments without the approval, encouragement, and enthusiastic support of the president. Marvin and Rouse identify the following five factors in federal agencies that "made substantial progress toward the development of PPB systems for policy decision-making":[17]

1. Active support, both formal and informal, of the agency head
2. Skilled leadership within the central analytic unit
3. Perception of PPB as essential to decision making
4. Qualified staffs
5. Sufficient staffs

Congressional attitudes toward PPB are neither clear nor uniform. "Individual members and committees have expressed a variety of attitudes varying from a desire to obtain direct outputs of PPB, to advocacy, to curiosity, to skepticism."[18]

Implementation of PPB in Education

The limited experience with PPB in education and the confusion attendant on its interpretation make it difficult to find a satisfactory case history. It is much too new to offer anything of significance at this point in time. Unfortunately, most programs start and end with a cost-accounting system labeled "program budgeting." The implementation model in the federal government could be readily adapted to the field of education. There are glimmerings that some are beginning to move on the project by defining objectives first and then going through the various phases of a sophisticated system outlined in the previous chapter.

Hartley offers the following suggestions to educational institutions seeking to implement PPB:[19]

1. Familiarize both instructional and fiscal administrators with program planning as a mode of thinking.

2. Transform your present summary operating budget into a summary program budget display.

3. Compute detailed costs for one particular program to serve as a model for all other programs.

4. Identify your objectives for a program, describe the performance indicators (such as tests), determine present accomplishments, identify six to eight ways to improve results, cost out alternatives, and show how some options can be phased into the program budget over a five-year period. This is in one form of systems analysis.

5. Prepare Five Year Education Plans (FYEP) that include curricular objectives, pupil projections, staff specializations, classroom needs, revenue estimates, and program budget projections.

6. Modify existing budget procedures for program budgeting, but do *not* abandon the present function: object budget code.

7. Do *not* expect a consultant to define your program structures. He should offer alternatives, but the actual program design should come from within the local district.

8. Allow sufficient time, perhaps two years, to phase in a program budget format. A full-scale PPBS may require five years. A hasty installation might create more problems than it solves.

9. Continue most of the existing accounting procedures and internal control devices. Develop cost-accounting and data-processing procedures.

10. Make certain that the professional staff and the community are informed of the advantages of program budgeting.

11. Do *not* expect program budgeting to reduce your overall costs, even though program budgeting is neutral on the issue of cost reduction. This concept will help you to allocate resources in the most efficient manner according to explicit program objectives.

12. Be aware of the possible skepticism, resistance, shortcomings, and limitations that program budgeting advocates may face.

13. Keep in mind the distinction between a conventional function-object budget, which emphasizes objects to be bought, and a program budget, which emphasizes programs to be accomplished.

14. Develop an analytic capability (cost-effectiveness studies and program analyses) so that decision makers in the district can be provided with detailed analyses of alternative courses of action before making decisions.

15. Prepare memos, directives, pamphlets, and other publications describing PPBS in your district and inform your faculty of the advantages of this concept.

16. Staff meetings should be devoted periodically to discussions of PPBS operating procedure problems, long-range goals, evaluation criteria, new program proposals, information systems, pertinent literature, and analytic capabilities.

17. As in-house capability increases, the operational role of the consultant group should be diminished.

18. Be prepared to challenge the assumptions underlying your district's operations. A good measure of the success of the PPBS process is the amount of discomfort it creates until you come to grips with the most persistent questions in your district.

Ristau demonstrates a feasible approach to involving teachers in the initiation of PPBS in a high school business education department.[20] His experimental model included the five processes of

orientation, development, acceptance, pricing, and analysis. His results produced an "idiographic and futuristic Business Education
Model for Methods and Procedures in PPBS." His participants were
generally unfamiliar with PPB at the start, but "teachers indicated
favorable attitudes toward the program budget" at the end. Among
his conclusions were that "teachers will respond to opportunities to
assume leadership roles in PPBS and to involve themselves meaningfully in PPBS to help preserve those ideals which are important to
their students and to the professional educator." This case of implementing PPBS with teacher involvement may hold promise in situations other than business education.

Summary

The 1960s may be remembered as the high point of the rhetoric
surrounding PPB. Pressures still exist for doing something about it
even though the enthusiasm has lessened. Although the early 1970s
were relatively quiet, the forces stimulating the installation of PPB in
education are likely to intensify by the end of the present decade.

Innovation is a process based on an invention, such as PPB, and is
concerned with improvement. General educational models may be
used to outline a general implementation approach for PPB. The five
stages for a PPB change model include the following sequence:
awareness, commitment, readiness, professional staff development, and
operations. The times help foster both awareness and the establishment of a commitment to install PPB. The two major outputs of the
readiness stage are a set of implementation strategies and resources to
fulfill strategies. PPB calls for special staff competencies and staff
additions. Formal implementation begins with operations.

The two basic strategies for PPB operations are the across-the-
board effort and the partial-and-evolutionary strategy. In the former
it is assumed that PPB can be adopted almost immediately and in all
agencies of the organization. This approach is seriously questioned,
because PPB is too complex, most schools lack the staff capability to
move quickly, and few would have the free resources to meet massive
initial costs. The federal government started with a PPB effort in the
air force, then moved it into the Department of Defense as a whole,
and some years later to other agencies and departments. This is not
the across-the-board strategy.

The more realistic approach is an evolutionary one calling for
installation of PPB in one agency or single program during a single
fiscal year. With success the numbers could be expanded in following

years. A fully implemented and sophisticated PPB system throughout the organization could be achieved within a five- or ten-year period. That amount of time would be necessary to develop a programmatic structure for education and the staff capabilities needed to implement the decision-making technology.

Some states may keep a parallel set of program and traditional budgets and accounts for at least a short period of time. This two-track system existed in the federal government for most of the 1960s. A true indication of the seriousness of state laws mandating PPBS would be a willingness to dedicate resources to implement the system and the repeal of all budgeting and accounting demands for educational institutions that are not consistent with PPBS.

PPB will call for new types of staff positions and capabilities. A central analytic staff is essential. The federal agencies that have made the most progress are those with the better and more recently prepared staff persons. It is important for key administrators as well as program budgeting specialists to understand and have skills in PPB. PPB training is offered in a limited but growing number of institutions of higher learning. Agencies like the AASA National Academy for School Executives and others offer short-term PPBS clinics; visitors to others reputed to be operating in PPB should proceed with caution. A general staff competency development model is presented. It includes the six stages of PPB awareness: interest, entry level skills and concepts, operational skills and concepts, refinement of skills and concepts, and professional competence.

PPB requires additional resources. Additional funds will have to be allocated from new sources of money or by transfers from reduced or eliminated programs in the organization. The minimum budget needed to implement the system will vary with the size of the organization. It is suggested that no less than $20,000 be dedicated annually in smaller systems to employ the necessary personnel and consultant services to get going in PPB. A much larger sum of $75,000 or more would be needed for the bigger systems. It is possible to move too fast as well as too slow in the implementation of PPB. The argument that PPB costs nothing may prove true in the long run if it proves to be an effective system, but it is fallacious in the short run.

Procedures for optimum implementation of PPB start with assessing the forces stimulating the adoption of PPB and end with preparing a PPBS strategy. Determining the cost-effectiveness of a PPB system itself is desirable. Obviously the system should be able to produce a contribution valued more highly than the investment of resources required to operate the system. Time and data are other resources needed in PPB implementation. There is a danger in promising more than can be delivered, and for that reason careful planning of capabilities is essential.

The federal government implemented PPB through a series of announcements and bulletins from the president and the Bureau of the Budget. These bulletins defined the substance of PPB and activities related to it. They called for the generation of three basic documents: program memoranda, multiyear program and financial plans, and special studies. The head of each federal agency was held responsible for installing PPB. All federal agencies were encouraged to develop staffs with analytical capabilities to implement the system. About 2,500 full-time equivalent employees in the federal government were dedicated to PPB in 1969. Recently the federal government reduced the large volume of support material required in an operational PPB system, thus, multiyear costing and cost-benefit analyses were recommended only for new policy decisions, not annually for all programs.

Five important factors in federal agencies that have made the most progress toward use of PPB were: active support from the agency head, leadership in the central analytic unit, attitudes toward PPB as being essential to decision making, qualified staff, and sufficient staff. Congressional attitudes toward PPB are neither clear nor uniform.

The limited experience with PPB in education and the lack of common interpretation of what it is provide no desirable implementation case history. Some suggestions for implementing PPB in education are presented.

Notes

1. S. J. Knezevich, *Administration of Public Education*, 2d ed. (New York: Harper & Row, 1970), pp. 79-80.

2. Egon G. Guba, "Methodological Strategies for Educational Change" (position paper for the Conference on Strategies for Educational Change, Washington, D.C.: November 8-10, 1965).

3. A. Wildavsky, "Rescuing Policy Analysis from PPBS," in *Public Expenditures and Policy Analysis*, ed. R. H. Haveman and J. Margolis (Chicago: Markham Publishing Co., 1970), p. 473.

4. K. E. Marvin and A. M. Rouse, "The Status of PPB in Federal Agencies: A Comparative Perspective," in *Public Expenditures and Policy Analysis*, p. 452.

5. Ibid., p. 455.

6. Ibid., p. 456.

7. Ibid., p. 450-51.

8. Ibid., p. 453.
9. Ibid.
10. Ibid., p. 455.
11. S. J. Knezevich, *Strategies for Educational Change: The Wisconsin R & D Center General Implementation and Staff Development Models for IGE/MUS-E,* Working Paper no. 93 (Madison, Wis.: Wisconsin R & D Center for Cognitive Learning, 1972), p. 31.
12. L. Merewitz and S. H. Sosnick, *The Budget's New Clothes* (Chicago: Markham Publishing Co., 1971), p. 2.
13. Ibid., pp. 301-303.
14. Ibid., p. 301.
15. Ibid., p. 302.
16. Marvin and Rouse, *op. cit.,* pp. 451-52.
17. Ibid., p. 459.
18. Ibid., p. 451.
19. Adapted and excerpted from H. J. Hartley, "Suggestions for Installing PPBS" (mimeographed remarks presented to a PPBS clinic sponsored by the AASA National Academy for School Executives, 1970).
20. R. A. Ristau, "The Development of a Business Education Model for Methods and Procedures in a Planning, Programming, and Budgeting System (PPBS)" (Ph.D. diss., University of Wisconsin, 1970).

Selected References

Bulletin 66-3. See Appendix A.
Bulletin 68-2. See Appendix C.
Wildavsky, A. "Rescuing Policy Analysis from PPBS." *Public Expenditures and Policy Analysis.* Edited by R. H. Haveman and J. Margolis. Chicago: Markham Publishing Co., 1970, pp. 461-81.

15. Problems and promises after years of trying: why it doesn't always work

PPB is entering its second decade as an operational management system. In spite of efforts elsewhere, most of the experience encountered during the first decade was recorded in the federal government. It is predicted that the system will move forward during the 1970s to other levels of government and educational institutions.

If the enthusiastic endorsement of PPB in the current literature is any indicator, its proponents are numerous. However, PPB also has its critics, some of whom appeared early in its history. They were relatively muted voices then, but new ones appear more frequently, and their voices are more strident and insistent. Part of this chapter will be dedicated to identification and analysis of the viewpoints of the critics of PPB. They help to outline the unfulfilled promises, the problems, and the reasons PPB does not always work as well as it should. Much of what is found in the previous chapters documents the viewpoint of its proponents.

At this time very few, if any, educational institutions have implemented a comprehensive PPB system. Some claim to be operating in the program budgeting mode, but in most cases it is closer to performance budgeting with stress on cost accounting and unit cost analysis. The last portion of this chapter will be dedicated to a discussion of why a system with so much promise appears to be moving so slowly in educational fields.

Critics of PPB in the Department of Defense

The April 1968 issue of *Armed Forces Management* included an editorial essay entitled, "Is PPBS All That Good?"[1] It quoted critics or at least individuals not as enthusiastic about PPB as were Secretary of Defense Robert McNamara and his systems analyst Alain Enthoven. To illustrate, Senator Jackson's Subcommittee on National Security and International Operations of the Senate Government Operations Committee was quoted as saying:

> PPB may for the first time identify (cost vs effectiveness) techniques as a "system," give them a special name, and advertise them, but the approach itself is as old as the problem of the buyer who would like to make two purchases and has money only for one.
>
> Some of the more enthusiastic advocates of PPBS seem to suggest that it can work miracles in all corners of government. But it is no magic wand.... Even in Defense the benefits of the PPB system have been overplayed by its proponents. It is not a statistical litmus paper, scientifically sorting good projects from bad. It may be used as easily to rationalize a decision as to make a rational choice. It is no substitute for experience and judgment, though men of experience and judgment may find it helpful.[2]

Perhaps the significant elements of this criticism are that PPB is not really new and that it may be used to rationalize a decision as well as to help choose the most prudent course of action. The fact that this is an excerpt from a Senate subcommittee report is significant.

The same magazine quoted another source, Professor Thomas Schelling of Harvard University, who testified before the Jackson Committee as follows: "A ... point I would emphasize is that PPBS works best, and historically has been mainly applied, in decisions that are largely budgetary." Schelling spoke mainly about efforts to use PPB in foreign affairs and added, "there is genuine concern that PPBS and other techniques of management that are essentially budgetary or quantitative may be not only of less positive value when applied to foreign affairs but even, through their tendency to distort criteria and to elevate particular kinds of analytical competence, to be of positive harm." Obviously, any technique may be misused and result in harm. This is not confined to program budgeting. It is perhaps true as well that McNamara may have latched onto PPBS, to quote Schelling again, not "merely to cut waste and to improve efficiency or to save money," but also to use this process of budgeting "to exercise what he believed to be his authority over military policy."[3] Schelling argued further that while PPB may have worked well in the Department of Defense "foreign affairs (of the State Department variety) is complicated and disorderly; its conduct depends mainly on the quality of people who have responsibility; decisions have to be based on judgments, often too suddenly to permit orderly analytical processes to determine those decisions."[4] There can be no question that the administration of any complex institution, particularly educational institutions, may encounter occasions when there is no time for in-depth analysis and a choice of action must be determined very quickly. PPB can do little to contribute to such situations, other than to suggest a rational problem-solving procedure.

The same somewhat critical essay concluded, however, that "few of even PPBS' strongest critics contend the system should be wiped out." The main argument was "that the system's limited effectiveness means it must be used not promiscuously but with considerable discretion."[5] It is relatively easy to assess the cost side of the cost-effectiveness equation, but extremely difficult to evaluate the merits on the "effectiveness side."

Armed Forces Management cited some unfortunate conclusions made as a result of PPB.[6] These included:

> 1. Reportedly, for example, some dozen different studies of a PPBS nature done early last spring [1967] on what would happen if the Arabs and Israelis went to war all concluded that, even if started under the worst possible set of circumstances for the Arabs, there was still no possibility that a war in the Middle East would end in anything but an Arab victory.
>
> 2. The F-111 was a product of this new management system.
>
> 3. PPBS advocates, in praising this system, have consistently misrepresented the facts in comparing the alleged precision of supply support in Vietnam relative to the "excessive procurements" during the Korean War.
>
> 4. PPBS was given a lot of credit for canceling some unwise decisions such as certain missile development in 1961-63, but, the argument goes, these would have been made even without the system.

Political Scientists as PPB Critics

Political scientists represent another class of PPB critics. Perhaps it was the invasion by economists of what may have been considered a private preserve of the political scientists, namely, governmental operations, that triggered this criticism. Whatever the accusations, they are worthy of special note. Early among the professors of political science who reacted with some concern, if not negatively, to

PPBS is Aaron Wildavsky. The very title of his article, "Rescuing Policy Analysis from PPBS," set the tone of his attack.[7] Wildavsky argued that PPBS was destined to run into serious difficulties at the very time this decision technology was being installed in many of the agencies of the national government. Writing about five years later, he concluded, "there is still no reason to change a single word of what I said then." He further declared that the planning programming budgeting systems had inflicted damage "to the prospects of encouraging policy analysis in American national government."[8] He conceptualized the aims of policy analysis as "providing information that contributes to making an agency politically and socially relevant."[9] Wildavsky claimed in earlier as well in more recent writings that, "program budgeting would run up against severe political difficulties." Among the predominant reasons for this is, according to his claim, that *"no one knows how to do program budgeting."*[10] He further considered it "tremendously inefficient," in spite of all the paper pushing with the annual program memoranda and the program and financial plans, because "data inputs into PPBS are huge and its policy output is tiny."[11] It was his opinion that the entire system resembles a Rube Goldberg apparatus.

He softened this sweeping criticism somewhat by saying he did not "mean to suggest that the introduction of PPBS has not led to some accomplishments."[12] Nonetheless, it was his argument that "PPBS discredits policy analysis," and that the "shotgun marriage between policy analysis and budgeting should be annulled."[13] It was Wildavsky's point of view that, "if we are serious about improving public policy, we will go beyond the fashionable pretense of PPBS to show others what the best policy analysis can achieve."[14]

Mosher was also of the opinion that PPBS was oversold.[15] Another political scientist, Bertram Gross, spoke about the dangers of what he called "paralysis by analysis."[16] Others referred to the economists promoting PPBS in government as "econologists." In assessing the impact of management science on political decision making, White declared, "whether known as PPBS, systems analysis, or operations research (each claims the others as either offsprings or siblings), the application of these and related technology has caused much controversy in federal civilian agencies, just as it has in defense and industrial settings."[17]

McGivney and Bowles continued in same vein but were supportive of PPBS as a decision tool. They insisted, however, that "while PPBS is a significant breakthrough for assessing relative economic-resource costs and benefits, there are relative social value and political-power

costs and benefits which are not taken into the balance of accounts."[18] They concluded that "the uncritical disciples of PPBS
have tended to ignore politics and political process while its critics
have not attempted to systematically explain its utility to the policy
making process."[19]

Merewitz and Sosnick devoted an entire volume to a critique of
planning programming and budgeting as well as benefit cost analysis.[20] While recognizing that in places they were very negative, they
claimed to be "reacting against what seems to us to be an over-
abundance of laudatory and superficial discussions of PPB." Instead
of "condemning PPB" they were "suggesting that some attention be
given to the negative side before expensive decisions to proceed"
were made.[21] Quickly identified were some of the semantic problems
encountered by those who seek to understand the substance of PPB.
They observed, as has been noted in this book, that PPB does not
have a standard definition and can mean "different things to different people."[22] It must be said that the criticisms leveled by Merewitz
and Sosnick are incisive, rational, and in many respects refreshing.
They do cast PPB and its benefits in a more realistic light.

Schick viewed PPB as "part of a larger movement of revision in
political study and adjustment in political practice." He concluded
that PPB "has had a rough time these past few years"; "confusion is
widespread"; "results are meager"; "publicity has outdistanced performance by a wide margin"; and "bureaus have produced reams of
unsupported, irrelevant justification and description."[23] He recognized that the "main impetus for PPB came from the new decisional
technologies associated with economic and systems analysis, not
from public administration or political science."[24] Modification of
budgeting practices precipitates shifts in politics. To Schick, "the
politico-budgetary world is much different from what it was in 1965
when PPB was launched, and it probably will not be the same
again."[25] Today budgeting is systems rather than process oriented.

The intrusion of the economist and his way of attacking problems
into positions of political influence through PPBS has had an impact.
It may have occurred at the right time in history, for "traditional
budget processes are unsuited for an active presidential role."[26]
Traditional budgeting kept much of the operational decisions in
lower echelons where the details of control were executed. The
emphasis on objectives, outcomes, and long-range planning coupled
with budgeting and analysis brought top echelons into a more
dynamic position in budgeting once again.

Although Schick recognized the impact of "systems budgeting"
with its distinctive "analysis of alternative opportunities," he felt

compelled to state that "PPB is an idea whose time has not quite come." PPB concepts "which took root in economics or planning will have to undergo considerable mutation before they can be successfully transplanted on political soil."[27] In short, PPB was introduced throughout the government before complete development of concepts, capability, conditions, resources, and techniques was accomplished. As a result, PPB in the federal government was said to be less a "majestic scrutinizing of objectives and opportunities" than a matter of going "through the motions of doing a program structure, writing a program memorandum, of filling in the columns of a program and financial plan."[28]

Another group of writers quoted a 1967 government memo that concluded that if "PPB develops into a contest between experts and politicians, it will not be hard to pick the winners. They will be the politicians in the Congress and the White House."[29] These same writers disagreed with the above conclusion and stated that "if a contest between PPB experts and politicians does develop, there may be no winners."[30] The qualitatively different problem-solving styles of politician managers and systems analysts complement each other rather than destroy one or the other.

Less rational and meaningful critiques of PPB appeared from other quarters in the early 1970s. Perhaps it is to the credit of PPBS that the far right extremists consider PPBS "a threat to human freedom" or one of the "weapons for mind control." Those at this end of the political spectrum fear enslavement of man "by force or by economics." PPB was, by some strange thought process, equated with computerization of the student and the inevitable curse of "complete programming of human behavior." Such reactions are difficult to counteract because so little truth is enmeshed with so much irrational and emotional argument.

Less extreme are some groups of teachers who have taken issue with PPBS and are actively resisting its implementation in educational institutions. In some cases absurdly high implementation costs are quoted by teacher groups as the basic objection to PPB. Such objections lack the crisp and rational attacks of the political scientists. They exist, however, and would-be implementers of PPB in educational institutions must expect such expressions to surface.

Why It Does Not Always Work

PPB has its strengths, as the economists tell us; but it has its limitations as well, as the political scientists are wont to remind us. It does not always work as well as some of the more enthusiastic supporters suggest. To begin with, it is a complex system. It requires understanding, a disciplined effort, and well-designed strategies to succeed. Many of the reasons why it does not work were stated more positively in previous paragraphs. To illustrate, it will not work if:

1. PPB is inadequately or incompletely conceptualized.

2. Top-echelon administrators refuse support or only mildly accept PPB.

3. Inadequate or no resources are dedicated to PPB.

4. Staff members are unprepared or are poorly prepared to meet its challenges.

5. Not enough staff strength and/or special capability is available to meet the operational demands of PPB.

6. Implementation timetables are unrealistic.

7. Limitations of PPB in the political arena go unrecognized.

8. PPB activities become ritualistic and considered ends in themselves.

9. Resource allocation decisions are allowed to drown in massive paperwork.

10. An attitude prevails in the organization that it cannot work or contribute much.

There is no royal road to PPB. All rational and scientific approaches are disciplined attacks on persistent problems. They require new capabilities and discipline. Zeal to change is not enough, for it soon dissipates and discontinuance may be just around the corner.

A new management system such as PPBS requires resources commensurate with its potentialities. PPB is not a cure-all. If too much is expected too soon, or more is promised than can be delivered, it may well be doomed to being a short-lived system.

The glamour that surrounds a novel approach is fading. PPB must depend more on its ability to deliver now than on the fact that it is new or achieved dramatic results someplace some years ago.

The political factors cannot be ignored. PPB may be seen as a mechanism for redistributing power through a political system rather than a rational approach to resource allocation decision making. Shifts in power balance within an organization will be resisted by those whose status may be reduced in the process. This suggests that a significant factor in the implementation of PPB may well be the retraining of those now in positions of power to use the strengths inherent in PPB.

PPB is less likely to work effectively when goal conflicts abound. It may help sharpen the issues surrounding the conflict, but it cannot define objectives with a high degree of precision in such situations. A programmatic structure is essential. Again, if the organization or institution is difficult to program, the system cannot work.

In summary, PPB cannot work without a commitment, without added staff with new capabilities, without resources, and without an environment conducive to its operations. But this is true of any management system or any significant change within an organization.

In the most sophisticated sense PPB is a complex resource allocation decision-making system that has much to offer to organizations confronted with demands for accountability and wiser use of resources. It may take longer than most people realize to implement. In the decades ahead it is destined to play a significant role in institutions dedicated to education. It is imperative that executives, administrators, and managers of educational institutions understand the range of its contributions and its potential, as well as its limitations. Skill in the use of PPB is an important asset to today's managers of educational institutions.

Summary

PPB is entering its second decade of implementation in management systems. Its proponents remain numerous. Nonetheless, its critics have increased, and their voices have become more strident. Some of the critics were around when the system was inaugurated in the federal government. Others have appeared on the scene more recently.

A magazine dedicated to management in the Armed Forces recorded some negative as well as positive evaluations of PPB. The Senate Subcommittee on National Security and International Operations considered PPB to be no magic wand. They felt that the benefits of PPB may have been overplayed by its proponents. They did not consider it to be a substitute for experience and judgment. Another expert testifying before the subcommittee questioned the role of PPB in such agencies as the Department of State and in such areas as foreign affairs.

It was indicated from other sources that studies of a PPB nature made some rather questionable decisions in such diverse areas as the outcome of the Arab-Israeli war, the development of the F-111 aircraft, and supply support during the Vietnam conflict. Likewise, it was felt by these sources that the system was given credit for a lot of decisions that doubtless would have been made the same way without it. In all fairness, few of even the most critical persons in the armed forces felt that PPB should be abandoned. They argued that it must be used with discretion rather than promiscuously.

Political scientists have been critical of an approach developed by economists in an area long considered the domain of the public administration branch of political science. One political scientist considered PPB to be tremendously inefficient and argued that no one knows how to do program budgeting. He sought to rescue policy analysis from PPB. He stressed that, for PPB to succeed, the political climate had to be right for it. Since PPB intruded on the policy-making process, it was essential to recognize the political forces influencing its operation.

Another set of writers devoted an entire book to a critique of planning, programming, and budgeting as well as cost-benefit analysis. They reacted primarily against superficial discussions, lack of standard definitions, and overselling of PPB, rather than condemning it outright.

Yet another political scientist felt that PPB introduced systems budgeting that was destined to change the budget process for all time. He felt compelled to say that its results are meager and that confusion abounds.

More recent critics have appeared, some from the far right political spectrum. In addition, some classroom teachers' groups have taken exception to the system. These kinds of criticisms of PPB are extremely vague and lack the precise rationality of the cogent arguments found among political scientists.

There is a danger of promising more than can be delivered or of assuming that PPB, as a system, has no limitations. Reasons are given why it might not work: it is a complex system; it cannot be started overnight; it demands a commitment from the top level and throughout the organization; to work, it requires staff capabilities and adequate resources. In addition, it calls for a disciplined implementation system. For all the criticisms, limitations of the systems, and difficulties in implementation, this book ends on the optimistic note that as a resource allocation decision system, program budgeting has much to offer. It is imperative for executives, administrators, and managers of educational institutions to understand it and to develop skills in implementing and operating it.

Notes

1. "Is PPBS All That Good?" *Armed Forces Management* 14, no. 7 (April 1968): 32-33.

2. Ibid., p. 32.

3. Ibid.

4. Ibid., pp. 32-33.

5. Ibid., p. 33.

6. Ibid.

7. A. Wildavsky, "Rescuing Policy Analysis from PPBS," in *Public Expenditures and Policy Analysis,* ed. R. H. Haveman and J. Margolis (Chicago: Markham Publishing Co., 1970), pp. 461-81.

8. Ibid., p. 463.

9. Ibid., p. 462.

10. Ibid., p. 467.

11. Ibid., p. 469.

12. Ibid., p. 470.

13. Ibid., p. 472.

14. Ibid., p. 479.

15. F. C. Mosher, "Limitations and Problems of PPBS in the States," *Public Administration Review* 29, no. 2 (March 1969): 160.

16. B. Gross, "The New System Budgeting," *Public Administration Review* 29, no. 2 (March 1969): 128.

17. M. J. White, "The Impact of Management Science on Political Decision Making," in *Planning-Programming-Budgeting,* 2d ed., ed. F. J. Lyden and E. G. Miller (Chicago: Markham Publishing Co., 1972), p. 396.

18. J. H. McGivney and B. Dean Bowles, "The Political Aspects of PPBS," *Journal of Planning and Changing* 3 (April 1972): 6.

19. Ibid., p. 11.

20. L. Merewitz and S. H. Sosnick, *The Budget's New Clothes* (Chicago: Markham Publishing Co., 1971).

21. Ibid., p. vii.

22. Ibid., p. 1.

23. A. Schick, "Systems Politics and Systems Budgeting," in *Planning-Programming-Budgeting,* p. 97.

24. Ibid., p. 86.

25. Ibid., p. 78.

26. Ibid., p. 87.

27. Ibid., p. 98.

28. Ibid., p. 97.

29. As quoted in C. W. Churchman and A. H. Schoinblott, "PPB: How Can It Be Implemented?" in *Planning-Programming-Budgeting,* p. 297.

30. Ibid.

Selected References

Gross, B. "The New System Budgeting." *Public Administration Review* 29, no. 2 (March 1969): 127-45.

"Is PPBS All That Good?" *Armed Forces Management* 14, no. 7 (April 1968): 32-33.

McGivney, J. H., and Bowles, B. Dean. "The Political Aspects of PPBS." *Journal of Planning and Changing* 3, no. 1 (April 1972): 3-12.

Merewitz, L., and Sosnick, S. H. *The Budget's New Clothes.* Chicago: Markham Publishing Co., 1971.

Mosher, F. C. "Limitations and Problems of PPBS in the States." *Public Administration Review* 29, no. 2 (March 1969): 159-65.

Schick, A. "Systems Politics and Systems Budgeting." In *Planning-Programming-Budgeting.* 2d ed. Edited by F. J. Lyden and E. G. Miller. Chicago: Markham Publishing Co., 1972, pp. 78-101.

White, M. J. "The Impact of Management Science on Political Decision Making." In *Planning-Programming-Budgeting,* pp. 395-423.

Wildavsky, A. "Rescuing Policy Analysis from PPBS." In *Public Expenditures and Policy Analysis.* Edited by R. H. Haveman and J. Margolis. Chicago: Markham Publishing Co., 1970, pp. 461-81.

Appendix A.   Bulletin 66-3

EXECUTIVE OFFICE OF THE PRESIDENT
BUREAU OF THE BUDGET
WASHINGTON, D.C 20503

BULLETIN NO. 66-3   October 12, 1965

TO THE HEADS OF EXECUTIVE DEPARTMENTS AND ESTABLISHMENTS

SUBJECT: Planning–Programming–Budgeting

1. *Purpose.* The President has directed the introduction of an integrated Planning–Programming–Budgeting system in the executive branch. This Bulletin contains instructions for the establishment of such a system. It will be followed by additional instructions, including more explicit policy and procedural guidelines for use of the system in the annual Budget Preview.

2. *Application of instructions.* This Bulletin applies in all respects to the agencies listed in Section A of Exhibit 1. The agencies listed in Section B of that Exhibit are encouraged to apply the principles and procedures for the development and review of programs to the extent practical. (In this Bulletin, the word "agency" is used to designate departments and establishments; the word "bureau" is used to designate principal subordinate units.)

3. *Background and need.* A budget is a financial expression of a program plan. Both formal instructions (such as those contained in Bureau of the Budget Circular No. A-11) and training materials on budgeting have stressed that setting goals, defining objectives, and developing planned programs for achieving those objectives are important integral parts of preparing and justifying a budget submission.

Under present practices, however, program review for decision-making has frequently been concentrated within too short a period; objectives of agency programs and activities have too often not been specified with enough clarity and concreteness; accomplishments have not always been specified concretely; alternatives have been insufficiently presented for consideration by top management; in a number of cases the future year costs of present decisions have not been laid out systematically enough;

and formalized planning and systems analysis have had too little effect on budget decisions.

To help remedy these shortcomings the planning and budget system in each agency should be made to provide more effective information and analyses to assist line managers, the agency head, and the President in judging needs and in deciding on the use of resources and their allocation among competing claims. The establishment of a Planning, Programming, and Budgeting System in accordance with this Bulletin will make needed improvement possible.

While the improved system is intended for year-round use within each agency, its results will be especially brought into focus in connection with the spring Preview. It should lead to more informed and coordinated budget recommendations.

4. Basic concepts and design.

a. The new Planning–Programming–Budgeting system is based on three concepts:

(1) The existence in each agency of an *Analytic* capability which carries out continuing in-depth analyses by permanent specialized staffs of the agency's objectives and its various programs to meet these objectives.

(2) The existence of a multi-year *Planning and Programming* process which incorporates and uses an information system to present data in meaningful categories essential to the making of major decisions by agency heads and by the President.

(3) The existence of a *Budgeting* process which can take broad program decisions, translate them into more refined decisions in a budget context, and present the appropriate program and financial data for Presidential and Congressional action.

b. Essential to the system are:

(1) An output-oriented (this term is used interchangeably with mission-oriented or objectives-oriented) program structure (sometimes also

called a program format) which presents data on all of the operations and activities of the agency in categories which reflect the agency's end purposes or objectives. This is discussed in more detail in paragraph 5, below.

(2) Analyses of possible alternative objectives of the agency and of alternative programs for meeting these objectives. Many different techniques of analysis will be appropriate, but central should be the carrying out of broad systems analyses in which alternative programs will be compared with respect to both their costs and their benefits.

(3) Adherence to a time cycle within which well-considered information and recommendations will be produced at the times needed for decision-making and for the development of the President's budget and legislative program. An illustrative cycle which does this is described in paragraph 9.

(4) Acceptance by line officials (from operating levels up to the agency head), with appropriate staff support, of responsibility for the establishment and effective use of the system.

c. The products of the system will include:

(1) A comprehensive multi-year *Program and Financial Plan* systematically updated.

(2) *Analyses,* including Program Memoranda, prepared annually and used in the budget Preview, Special Studies in depth from time to time, and other information which will contribute to the annual budget process.

d. The over-all system is designed to enable each agency to:

(1) Make available to top management more concrete and specific data relevant to broad decisions;

(2) Spell out more concretely the objectives of government programs;

(3) Analyze systematically and present for agency head and Presidential review and decision possible alternative objectives and alternative programs to meet those objectives;

(4) Evaluate thoroughly and compare the benefits and costs of programs;

(5) Produce total rather than partial cost estimates of programs;

(6) Present on a multi-year basis the prospective costs and accomplishments of programs;

(7) Review objectives and conduct program analyses on a continuing, year-round basis, instead of on a crowded schedule to meet budget deadlines.

e. The entire system must operate within the framework of over-all policy guidance—from the President to the agency head, and from the agency head to his central planning, programming, and budgeting staffs and to his line managers. Fiscal policy considerations and other aspects of Presidential policy will be provided by the Bureau of the Budget in accordance with the President's program. Modifications will also have to be made from time to time to reflect changing external conditions, Congressional action, and other factors.

5. *The program structure.*

a. An early and essential step for each agency is the determination of a series of output-oriented categories which, together, cover the total work of the agency. These will serve as a basic framework for the planning, programming, and budgeting processes (including work on systems analysis, reporting, evaluation of accomplishments, and other aspects of management) and for relating these processes to each other. The following principles should guide the development of such output categories.

(1) *Program categories* are groupings of agency programs (or activities or operations) which serve the same broad objective (or mission) or which have generally similar objectives. Succinct captions or headings describing the objective should be applied to each such grouping. Ob-

viously, each program category will contain programs which are complementary or are close substitutes in relation to the objectives to be attained. For example, a broad program objective is improvement of higher education. This could be a *program category,* and as such would contain federal programs aiding undergraduate, graduate and vocational education, including construction of facilities, as well as such auxiliary federal activities as library support and relevant research programs. For purposes of illustration and to aid understanding, Exhibit 2 shows some program structures as they might be applied to two organizational units within different agencies; the same approach, of course, applies to the agency as a whole.

(2) *Program sub-categories* are sub-divisions which should be established within each program category, combining agency programs (or activities or operations) on the basis of narrower objectives contributing directly to the broad objectives for the program category as a whole. Thus, in the example given above, improvement of engineering and science and of language training could be two program sub-categories within the program category of improvement of higher education.

(3) *Program elements* are usually sub-divisions of program sub-categories and comprise the specific products (i.e., the goods and services) that contribute to the agency's objectives. Each program element is an integrated activity which combines personnel, other services, equipment and facilities. An example of a program element expressed in terms of the objectives served would be the number of teachers to be trained in using new mathematics.

b. The program structure will not necessarily reflect organization structure. It will be appropriate and desirable in many cases to have the basic program categories cut across bureau lines to facilitate comparisons and suggest possible trade-offs among elements which are close substitutes. It is also desirable to develop program formats which facilitate comparisons across agency lines (e.g., in urban transportation and in recreation).

c. Basic research activities may not be and frequently are not mission or output oriented. Whenever this is the case, such activities should be identified as a separate program category or sub-category as appropriate. However, applied research and development is usually associated with a specific program objective and should be included in the same program category as the other activities related to that objective.

d. To facilitate top level review, the number of program categories should be limited. For example, a Cabinet Department should have as many as fifteen program categories in only a rare and exceptional case.

e. Program categories and sub-categories should not be restricted by the present appropriation pattern or budget activity structure. (Eventually, however, it may be necessary and desirable for the "Program by Activity" portion of the schedules in the Budget Appendix to be brought into line with the program structure developed according to this Bulletin.)

6. *The Multi-year Program and Financial Plan.*

a. The entire process is designed to provide information essential to the making of major decisions in a compact and logical form. A principal product of the process will be a document, the Multi-Year Program and Financial Plan of the agency.

b. Thus, the process is concerned with developing for agency head review, and, after his official approval or modification, for Bureau of the Budget and Presidential review (as summarized in Program Memoranda, per paragraph 7c) a translation of concretely specified agency objectives into combinations of agency activities and operations designed to reach such objectives in each of the stated time periods.

c. The Program and Financial Plan will:

(1) Be set forth on the basis of the program structure described in paragraph 5, above.

(2) Cover a period of years, usually five, although the number will vary with the considerations pertinent to particular agencies; for example, a longer time span would be appropriate for timber production and for large multiple-purpose water resource projects. The multi-year feature is not to be compromised by the expiration of legislation at an earlier date, since extension or renewal, with possible modification, of the legislation should be reflected in the plan.

(3) Include activities under contemplated or possible new legislation as well as those presently authorized.

(4) Show the program levels which the agency head thinks will be appropriate over the entire period covered by the multi-year plan.

(5) Express objectives and planned accomplishments, wherever possible, in *quantitative* non-financial terms. For example, physical description of program elements might include the additional capacity (in terms of numbers to be accommodated) of recreational facilities to be built in national forests, the number of youths to be trained in Job Corps camps along with measures of the kinds and intensity of training, the number of hours of Spanish language broadcasts of the Voice of America, the number of children to receive pre-school training, and the number of patients in federally-supported mental hospitals. In some programs, it may not be possible to obtain or develop adequate measures in quantitative physical terms such as these but it is important to do so wherever feasible. In any case, objectives and performance should be described in as specific and concrete terms as possible.

(6) Where relevant, relate the physical description of federal programs to the entire universe to be served. For example, a poverty program plan directed at aged poor should describe not only the numbers receiving specific federal benefits but might well show what proportion of the entire aged poor population is being benefited.

(7) Associate financial data with the physical data to show the cost of carrying out the activity described. Cost data should be expressed in systems terms. That is, *all* costs—such as capital outlay, research and development, grants and subsidies, and current costs of operations (including maintenance)—which are associated with a program element should be assigned to that element. These component costs generally can be derived from existing appropriation and accounting categories. Where there are receipts, such as the collection of user charges or proceeds from sales of commodities or other assets, an estimate of receipts should also be included.

(8) Translate the costs and receipts used for analytic purposes, as described in the preceding subparagraph, into the financial terms used in federal budget preparation, presentation, and reporting.

d. The Program and Financial Plan as approved by the agency head will be submitted to the Bureau of the Budget. The Bureau of the Budget will also be kept abreast of significant revisions and updatings (see sub-paragraphs *e* and *f*, immediately below).

e. The Program and Financial Plan, as approved or modified by the agency head in conformity with guidance received from the Bureau of the Budget and the President (usually following the annual spring Preview), will form the basis for the agency's budget requests. Therefore, it should not be changed except in accordance with a procedure approved by the agency head. Appropriate arrangements should be made for participation of the Budget Bureau in significant changes.

f. Provision will be made for a thorough reappraisal and updating of the Program and Financial Plan annually. In this process, one year is added on to the plan. Other changes to the plan are to be expected from time to time and a procedure may be useful for making minor changes to the plan without requiring agency head approval.

7. *Analysis.* An analytic effort will be undertaken to examine deeply program objectives and criteria of accomplishments. Whenever applicable this effort will utilize systems analysis, operations research, and other pertinent techniques. The analysis should raise important questions, compare the benefits and costs of alternative programs and explore future needs in relationship to planned programs. The sources of data used will be many, including most importantly, the Program and Financial Plan, special studies done throughout the agency, and budget, accounting and operating data. It is important to have continuity in the work of staffs doing this work and to build expertise in them over a period of years. As expertise is developed, more and more of the agency's activities can be subjected to these analytical techniques.

a. *Special Studies* on specific topics should be carried out in response to requests by the agency top management, the Budget Bureau, or at the initiative of the analytic staff itself. Suggestions should also be made by line operating managers. The special studies may involve intensive examination of a narrow subject or broad review of a wide field. The broad program studies envisioned here will often be hampered by a dearth of information and gaps in our knowledge which can be filled only by project studies and other micro-economic studies. Nevertheless, these broad studies should be assigned top priority in the agency's analytic effort.

b. *Questions* should be posed by the analytic staffs to other elements of the agency on program objectives, measures of performance, costs and the like.

c. A broad *Program Memorandum* should be prepared annually on each of the program categories of the agency. The Program Memorandum will summarize the Program and Financial Plan approved by the agency head for that category and present a succinct evaluation and justification. It should appraise the national needs to be met for several years in the future (covering at least as many years as the Program and Financial Plan), assess the adequacy, effectiveness, and efficiency of the previously approved plan to meet those needs, and propose any necessary modifications in the previously approved plan, including new legislative proposals. Thus, the Program Memorandum should:

(1) Spell out the specific programs recommended by the agency head for the multi-year time period being considered, show how these programs meet the needs of the American people in this area, show the total costs of recommended programs, and show the specific ways in which they differ from current programs and those of the past several years.

(2) Describe program objectives and expected concrete accomplishments and costs for several years into the future.

(3) Describe program objectives insofar as possible in quantitative physical terms.

(4) Compare the effectiveness and the cost of alternative objectives, of alternative *types* of programs designed to meet the same or comparable objectives, and of different *levels* within any given program category. This comparison should identify past experience, the alternatives which are believed worthy of consideration, earlier differing recommendations, earlier cost and performance estimates, and the reasons for change in these estimates.

(5) Make explicit the assumptions and criteria which support recommended programs.

(6) Identify and analyze the main uncertainties in the assumptions and in estimated program effectiveness of costs, and show the sensitivity of recommendations to these uncertainties.

d. In sum, the analytic effort will:

(1) Help define major agency objectives and subobjectives.

(2) Analyze and review criteria by which program performance is measured and judged, and help to develop new, improved criteria.

(3) Compare alternative programs, both in terms of their effectiveness and their costs, old as well as new.

(4) Develop reliable estimates of total systems costs of alternatives over the relevant span of years.

(5) Analyze the validity of cost data.

(6) Identify and analyze program uncertainties; test the sensitivity of conclusions and recommendations against uncertain variables.

(7) Carry out systems analyses to aid in making program choices.

8. *Relation of the system to the budget process.*

a. Two products of the system will be utilized in the spring Budget Preview: the Program Memoranda (which incorporate in summarized form the relevant portions of the Program and Financial Plan) and Special Studies.

b. All annual budget requests in the fall will be based on and related to the first year of the current multi-year Program and Financial Plan, subject to such modifications as may be required by changing circumstances since the plan was last reviewed and approved by the agency head. Within this framework the detailed formulation and review of the budget will take place.

c. The introduction of the Planning, Programming, and Budgeting system will not, by itself, require any changes in the form in which budget appropriation requests are sent to Congress. Further, this Bulletin is not to be interpreted to set forth changes in the format of annual budget submissions to the Budget Bureau. Circular No. A-11 will be revised as needed to provide guidance on such budget submissions.

d. Over the next few years agency operating budgets used to allocate resources and control the day-to-day operations are to be brought into consistency with the Program and Financial Plan. Performance reports that show physical and financial accomplishments in relation to operating budgets should also be related to the basic plan.

e. The Planning, Programming and Budgeting functions are closely related and there must be close coordination in the work of the various staffs.

9. *An illustrative annual cycle.* Program review is a year-round process of re-evaluating and updating program objectives, performance, and costs. The annual cycle described below is presented for purposes of illustration and will be refined and changed over time. It is intended to identify check-points to assure that essential steps are taken and that current reviews, revisions and recommendations are given consideration at appropriate times in the budget cycle. Insofar as this schedule affects internal agency operations and does not affect Bureau of the Budget scheduling, it may be modified by each agency head to suit his needs. The illustrative annual cycle shows in outline form how the system would work after it is established and operating for an agency participating in the Preview.

January. Changes are made by the agency to the prior multi-year program plan to conform to Presidential decisions as reflected in the budget sent to the Congress.

March. By March bureaus or similar major organizational units within the agency will submit to the agency head their current appraisals of approved program objectives and multi-year plans and their proposals for (a) needed modifications, including measures to meet new needs and to take account of changing and expiring needs, and (b) extension of plans to cover an added year (e.g., 1972). The Director of the Bureau of the Budget will advise the agency head of any change in the over-all policies and objectives upon which the currently approved plan is based.

April. On the basis of instructions from the agency head following his review of bureau submissions, bureaus develop *specific* program plans.

May. Analytic staffs complete Program Memoranda. Agency head reviews program plans and approves Program Memoranda for submission to the Bureau of the Budget. He may want to assign additional studies on the basis of this review.

May–June. The budget preview is conducted by the Bureau of the Budget. The basic documents for this preview are the Program Memoranda prepared by agencies which are to be submitted to the Bureau of the Budget by May 1, and Special Studies to be submitted over a period of several months preceding this date. Presidential guidance will be obtained, where necessary, on major policy issues and on the fiscal outlook.

July–August. Appropriate changes to program plans are made on the basis of the guidance received and of congressional legislation and appropriations. Budget estimates, including those for new legislative proposals, are developed on the basis of the first year of the currently approved program plans (e.g., 1968).

September. Budget estimates and agency legislative programs are submitted to the Bureau of the Budget.

October–December. Budget Bureau reviews budget estimates, consults with agencies, and makes its recommendations to the President. Presidential decisions are transmitted to agencies, the budget is prepared for submission to Congress, and the legislative program is prepared.

January. Changes are again made by the agency to the multi-year program plan to conform to Presidential decisions as reflected in the budget sent to the Congress.

10. *Responsibility and staffing.*

a. Personal responsibility for the Planning, Programming, and Budgeting system rests with the head of each agency. Since planning, programming, and budgeting are all essential elements of management, line managers at appropriate levels in the agency must also take responsibility for, and participate in, the system. Responsibility should be so fixed that the agency head receives the recommendations of his principal managers (e.g., bureau chiefs) on program plans as well as on the findings and recommendations of centrally prepared analytical studies. Similarly, arrangements should be made for obtaining original suggestions, and views from other echelons in a manner consistent with the assignment of responsibility and authority.

b. Specialized staff assistance is also essential in all but the smallest agencies. Such assistance will be especially useful in the preparation and review of Program and Financial Plans and in the preparation of the appropriate analytical studies. Each agency will, therefore, establish an adequate central staff or staffs for analysis, planning and programming. Some bureaus and other subordinate organizations should also have their own analytical planning and programming staffs.

c. No single form of organization is prescribed since agency circumstances differ. Planning–Programming–Budgeting activities are functionally linked but it is not essential that they be located in the same office so long as they are well coordinated. However, it is important that the head of the central analytic staff be directly responsible to the head of the agency or his deputy.

11. *Initial action under this Bulletin.* The head of each agency listed in Exhibit 1 should see that the following steps are taken by the dates indicated. It is recognized that this is a tight schedule. Nonetheless, the President's interest in the prompt establishment of the new Programming, Planning, and Budgeting system requires that each agency exert every possible effort to adhere to this schedule.

a. *Within 10 days* after issuance of this Bulletin—the agency head should designate an official to be responsible for the development of the Planning–Programming–Budgeting system for the entire agency and inform the Bureau of the Budget of his choice.

b. *By November 1, 1965*—each agency head should have tentatively decided, in cooperation with the Bureau of the Budget, the broad program categories to be used initially in the system. Bureau of the Budget staff are prepared to make suggestions on these categories.

c. *By December 31, 1965*—agency instructions, procedures, or regulations for the Planning–Programming–Budgeting system should be issued, and a copy forwarded to the Bureau of the Budget. If is is not possible to have these in polished form by this date, they should be issued at least in such form as will allow the agency to proceed without delay on the steps necessary to produce the material required by May 1, 1966, with the more complete and polished instructions or regulations issued as soon as feasible but not later than March 31, 1966.

d. *By February 1, 1966*—each agency head should have approved the basic program structure (including program categories, program sub-categories, program elements, and the non-financial units for measuring program objectives and accomplishments in quantitative terms) to be used in the program plan.

e. *By April, 1, 1966*—a comprehensive, multi-year Program and Financial Plan should be completed for consideration and review by the agency head. The Program and Financial Plan, as approved by the agency head, will be forwarded to the Bureau of the Budget.

f. *By May 1, 1966*—for the spring Preview, Program Memoranda described above will be forwarded to the Bureau of the Budget. By this date or earlier, Special Studies will also be forwarded. More specific guidance and instructions will be provided by the Bureau of the Budget.

Exhibit 1
BULLETIN NO. 66-3

A. *AGENCIES TO BE COVERED BY THE PREVIEW*

Department of Agriculture
Department of Commerce
Department of Defense—separate submission for:
    Military functions (including Civil Defense)
    Corps of Engineers, Civil functions
Department of Health, Education, and Welfare
Department of Housing and Urban Development

Department of Interior
Department of Justice
Department of Labor
Post Office Department
Department of State (excluding Agency for International Development)
Treasury Department
Agency for International Development
Atomic Energy Commission
Central Intelligence Agency
Federal Aviation Agency
General Services Administration
National Aeronautics and Space Administration
National Science Foundation
Office of Economic Opportunity
Peace Corps
United States Information Agency
Veterans Administration

B. *OTHER AGENCIES FOR WHICH A FORMAL PLANNING–PROGRAMMING–BUDGETING SYSTEM IS ENCOURAGED*

Civil Aeronautics Board
Civil Service Commission
Export-Import Bank of Washington
Federal Communications Commission
Federal Home Loan Bank Board
Federal Power Commission
Federal Trade Commission
Interstate Commerce Commission
National Capital Transportation Agency
National Labor Relations Board
Railroad Retirement Board
Securities and Exchange Commission
Selective Service System
Small Business Administration
Smithsonian Institution
Tennessee Valley Authority
United States Arms Control and Disarmament Agency

Exhibit 2
BULLETIN NO. 66-3

PROGRAM CATEGORY EXAMPLES

Coast Guard

Present Appropriation Structure

General and Special Funds:

Operating expenses
Acquisition, construction and improvements
Retired pay
Reserve training

Intragovernmental Funds:

Coast Guard Supply Fund
Coast Guard Yard Fund

Present Activity Schedule
Vessel Operations
Aviation Operation
Shore Stations and Aids Operations
Repair and Supply Facilities
Training and Recruiting Facilities
Administration and Operational Control
Other Military Personnel Expense
Supporting Programs

Proposed Program Structure

Search and Rescue
Aids to Navigation
Law Enforcement
Military Readiness
Merchant Marine Safety
Oceanography and Other Operations
Supporting Service

PROGRAM CATEGORY EXAMPLES

Forest Service

Present Appropriation Structure

Forest protection and utilization
Cooperative range improvements
Forest roads and trails
Access roads
Acquisition of lands for national forests:

Superior National Forest
Special Acts
Cache National Forest
Wasatch National Forest

Assistance to States, tree planting
Expenses, brush disposal
Roads and trails for States
Other Forest Service permanent appropriations

Proposed Program Structure

Timber Production
Outdoor Recreation
Natural Beauty
Wildlife
Water
Forage
Minerals and Mining
Research
Other

Appendix B. Supplement to Bulletin 66-3

EXECUTIVE OFFICE OF THE PRESIDENT
BUREAU OF THE BUDGET
WASHINGTON, D.C. 20503

SUPPLEMENT TO BULLETIN NO. 66-3   February 21, 1966

TO THE HEADS OF EXECUTIVE DEPARTMENTS AND ESTABLISHMENTS

SUBJECT: Planning—Programming—Budgeting

1. *Purpose.* Bureau of the Budget Bulletin No. 66-3 outlined the concept of an integrated Planning–Programming–Budgeting system. Pending the consolidation of all instructional materials on the Planning–Programming–Budgeting system in a circular issuance, this Supplement is being issued to provide necessary details on two of the central documents in this system, the Program and Financial Plans (PFP) and Program Memoranda (PM). Both the Financial Plans and the Program Memoranda are to be forwarded by May 1, 1966, to the Bureau of the Budget by the agencies listed in Part A of Exhibit 1 of Bulletin 66-3. These documents will form the basis for this year's Spring budget preview.

2. *Constraints.* No explicit financial guidelines or constraints are provided to agencies. Each agency head is to recommend the mix and level of programs for his agency. However, the basis of program decisions is *choice* among alternatives, and assessment of priorities. Future federal budgets, as past ones, cannot provide unlimited resources—choices will have to be made. It is important that the Program and Financial Plans and Program Memoranda be prepared with as much attention paid to reducing and modifying obsolete and low priority programs as expanding others and introducing new ones.

3. *Program and Financial Plans.*

    a. *Composition.* Each Program and Financial Plan should consist of three parts:

    Part I will tabulate program output.

    Part II will tabulate program costs and other financial data, in a format paralleling that of Part I.

    Part III will include special tabulations.

The Plan will consist only of these tables, together with such brief explanatory notes as may be necessary. All descriptive and analytic material will be included in the Program Memoranda.

(1) *Part I. Tabulation of Program Output.* The Program Output tabulation will consist of tables showing agency physical outputs. Stub headings of the tables are the program categories, sub-categories and elements of the agency's program structure. All categories, sub-categories and elements approved by the agency head should be shown. Activities requiring legislation should be so noted. The column headings should be fiscal years—FY 1965 through FY 1967, plus FY 1968 through the last fiscal year of the planning period (FY 1972 in the case of those agencies developing five-year plans).

One principal indicator of physical output or services rendered will be shown for each program element. The output measure chosen should be that which is the most important single quantitative measure of program performance. For urban highway construction, for example, output might be number of lane-miles of highways built. For an on-the-job training program, it might be number of workers trained.

Using the on-the-job training example, the program output table would look as follows, assuming that the program category was "Manpower Development Assistance," the sub-category, "Manpower Training," and the element, "On-the-job Training":

	FY							
	65	66	67	68	69	70	71	72
I. Manpower Development Assistance								
A.								
B. Manpower Training								
1.								
2. On-the-job training (No. of workers trained—000)	XX	XX	XX	XX	XX	XX	XX	XX

In the majority of cases no single measure of output is satisfactory. In the case of the urban highways, for example, some measure of traffic-handling capacity might be needed as well as a statement of lane-mileage. Similarly, in the case of Manpower Training, some measure of the number of hours of training per worker, or training costs per worker, or the intended effect of training on earning capacity might be shown. In all such cases, the agency should submit, as part of the special tabulations in Part III, additional tables showing these supplementary measures of output.

(2) *Part II. Financial Tabulations.* The first tabulation in this part should be a Program Cost tabulation which will have the same stub and column headings as the Program Output tabulation. The total federal program costs shown for each year should be based on the system cost concept described in the Bureau of the Budget Bulletin No. 66-3. It should display the total agency costs, required to achieve the comparable output shown in Part I, whether funded through appropriations, trust funds, revolving funds, or otherwise. Where the accounting system of the agency is oriented towards the present appropriation and activity structure and is unable to produce program cost data with precision, costs should be estimated as closely as possible.

The cost tabulation for on-the-job training would appear as follows:

	FY	($ rounded to tenths of millions)						
	65	66	67	68	69	70	71	72
I. Manpower Development Assistance								
A.								
B. Manpower Training								
1.								
2. On-the-job training . . .	XX	XX	XX	XX	XX	XX	XX	XX

Totals and sub-totals should be shown for program categories and sub-categories.

The services performed by one agency for another should be reflected in the plan of both agencies. For example, administrative support services provided overseas to another agency by the State Department on a reimbursable basis would be shown as a cost in the serviced agency's Program and Financial Plan, and as a cost and an output in the State Department's Program and Financial Plan.

Data on the New Obligational Authority and Expenditure implications of the proposed programs need not be forwarded to the Bureau of the Budget, unless specifically requested. Such data should be developed in the form which is most convenient for each agency.

(3) *Part III. Special Tabulations.* Many agencies will be asked to tabulate revenues received, and to show major capital investment plans. For some agencies, tables on federal manpower requirements and sources of financing may be required. As noted above, it will also be desirable in the case of some programs to identify measures of program output in addition to those listed in Part I. The Bureau of the Budget will work out with each agency the special tabulations to be included.

b. *Other information.* Other information may be required later. The schedule for developing this information will be worked out by the Bureau of the Budget separately with each agency. Some of the tables in this category are:

(1) Tabulations of state and local government programs (or in the case of some foreign affairs agencies, foreign programs) and in some cases activities of the private sector (including federal corporations) where these are closely related to federal government programs.

(2) Program element data sheets—one for each program element—which will provide a brief factual description of each element.

(3) A crosswalk between the costs shown in program terms in Part II, and the agency appropriation accounts and other sources of financing, together with a reconciliation of total program costs under each source of financing to new obligational authority and expenditures.

4. *Program Memoranda.* Bulletin 66-3 provided that a Program Memorandum is to be prepared annually on each of the program categories shown in the Program and Financial Plan. Certain exceptions can be made, however. Unless specifically requested, Program Memoranda need not be submitted for any residual category; e.g., "General Support" or "Other." Additionally, where no major program choices appear to be open, or where a joint analysis of several program categories appears preferable, separate Program Memoranda may not be required. In each such case, however, the decision should be taken after consultation with the Bureau of the Budget.

The Program Memorandum for a particular program category provides the analytic backup for the programs described in the Program and Financial Plan. These Memoranda should serve as basic planning documents not only by agency top management and the Bureau of the Budget but throughout the agency. Moreover, they should be regularly updated so that at any given time they provide a current statement of agency objectives and programs. They will provide the focus for the Bureau of the Budget's Spring Preview.

On the basis of Bureau of the Budget comments and of continuing internal .agency review, these Memoranda should then be modified as background to FY 1968 budget proposals. The Memoranda, as modified, together with the decisions taken in the President's budget recommendations, will form the point of departure for the Memoranda to be submitted in the Spring of the following year. The Memoranda will thus be the focal points for the continuous development, refinement, and change of concepts and programs.

a. *Format and content.*

(1) Program Memoranda should be prepared in the form of Memoranda from the agency head to the Director of the Bureau of the Budget.

(2) Part I should (a) state the recommendations made, noting the relation of such recommendations to those of the prior year; (b) summarize the Memorandum, including the alternatives analyzed, in not more than two pages; and (c) include a copy of the PFP for the program category.

(3) Part II should present the factual and analytic basis for the program proposals. It should be a hard, quantitative analytic document, not an essay, and not merely a budget justification. It should (a) specify national needs in the area covered by the memorandum; (b) define the agency's objectives with respect to those needs in precise and concrete terms; (c) analyze the probable effectiveness and the long-term costs of the programs proposed to attain those objectives; (d) outline and compare alternative programs for meeting the same objectives; and (e) make clear and precise the priorities within program sub-categories and categories and state the relative emphasis among broad program categories. In the course of this presentation the assumptions and the criteria used must be made explicit. Where relevant factors have not yet been ade-

quately analyzed, they must be identified, and an indication given of the nature of the data needed or the studies still to be performed.

Where special studies or other analyses of particular pertinence have been completed, they may be made appendices to the Program Memoranda.

b. *Length.* There is no fixed requirement as to length, but thorough coverage of an important program category, including tables, will ordinarily take from 20 to 50 pages, single spaced.

c. *Method.*

(1) In general, there are more important questions deserving analysis than there is analytic capacity available to do the work. The Program Memoranda should focus on the central questions. In some cases these have been identified in the program issues posed by the Bureau of the Budget. Choices on which subjects should be given highest priority should be decided after consultation with Bureau of the Budget staff.

(2) The Memoranda should be as specific and as quantitative as possible. Broad, general statements of national needs, such as the "development of a safe and efficient civil aviation system" or the "elimination of poverty," though adequate for some purposes, cannot form a basis for analysis. The adequacy of specific programs cannot be assessed unless their goals are stated precisely—quantitatively wherever possible—and the time span for their accomplishment is specified. Correspondingly, specific goals should not be adopted until the costs of achieving them have been assessed.

(3) In many cases program analysis can be greatly assisted by a development of a formal program model. Such a model would show, usually on the basis of statistical data, the relationship of outputs the program inputs. All such models are simplified versions of the phenomena being described, but they help clarify the effectiveness of existing programs, and of possible new programs.

(4) The Memoranda must carefully identify assumptions. Some assumptions will be about facts; for example, the level of economic activity or the rate of family formation. Others will be assumptions about values; for example, the specific level of health to which our Indian

population should be brought. Some indication should be given of the degree to which alternative assumptions affect conclusions.

(5) It will often be desirable to analyze explicitly the effect on program choice of making alternative assumptions.

(6) It is often useful to discuss program uncertainties about future programs. In general, the further into the future a program is projected, the greater the uncertainty about needs and objectives—but also the greater the range of options. For this reason it may be useful to outline a strategy in which certain actions are taken now which both keep open future options and help provide the data or analysis needed to eventually choose between them. The reduction of uncertainty by data gathering, by research or simply by the passage of time may then make possible wiser choices than could now be made, and those choices will still be open because the decisions made now were designed to keep them open.

(7) Where estimates of effectiveness or cost are uncertain, it is sometimes illuminating to do a "breakeven analysis," that is, an analysis which compares the uncertain program with one on which there are adequate data. For example, an unproven mail sorting machine of known costs might be compared with existing mail sorting methods by calculating the performance which would make the new machine just competitive with the old methods. Conversely, if the mail sorting ability of the new machine were specified, one could calculate how much the Post Office could pay for it and be as well off as with existing methods.

(8) Quantification should not be attempted where it is inappropriate or meaningless. In many cases, the effectiveness of programs is difficult to quantify; for some activities, it is impossible. Even in these cases, however, cost can be estimated, and a more precise knowledge of program costs can provide a partial basis for the over-all judgments which are made in any event. As in the case of the Program and Financial Plan, all costs shown should by systems costs; i.e., all costs incurred in the production of a given output or service.

d. *Legislative implications.* New programs proposed in the Program Memoranda will often require authorizing legislation. The Program Memoranda should, where possible, outline the essential features of the required legislation including timing.

5. *Handling of documents.* The Program and Financial Plans and Program Memoranda will be submitted to the Bureau of the Budget in 25 copies. These documents will be handled in accordance with Bureau of the Budget Circular No. A-10, "Responsibilities with Respect to the Budget."

6. *Inquiries.* Questions on format and substance that arise during the course of preparing agency Program and Financial Plans and Program Memoranda should be brought to the attention of Bureau of the Budget examining staff for assistance and advice.

CHARLES L. SCHULTZE
Director

Appendix C. Bulletin 68-2

EXECUTIVE OFFICE OF THE PRESIDENT
BUREAU OF THE BUDGET
WASHINGTON, D.C. 20503

BULLETIN NO. 68-2   July 18, 1967

TO THE HEADS OF EXECUTIVE DEPARTMENTS AND ESTABLISHMENTS

SUBJECT: Planning–Programming–Budgeting (PPB)

1. *Purpose.* This Bulletin contains current guidelines for the continued development of integrated Planning–Programming–Budgeting (PPB) systems within agencies of the executive branch. It is not intended to change the instructions for the preparation of the 1969 budget previously communicated by letter to the agencies listed in section 1 of the Attachment, and it is consistent with the current revision of Bureau of the Budget Circular No. A-11. This Bulletin replaces Bulletin No. 66-3 and the supplement thereto.

2. *Application of instructions.* The Bulletin applies in all respects to the agencies listed in section 1 of the Attachment. It is applicable not later than January 1, 1968, to the agencies listed in section 2. Agencies listed in section 3 should prepare to develop and integrate their planning and programming with budgeting as fully as practicable, but specific time limits are not prescribed herein. Bureau staff will be available for consultation on the nature, extent, and timing of the application of these instructions to the agencies listed in section 3.

3. *Principal objective of PPB.* The principal objective of PPB is to improve the basis for major program decisions, both in the operating agencies and in the Executive Office of the President. To do this, it is necessary to have clear statements of what the decisions are and why they were made. Program objectives are to be identified and alternative methods of meeting those objectives are to be subjected to systematic comparison. Data are to be organized on the basis of major programs, and are to reflect future as well as current implications of decisions. As in the case of budgeting generally, PPB applies not only to current programs, but to proposals for new legislation. The budget is the financial expression of the underlying program plan. The budget review will therefore be conducted *primarily in program terms* for each agency to which this Bulle-

tin applies. It is essential that the Program Memoranda, Program and Financial Plan, and Special Studies provide adequate bases for these decisions. The budget, however, is submitted and must be justified to the Congress in terms of individual appropriations. The program decisions must, therefore, be translated into appropriation requests, and the relationship of these requests to the program decisions must be clearly set forth.

4. *Elements of the system.* The PPB system is built upon three types of documents:

a. *Program Memoranda* (PM) which succinctly present the agency head's major program recommendations to the President within a framework of agency objectives, identify the alternatives considered, and support the decisions taken on the basis of their contribution to the achievement of these objectives;

b. A comprehensive multi-year *Program and Financial Plan* (PFP) which is periodically updated and presents in tabular form a complete and authoritative summary of agency programs (initially those recommended by the agency head and, subsequently, those adopted by the President) in terms of their outputs and costs; and

c. *Special Studies* (SS) which provide the analytic groundwork for decisions reported in the Program Memoranda.

The Program Memoranda and the PFP are organized around a program structure.

5. *Program structure.* The program structure groups the activities of an agency into a set of program categories that facilitates analytic comparisons of the costs and effectiveness of alternative programs. Individual program categories establish the scope of the related Program Memorandum. The program categories should, therefore, be chosen so far as possible to permit a self-contained analysis of programs with common outputs or with common objectives.

a. The program categories used in each agency should provide a suitable framework for considering and resolving the major questions of mission and scale of operations which are the proper subject of decision at the highest level within the agency and within the Executive Office of the President. These program categories will not necessarily be consistent with appropriation categories or with organizational structures.

b. Normally, an agency will have between five and ten major program categories. Most program categories will contain one or more subordinate levels, called sub-categories and program elements. Some of the sub-categories and program elements will complement others within the same main category. Some may be competitive with others.

c. Each agency is responsible for proposing its own program structure and for reviewing it regularly and proposing its amendment where appropriate. The Bureau of the Budget should be consulted with respect to program structure and its approval obtained for changes therein.

d. The Bureau of the Budget will provide leadership in seeking to fit agency program structures into a government-wide structure. As progress is made in this effort, agencies may be asked to adjust their structures to permit achieving a comprehensive and compatible structural pattern across agency lines.

6. *The Program Memoranda.* Each agency should prepare a Program Memorandum (PM) for each program category.

The Program Memoranda should outline the broad program strategy upon which the agencies' plans and programs are to be built for the future years and provide background for the development of annual budget and legislative programs. They define long-range goals and objectives and anticipated program accomplishments.

a. With respect to the *annual* budget and legislative processes the Program Memoranda serve two major purposes:

(1) They contain the major program recommendations of each agency for the upcoming budget, and define authoritatively the strategy underlying those program recommendations. As such they convey the tentative program recommendations of the agency head, and also provide internal guidance for the preparation of the agency's detailed budget submission. For this purpose, the Program Memoranda must record all of the major program decisions within each category.

(2) In addition to showing *what* choices have been made, the Program Memoranda should make clear *why* particular choices have been made, by identifying agency objectives in a measurable way, and comparing alternative programs in terms of their costs and their achievement of the objectives. In short, the Program Memoranda should provide an *explicit* statement of program strategy, with the basis for major program decisions explicitly stated. The documents should be concise enough to be used directly by agency heads and by the Director of the Bureau of the Budget.

b. The basic PM should stand on its own and in no case should it be longer than twenty pages. It should be prefaced by a two- or three-page summary.

c. The treatment of decisions in the Program Memoranda may vary. Wherever there are major policy issues relating to a program, the Program Memorandum should, at least, identify the issues in terms of the alternative courses of action among which choices must be made and the recommended course of action. Wherever possible, it should summarize the analytic basis for the choice. Where Special Studies carry the detailed analysis and have been made available, a Program Memorandum need only summarize the findings, making reference to the study reports without repeating their contents. Supporting analyses may also be contained in separate appendices to the basic PM.

d. The limits imposed by the availability of analytic staff resources or other circumstances may in some cases make ,it impossible to provide full treatment of alternatives and their analysis in each Program Memorandum. Such instances will diminish as the PPB system is developed. Nevertheless, since the Program Memoranda are to constitute the principal basis for major program decisions in the budget review process, it is essential that such decisions in each program category be recorded in the PM and that the reason for the decisions be stated. Minor decisions will, of course, be reflected in the PFP and all decisions will be reflected in the appropriation requests. This selectivity will not only produce desirable brevity in the Program Memorandum, but will also permit the focusing of the limited number of studies that can be done on the issues where they can have the greatest effect.

e. When a program is an experimental one or a demonstration, the PM should clearly identify this fact. If it is necessary to proceed for more than one year on an experimental or demonstration basis, the PM should indicate why a decision to start a full-scale program is being postponed, what is being done to reach a conclusion on expansion or termination, and the date when a decision is expected.

f. The PM should deal explicitly with the legislative implications of the alternatives presented in it.

7. *Multi-year Program and Financial Plan.* The PFP presents in tabular form, and for a period of several years, pertinent data relating to the outputs, cost, and financing of agency programs. These data are to be presented in a set of tables that reflect the decisions on agency programs contained in the Program Memoranda as well as minor program decisions not set forth there. The PFP should show the future implications of current decisions. The output and costs are to be shown for each program element, grouped in terms of the program structure by category and sub-category, and for each year of the planning period covered by the PFP—the fiscal year just past, the current year, and the budget year, plus at least four future years.

a. *Presentation of future year data.* The years beyond the budget year are included primarily to show the future implications of current (past and present) decisions. This projection, therefore, is not designed to predict comprehensively future budget totals for agencies or for major programs.

(1) This approach permits, on the output side, a showing of the expected results of development or demonstration projects and the fruition of multi-year investment projects; and, on the cost side, a reflection of future requirements that are the results of program decisions for the budget year. For current decision-making purposes, this will make a more effective presentation where program levels are prescribed by law, where a program involves investments and future operating costs spread over several years, where program levels are determined by factors outside government control (such as increases in population), or where a program is undertaken as an experiment or demonstration to provide a basis for future program decisions.

In the latter case, the PFP should identify, by a footnote, the year in which the next decision will be required on the program. Thus, if the current decision does not provide for full-scale operation of a program, costs and outputs should not be projected beyond the next decision point. (For major program decisions, the expected cost and output of the full-scale program, the evidence being accumulated to warrant expansion or termination, as well as the timing of the next decision point should, of course, be discussed in the PM.)

(2) Where an existing program is expected to continue throughout the planning period, but no decision has been made as to its future level, it should be shown at its current levels unless (a) mandatory or built-in changes are required under existing law, by uncontrollable workload, or by demographic or other factors, or (b) explicit justification for some other pattern is provided in the Program Memorandum (or if the decision is a minor one, reflected succinctly in a footnote to the PFP).

(3) The PFP therefore is to show the implications of current decisions and will not necessarily reflect accurate estimates of agency budget totals for the years beyond the budget year, because it omits new programs not yet recommended and fails to reflect program level changes, including the termination of some existing programs, decisions which are not part of the current budget cycle. The fact that the PFP is designed to show the future implications of current decisions is *not* meant to imply that in Program Memoranda or Special Studies, or for their own internal use, agencies should not develop and evaluate alternative individual program policies, costs, and outputs for a five-year period. They are encouraged to do so. The PFP, itself, however, is meant to be a record of the present and future budgetary and output consequences of the current year's decisions. In brief, the long-run program strategy outlined and analyzed in the Program Memoranda need not—and in many cases should not—be confined to decisions taken in the coming budget. The data shown in the PFP, however, should.

b. *Outputs.* Table I of the PFP will display outputs—that is, a quantitative measure of end products or services produced by a program element. Where it is meaningful to do so, outputs should be aggregated by sub-category and category of the program structure.

(1) Outputs by program element in Table I are to reflect the best measure of what is produced by that element. Outputs will not necessarily measure the achievement of a program objective, nor the benefits of the program. Such measures are vital to the PPB process—they should be identified as soon as practicable, and should be given full considera-

tion in the Program Memoranda and Special Studies. Wherever meaningful measures of achievement and effectiveness are available for a program, the PFP should display them either on a separate line in Table I, properly identified, or by means of a supplementary table. In certain cases, such as research programs, where meaningful measures of output cannot be defined, the best available quantitative non-financial descriptions of the program should be used (e.g., the number of projects initiated, continued, and completed, number of research workers engaged, or the number of researchers trained).

(2) In some cases—a recreation program, for example—costs in the PFP may best be related to the capacity of proposed recreation facilities, and this might serve as the best output measure. Attainment of the objective of the program, however, may best be shown by a measure of the use of the facilities—which is an important factor for decision-making on the program. Both of these measures, therefore, are relevant and appropriate for presentation.

(3) In the case of an on-the-job training effort, the simplest measure of output in relation to cost might be the number of workers trained, or the student weeks of training supplied. The number of workers trained might also have added significance since it may reflect the diminution of dependence on public assistance. But the ultimate purpose of the program presumably is to improve the earning capacity of the worker trained. The best measure of the success of the effort, therefore, might be the increase in income that results from the training. It is possible that a program which showed "low output"—in terms of the numbers of workers trained—might be more effective on this criterion because it was better taught, or focused on skills in shorter supply, than a program that showed a higher "output."

(4) In short, where objectives are complex, as they often are for government programs, it may be impossible to find a single, conceptually clear output measure that will satisfy all the needs of decision-making on a program. Basically, the PFP should show measures of what is produced as a result of a program effort, supplemented where appropriate by one or two other measures of achievement and effectiveness, with the relationship of these measures and the pertinent costs explained in the PM's and Special Studies.

c. *Costs.* Parallel to the display of output in Table I, Table II of the PFP presents a tabular statement of financial requirements in terms of program costs to be incurred for program activities. In addition to the display of program costs for each program element, the NOA requirements for the budget year for each program category should be set forth. Differences between budget year NOÁ and program cost that are greater than 10 per cent of the larger item should be explained in a footnote. The definitions of "program cost" and "NOA" are those established by Circular No. A-11 for the program and financing schedules in the budget appendix. (Agencies desiring to use any other financial concept in lieu of program costs should consult the Bureau of the Budget.)

(1) The financial data presented in the PFP for each program element should reflect total program costs inclusive of the program-oriented research and development, investment, and operating costs required to produce the ouptut shown in Table I. Where there exists a significant difference between the total program costs and the costs funded by the particular federal agency, both the cost to the given agency and the total net cost to other agencies, other units of government, the private sector, or other sources, should be identified and shown in three separate lines—one for the given agency, one for other federal agencies, and the third for all other sources.

(2) For programs financed with earmarked receipts or with their own generated receipts, such as loan programs, government corporation activities, and revolving funds, Table II of the PFP should show the total level of resources committed or applied, as well as cost to the government and obligational authority. In difficult or unusual cases, the agency should consult with the Bureau of the Budget on this display.

(3) It should be noted that costs in the PFP are defined in a more limited sense than the costs which may—and usually should—be utilized in the Program Memoranda or in Special Studies. For decision-making purposes, the analysis of a problem should include the consideration of economic opportunity costs, marginal costs, and systems costs.

(4) For the year immediately past, the presentation is to be based upon cost data that are adequately supported in the agency accounting system. Where the maintenance of specific accounts for program classifications is not justified as an efficient and practical approach, cost

data for the past year may be developed through cost allocation or analysis techniques: in such cases there should be a technical note appended to the PFP to indicate the techniques used. Cost distribution practices should be so developed as to provide a suitable basis for program decisions and to provide to the managers concerned reliable information that will permit them to evaluate results actually obtained in relation to the resource allocation decisions made under PPB.

d. *Reconciliation of program costs to appropriations.* The PFP will include as Table III a reconciliation—a "cross-walk"—of the NOA shown for the budget year in the PFP, with NOA estimates by appropriation and fund account. However, this table need not necessarily go to the level of program element; and translation can be done at the level of program category or sub-category, whichever is appropriate. Similarly, for this purpose, appropriations of funds which are grouped into a single "building block" under Circular No. A-11 (for example, certain relatively inactive accounts) may also be so grouped for the purposes of this tabulation. The purpose is to provide a reconciliation between program costs and the budget submission, sufficient to insure that the budget submission is consistent with the intent of the program decisions. The PFP constitutes a link between the marginal systems costs in the PM that are pertinent to decision-making, and the financing needed to carry out programs.

8. *Special Studies.* Special Studies are a vital element of PPB. By providing the analytic basis for decisions on program issues in the PM, they determine the quality of the PPB system's contribution to the decision-making process. Special Studies will, in general, formulate and review program objectives in terms useful for making program comparisons; they will review in terms of costs and benefits the effectiveness of prior efforts, compare alternative mixes of programs, balance increments in costs against increments in effectiveness at various program levels with attention to diminishing returns and limitations of physical resources, and assess the incidence of benefits and costs as well as their totals. Normally, a Special Study will not be co-extensive with a program category. Most will deal with specific phases of a program; some studies will cut across program category lines. In every case a Special Study will contain specific recommendations for future action. There is no fixed length or format for Special Studies.

A Special Study should normally be made whenever a proposal for major new legislation is involved. Such a study should spell out the purposes, costs, and expected accomplishments under the legislation, and the alternatives considered for accomplishment of the purpose.

9. *Timing for production of documents.* PPB is a continuous process. The analytic work cannot produce once-and-for-all answers. Successive analyses should assist in producing successively better government decisions and in responding to new initiatives and changing circumstances. The decisions to which PPB contributes are basically incorporated in two annual processes—the annual executive budget of the government and the annual legislative program of the President. Consequently, it is necessary that the preparation and presentation of PPB documents fit the schedules for these two processes. Similarly, the documentation under this instruction should be coordinated with and be consistent with the submissions made under Circular No. A-11 on the budget and Circular No. A-19 on legislation. In fact, the PM and the PFP are integral parts of each covered agency's budget submissions.

The timing for the major documents is as follows:

a. *Program Memoranda.* Program Memoranda will be drafted each year for each program category. The Bureau of the Budget will identify well in advance certain issues it may wish to have especially considered. The Bureau of the Budget will also generally indicate a staggered schedule of dates for the submission of draft Program Memoranda, usually over the period from February 15 through July 15. The draft Program Memoranda should contain or be accompanied by tables showing for the planning period the output and cost data covering at least the major issues dealt with in the PM for the given program category.

Wherever possible, the Bureau will respond to the draft PM with comments on recommendations and supporting rationale. Revisions should then be made in the PM to reflect the agency head's consideration of the Bureau's comments and to reflect any further developments in the agency analysis. The PM should then be submitted in final form by September 30.

b. *Program and Financial Plan.* The Program and Financial Plan is to be prepared annually and transmitted to the Bureau by September 30. It should be consistent with the Program Memoranda and the rest of the budget submission which is due at the same time.

The PFP should be revised as necessary for use within the agency to reflect major changes in the program plans taking place, but submission of any such revised PFP to the Bureau of the Budget is not required as a routine matter. The PFP should be revised for consistency with the President's budget in January. Where congressional action on the agency budget is completed appreciably ahead of September 30, a further revision would be appropriate to reflect such action.

c. *Special Studies.* Agencies should maintain a continuing program of Special Studies. These may extend over more than one year of the budget cycle and need not follow a uniform time pattern.

(1) A list of Special Studies contemplated by the agency should be submitted to the Bureau of the Budget not later than January 15, covering the new calendar year. The Bureau may make additional suggestions with reference to proposed studies, giving particular emphasis to studies which may be needed for the forthcoming budget cycle each year, and the dates by which such studies should be submitted. Special studies requested by the Bureau, and such others as the agency head believes appropriate for submission, should be forwarded to the Bureau as soon as they have been reviewed by the agency head. The Bureau of the Budget will give substantive and technical comment as promptly as feasible.

(2) Draft Program Memoranda and Special Studies should be submitted to the Bureau of the Budget in six copies, or such other number as may be requested by Bureau representatives. Each final PM and PFP should be submitted in the same number as is specified in Circular No. A-11 for annual budget submissions, or in such other number as Bureau of the Budget representatives may specify.

10. *Illustrative annual cycle.* In summary, a typical annual cycle is as follows:

September: Agency submits PM's in final form, PFP's, the annual budget, and the annual legislative program to the Bureau of the Budget.

October–   Bureau reviews and recommends to the President; Presi-
December: dential decisions made and communicated to the agency.

January:	Executive budget is presented to the Congress; major elements in the legislative program are indicated in the State of the Union message, the budget message, the economic report, or in other communications to Congress.
January:	Agency reviews special study program and submits proposed list for the calendar year to the Bureau.
January:	Agency updates the PFP to conform to the executive budget.
February:	Bureau indicates to agency its request for Special Studies and for issues to be covered in Program Memoranda during the upcoming budget cycle.
February–July:	Agency brings Special Studies to completion and prepares drafts of Program Memoranda.
April–August:	Budget Bureau responds on Special Studies and draft Program Memoranda.
July–September:	Agency head makes final decisions on his program recommendations; agency revises draft Program Memoranda; agency updates PFP, adding one year and making it conform to agency head recommendations.
Year around:	Special Studies are begun, carried on and completed, as appropriate.

11. *Responsibility, staffing and training.* Responsibility for the development and use of Planning-Programming-Budgeting systems rests with the head of each agency. Since planning, programming and budgeting are all essential elements of management, it is necessary that line managers at appropriate levels participate in the system. Management responsibility should be so fixed that the agency head receives the recommendations of his principal managers on all major program issues. It may be desirable to provide principal managers with small analytic staffs to insure their meaningful participation in Special Studies and other analytic work. Similar arrangements for obtaining the views of other echelons may be made, consistent with the agency's assignment of responsibility.

a. Whether or not analytic staffs are provided the principal managers, each agency should establish a specialized analytic staff reporting directly to the agency head or to his deputy. The principal duties of this staff will be to coordinate the analytic and planning work done in the subordinate bureaus or other organizations of the agency; to initiate and conduct Special Studies; where appropriate, to provide first drafts of Program Memoranda; and to supervise or monitor research for program analysis.

b. Each agency should take such action as is needed to provide, within the management system of the agency, for an automatic provision of pertinent data on the results of the resource allocation decisions made under PPB. Agency information systems should be designed to provide timely data on outputs and costs in budget execution—suited to the needs of the managers concerned with agency programs—so that programs may be effectively carried out according to plans and related operating budgets, and to provide information useful for planning and programming in the next cycle of operations.

c. To make PPB a fully effective system, a general understanding of the methods and purposes of PPB must be created throughout the agencies. Agencies are, therefore, encouraged both to make maximum use of the various training and educational programs offered through the Civil Service Commission, and also to establish their own internal orientation and training courses.

CHARLES L. SCHULTZE
Director

Attachment

Section 1
 Department of Agriculture
 Department of Commerce
 Department of Defense—separate submission for:
  Military functions (including Civil Defense)
  Corps of Engineers, Civil functions
 Department of Health, Education, and Welfare
 Department of Housing and Urban Development
 Department of the Interior
 Department of Justice

Department of Labor
Post Office Department
Department of State (excluding Agency for International
    Development)
Department of Transportation
Department of the Treasury
Agency for International Development
Atomic Energy Commission
Central Intelligence Agency
General Services Administration
National Aeronautics and Space Administration
National Science Foundation
Office of Economic Opportunity
Peace Corps
United States Information Agency
Veterans Administration

Section 2

Civil Service Commission
Federal Communications Commission
Federal Power Commission
Federal Trade Commission
Interstate Commerce Commission
Securities and Exchange Commission
Small Business Administration
Tennessee Valley Authority

Section 3

Export-Import Bank of Washington
Federal Home Loan Bank Board
Federal Mediation and Conciliation Service
National Labor Relations Board
Railroad Retirement Board
Selective Service System

PPBS and systems management glossary

ACCOUNT. A specific financial record containing information on a resource or a financial transaction related to a specific asset, liability, expenditure, budgetary item, etc., identified within its title.

ACCOUNTING. The process of classifying data for record keeping: the system of classifying and summarizing financial receipts, expenditures, and related transactions.

ACRONYM. A "word" formed from the first letters of a series of words. Some acronyms are pronounced as any other word, others such as PPBS, are recited letter by letter.

ALLOCATION. Process of apportioning resources among one or more programs or functions to achieve a specific objective: to assign or distribute means among various purposes.

ALTERNATIVES. A set of options or choices available: specific and different courses of action available to accomplish objectives: means for achieving objectives: feasible strategies for a problem.

ANALYSIS. A systematic separation of a complex structure or problem into its essential components to ascertain the relationships among elements and the whole: a process for clarifying a complex vehicle by reducing it to its basic components: the application of systems techniques to ascertain the relationships among various factors such as costs and benefits.

AUDITING. Process of systematic examination, verification, and review of conditions and operation to ascertain true status.

BASE-CASE. A description of conditions as existing at a given or the present point in time.

BENEFIT-COST ANALYSIS. See COST-BENEFIT ANALYSIS.

BUDGETARY PROCESS. Steps or phases in developing a budget document such as preparation, presentation, adoption, execution, and appraisal.

COST. An outlay or an expenditure to achieve an object or objective, an indicator of resources consumed to reach a given condition: may be measured in dollars, time, or opportunities foregone.

COST ACCOUNTING. A branch of accounting concerned with searching out and reporting all elements of costs incurred or identifying all resources consumed in executing a specific activity or a unit of work.

COST-BENEFIT ANALYSIS. Systematic examination of an alternative as determined by the economic value (advantages) of the alternative as related to its economic costs (disadvantages): an analytical approach to solving problems of choice where both costs and benefits are measured and analyzed in monetary terms. The outcome is expressed as an index score or ratio of benefits divided by costs.

COST-EFFECTIVENESS ANALYSIS. Systematic examination of an alternative in terms of its advantages as measured by a fixed level and quality of an outcome, and disadvantages, as measured by the economic cost. The measure of desirability (effectiveness) is *not* the same as the measure of costs. The index or ratio shows the costs of various alternatives that produce the same degree of effectiveness.

COST-EFFECTIVENESS CURVE. An S curve drawn to show the relationships between costs, computed along the X axis, and effectiveness, computed along the Y axis.

COST, INCREMENTAL. An increase of a specified quantity or unit of value, expenditure, or resources consumed to produce the next unit of something: a fixed sum expended. Synonym: marginal cost.

COST, LIFE CYCLE. Total expenditure of resources for a project from the point of inception to its termination. Terminal dates may be arbitrarily set if the life cycle is in excess of the determined long-range planning structure. The three major cost categories are: (1) research and development, (2) investment costs, and (3) operating costs.

COST, OPPORTUNITY. Economic value of opportunities foregone: the value of a resource in its best alternative use: the alternative opportunity benefits that are sacrificed as the result of a decision.

COST, SUNK. The resources consumed in the past (usually for buildings and equipment, which have been depleted or cannot be salvaged for use in future operations). Such resource expenditures are not relevant to a current decision concerning the future; only the future costs are important.

COST-UTILITY ANALYSIS. Similar to cost-benefit and cost-effectiveness analysis, but the output is measured in terms of usefulness agreed on by some authoritative panel or others.

CRITERION or CRITERIA. A standard or standards on which judgment is to be based: a test of relative degrees of desirability among alternatives: standards by which a course of action is evaluated: something set up and established by authority as a rule for the measure of quantity, quality, value, etc.

CROSSWALK. The expression of the relationship between program structures: a table with the rows of the table listing the program categories and the columns showing the appropriations and budget activities.

CYBERNETICS. The field of technology involved in the comparative study of the control and intracommunication of information: handling machines and the nervous systems of animals and man in order to understand and improve communication.

EFFECTIVENESS. The degree to which a program achieves its stated objectives: a measure of desired effect in qualitative terms in relation to a criterion.

ERMS (EDUCATIONAL RESOURCES MANAGEMENT SYSTEM). An acronym for the conceptual schema developed by the Research Corporation of the Association of School Business Officials, which describes the application of the planning-programming-budgeting-evaluating system concept to education.

EVALUATING. The process of determining or fixing a value to something; assessing the attainment of objectives and, therefore, the worth of a program: judging according to a criterion.

EXTERNALITY. A side effect from a planned activity for which there is no specific or economic market.

FISCAL MANAGEMENT CYCLE. A sequence of financial activities that starts with the budget, continues with accounting and auditing, and terminates with reporting.

FUNCTION. A major group of related actions that contribute to a larger action.

FUNCTIONAL-CHARACTER CLASSIFICATION. An accounting classification system in which expenditures are systematized by functions or character of work facilitated.

GOAL. A broad objective to be achieved: a broad outcome pointing to a direction to be pursued: a generation on a terminal point.

INCREMENT. A fixed increase; a gain in a unit of value.

INCREMENTAL BUDGETING. A method of developing future budgets by starting with present or base level of expenditures for the present or previous years and stipulating no increment or an additional unit expressed in dollars or percentage of gain: the traditional budget development procedures as opposed to zero base budgeting. Synonym: comprehensive budgeting.

INDICATOR (PERFORMANCE or OUPUT). A measure of the condition or a characteristic of a performance or an output: may be by indirect or direct observation with or without a sensitive instrument.

INPUT. A resource consumed or available to pursue an activity or an objective: component of a production process: energy of a system or contribution of a valued resource to a function.

INTERFACE. The point where two or more streams of activity merge and meet: the area or point of interaction between two or more systems or subsystems.

LINEAR PROGRAMMING. A mathematical technique for optimizing the overall allocation of resources to various activities where constraints are such that not all activities can be performed optimally. A requirement is that the relationship between the activities and the constraints and objectives be linear in a mathematical sense. The objective is to maximize or minimize some function. The decision problem is solved by finding the levels of the various activities that maximize or minimize the objective function that satisfies all constraints.

LINE-ITEM BUDGET. A traditional budget based on objects of expenditure. Each object such as salaries paid or supplies to be purchased is placed on a separate line in the budget.

MANAGEMENT-BY-OBJECTIVES (MBO). Management that emphasizes the achievement of predetermined objectives at some future point in time. Some also see it as a manager appraisal system based on outcomes achieved rather than personal traits.

MANAGEMENT INFORMATION SYSTEM (MIS). A computer-based system containing data relevant and essential to the management of an organization.

MARGINAL COST. Total cost of producing one additional unit of production or service beyond a given base.

MATRIX. A rectangular array of mathematical quantities by rows and columns used to facilitate the study of problems in which the relation between the contrasting terms is fundamental.

MODEL. A representation of reality, a simplified version of the real world: synonymous with theory, therefore, a cluster of interlocking and interactive concepts systematized into an abstracted intellectual pattern capable of interpreting generalizable trends and interrelationships that prevail within reality.

MULTIYEAR PROGRAM AND FINANCIAL PLAN. The casting of the budget document to show expenditures for several, usually five, fiscal periods rather than one. It shows the future implications of current educational program decisions. Expenditures are based on programs as well. Comprehensive summary of agency programs showing outputs, costs, and financing. Sometimes called the "program budget."

OBJECT OF EXPENDITURE. Specific service, item, or commodity obtained as an outcome of making a specific expenditure. Salaries, supplies, materials, and purchased services are illustrations of objects of expenditure.

OBJECTIVE. A statement of a specific outcome or terminal condition to be achieved: outcomes that include very specific directions or challenges to be met: a future-oriented strategic position to be achieved by an organization.

OBJECTIVE PERFORMANCE. A well-defined statement of educational outcome that includes descriptor phrases about expected terminal behavior, conditions, and criteria.

OPERATIONS RESEARCH (OR). A scientific analysis approach to problem solving that stresses quantitative analysis and mathematical models as a way to discover the optimum solution: a technique that emphasizes applied mathematics such as linear programming. Objectives and assumptions are accepted as constraints and not questioned as is done in systems analysis.

OPTIMIZATION. A mathematical procedure used to determine the best mix of inputs to meet an objective: a strategy to maximize objectives.

OUTCOME. A generic term that embraces all statements of ends to be achieved such as mission, goal, and objective: a product or result gained: result obtained from input of resources.

OUTPUT. The result of a process consuming inputs: that which is produced.

PLANNING. A process of preparing a set of decisions for action in the future, directed at achieving goals by optimal means. Two outcomes of the planning dimension of PPB are objectives and alternatives to fulfill objectives.

PPBADERS. An acronym, developed by S.J. Knezevich, for the following processes included in program budgeting: planning, programming, budgeting, analyzing, deciding, recycling system: a more comprehensive list of PPB processes.

PPBES (see also PPBS and RADS). Acronym developed by the Research Corporation of the Association of School Business Officials, for the planning-programming-budgeting-evaluating system; an extension of PPBS that includes the evaluating process.

PPBS (see also PPBES and RADS). Acronym for the planning-programming-budgeting system developed by RAND Corporation and installed and popularized by the United States Department of Defense: an integrated system to facilitate planning and decision making.

PERFORMANCE BUDGETING. A management-oriented budgeting approach that casts budget accounts in functional classification systems and seeks to assess work efficiency: retrospective in outlook.

PROGRAM. To cluster a series of interdependent, closely related activities or inputs around a common objective or set of allied objectives.

PROGRAM ACCOUNTING. Accounting by the purpose or objective to which the fiscal transaction is to contribute placed in a multiyear time frame: recording and classifying resource expenditures around one or more outcomes.

PROGRAM BUDGET. A budget document in a "programmatic format," that is, aggregation of expenditures around identified objectives in a multiyear time frame.

PROGRAM BUDGETING. Synonym for PPBS preferred by some developers of such ideas such as Novick.

PROGRAM CATEGORY. A cluster of activities identified with fairly broad objectives or goals.

PROGRAM ELEMENT. A subdivision of a program subcategory: a second level of breakdown from the program category level: a discrete program classification (item) that facilitates the process of quantifying the several characteristics (properties) of the program.

PROGRAM MEMORANDA. A document that contains succinct descriptions of output-oriented categories (programs) that cover the work of an agency for the budget period. It may include information on recommended changes, the needs to which program is addressed, the objectives of the program, required resources, the expected effectiveness, and the target population. Originally intended to be filed annually, now confined to new or significantly modified programs. A justification statement for budget requests.

PROGRAMMING. The process of translating objectives into related activities and resources into programs: developing programmatic formats.

PROGRAM STRUCTURE. An organizational structure based on activities related to objectives rather than on functions, regions, or type of product.

PROGRAM SUBCATEGORY. A major subdivision of a program category based on objectives more specifically and narrowly defined than for a program category.

PRORATING. A process of dividing and assigning a single cost to several services or functions benefiting from the expenditure. Techniques are arbitrary and are based on such factors as time, mileage, or hour consumption.

RADS (see also PPBS and PPBES). Acronym, originated by S. J. Knezevich, meaning Resource Allocation Decision System; similar to PPBS and ERMS but focuses on the end result rather than processes used within the system.

RESOURCE. Available means to pursue an end: computable wealth assigned to a purpose: inputs available to the school system for use in attaining its objectives.

RESOURCE, HUMAN. Individual identified as a potential talent by reason of knowledge or experience and willingness to integrate specialty with the accomplishment of an objective.

SPECIAL STUDIES. Cost-effectiveness analysis of program alternatives for further justification of resource allocation decisions. Used in federal government bulletins on PPBS.

SUBJECTIVE MEASURES. Impressionistic observations of the comparison of outputs with the criteria of related objectives for which outputs were produced.

SUBOPTIMIZATION. Selection of the best alternative course of action that pertains to a subproblem, that is, to only part of the overall problem or objective. Usually necessary because alternatives at all the various levels of decision making cannot be analyzed simultaneously before decisions must be made at some levels. Also referred to as any intermediate stage in a long-run goal attainment program.

SUBPROGRAM. A division of a program category. It combines activities on the basis of objectives within the broader objectives of the program category.

SUPPORT SERVICES. Services contributing to or essential to agents engaged in direct production or service, such as administrative, technical, and logistical functions that facilitate and enhance teaching or learning objectives. Important adjuncts for the fulfillment of objectives.

SYSTEM. An array of components designed to accomplish a particular objective according to plan: a cluster of interactive and interdependent components that focus on one or more related objectives.

SYSTEMS ANALYSIS. A continuous cycle of activities based on defining objectives, designing alternatives to achieve objectives, evaluating alternatives on a systematic basis, using models of the unit under study, employing interdisciplinary teams for analysis, and using scientifically oriented decision procedures: a method of inquiry or way of looking at problems: a highly rational approach to analysis emphasizing the tools of economics: quantitative analysis approaches even under uncertain conditions.

SYSTEMS APPROACH. A rational approach for designing a system to attain specific objectives: a set of techniques for resolving problems through the scientific method and use of models and quantitative analysis techniques.

SYSTEMS MANAGEMENT. Administration or management of organizations based on or consistent with the systems approach.

TRADE-OFF ANALYSIS. The weighing, on the basis of selection criteria, of the use of alternative approaches to attain an objective with the intent to select a "best" alternative.

UNIT COST ANALYSIS. A branch of accounting that seeks to determine output per standard measurable unit: related to cost-accounting.

ZERO-BASE BUDGETING. Justification from zero with the continuation of every program in the budget questioned and documented; consideration of basic level or present funding as well as incremental changes for next fiscal period. Contrasts with incremental budgeting.

Index

Accountability, 57-59
Accounting
  defined, 148-49
  systems, 149-67
Acronyms, 2
Across-the-board strategy,
  258-60
Adams, B. K., 121
Airforce, 17, 18
Alternative operation strategies,
  258-60
Alternatives, 172-74
American Association of School
  Administrators (AASA), 23,
  256, 261, 269
Analysis, cost, 171-79, 182-222
  cost-benefit, 183-85, 206-208,
  218-19
  cost-effectiveness, 183-86, 194,
  203-206
  cost-utility, 183-85
  danger and constraints, 217-22
  levels of, 186-88
  philosophical criteria for, 188-89
  programmatic structures and,
  189-93
  quantitative, 194-222
Appraisal, 236-50

Association of School Business
  Officials, 246-48. *See* RC-ASBO

Bach, R. H., 229-35
Benefit-cost analysis, 15, 172
Bell Laboratories, 16
Bernabei, R., 41-42, 51
Bloom, B., 40-41, 51
Bowles, B. D., 230, 235, 275, 281
Brown, A. L., 81, 107, 108
Budget
  calendar, 114
  definitions, 110-12
  document, 111-13
  performance. *See* Performance
  budgeting
  program. *See* Program budgeting
  reforms, 115-18
  triangle, 113-15
  types of, 116, 136-38
  zero-base. *See* Zero base budgeting
Budget and Accounting Act, 16, 110,
  117
Budgetary process, 110-15
Budgeting, 109-45
  and other fiscal instruments,
  118-20
  classifications, 118

Budgeting (continued)
    cycle, 118-19
    history, 16-18, 110-12, 115-18
Bulletin 66-3, 14, 15, 74, 77, 102,
        182, 187, 189, 258, 264, 265,
        271, 284-300
    Supplement to, 301-309
Bulletin 68-2, 15, 182, 189, 264,
        265, 271, 310-24
Bulletin 68-9, 15
Bureau of the Budget, 15, 225, 265
Burkhead, J., 27, 121, 122

Callahan, R. E., 170
Carlson, J. W., 187-88, 222, 224
Carpenter, M. B., 180, 186, 222
Center for Vocational and Technical
        Education, 22, 208
Change, 253-54. *See* Innovation
Churchman, C. W., 281
Comprehensive budgeting. *See* Zero
        base budgeting
Controlled materials plan, 17
Cost(s), 147, 160-61. *See also*
        Expenditure accounting
Cost-benefit analysis. *See* Analysis,
        cost effectiveness
Cost-effectiveness curves, 194-203,
        213-17
Cost-utility analysis. *See* Analysis,
        cost-utility
Cotton, J. F., 27, 33-34, 38, 173,
        180, 181, 183, 186, 210, 212,
        214, 216, 222, 223, 225, 234
Curtis, William H., 13, 22, 27, 107,
        108

Dade County, Florida, 22
Deno, S. L., 45-46, 51
Department of Agriculture, U.S., 15,
        18, 19, 139-43
Department of Defense, U.S., 15,
        19, 32, 90-92, 174, 255, 258,
        268, 273-74
Decision making, 171-72, 225-30
Decision technology, 224-34
Deferred benefits, 194
Dewey, John, 172-72, 178, 226,
        233, 234, 253
Diffusion, 253, 254

Downey, L. M., 108
Dror, Y., 31-32, 38
Drucker, Peter, 53, 60, 62, 70
Duke, W. R., 248-49, 251
Dupuit, Jules, 15
Dyer, J. S., 251

Economic
    analysis, 9
    terms, 9
Edison, Thomas A., 16
Effectiveness levels, 212-17
Enke, E. L., 148, 169, 170
Enthoven, A. C., 173, 175, 180, 273
EPPBS, 2
ERIC, 10, 248, 251
ERMS, 5
Evaluation, 241-46
    instrument, 243-46
    PPBS operations, 241-43
Expenditure accounting, 149-56

Fiscal control, 116-18
Fiscal management cycle, 113
Fisher, G. H., 171, 179, 180, 184,
        185, 222, 223, 232, 235
Ford Motor Company, 19
Fowlkes, J. G., 27, 121, 122, 169,
        170

General Motors, 17, 19
Glossary, 325-30
Goals. *See* Objectives or Outcomes
GOPBS, 30
Gross, Bertram, 275, 281
Guba, E. G., 254, 270
Guba-Clark model, 254

Haggart, S. A., 180, 189-94, 222,
        223
Hammann, A., 139, 140, 141, 145,
        146
Hammond, J. S. III, 229-30, 235
Hartley, H. J., 23, 27, 251, 266,
        271
Hatry, H. P., 27, 33-34, 38, 85, 108,
        173, 180, 181, 183, 186, 210,
        212, 214, 216, 222, 223-24,
        225, 234
Haveman, R. H., 8, 13, 223

Held, V., 107, 121
Hicks, J., 222
Hirsch, W. Z., 21
Hitch, Charles J., 5-6, 18-19, 27, 32
Hoffman, F. S., 13, 225, 234
Holstein, W. K., 229, 235
Hoover Commission, 18, 124-25
Howell, R. A., 55-56, 70
Hoye, R. E., 251
Huff, R. H., 145

Incremental budgeting, 135
Individually guided education (IGE),
    40-100
Individually prescribed instruction
    (IPI), 40, 100
Implementation, 242-50, 255-60,
    262-70
Innovation, 253-58
Instructional objectives exchange
    (IOX), 41

Jackson, H. (Senator), 273
Jenkins, J. R., 45-46, 51
Jernberg, J. E., 115
Johnson, L. B., 14, 15, 19, 20, 224,
    255, 258

Kaldor-Hicks criterion, 189
Key, V. O., 130, 145, 146
Knezevich, S. J., 13, 27, 107, 108,
    121, 122, 169, 170, 234, 270,
    271
Krathwohl, D. R., 40-41, 51

Leles, S., 41-42, 51
Levinson, H., 55, 70
Lindman, E. L., 152, 156, 169, 170
Little criterion, 189

Macleod, R. K., 161, 170
McGivney, J. H., 38, 223, 230, 235,
    275, 281
McGregor, Douglas, 53-54, 70
McKean, R., 19, 27
McNamara, R. S., 6, 18-19, 255, 273
Management by objectives (MBO),
    52-69
Marginal analysis, 175-76, 179
Margolis, J., 223

Marvin, K. E., 222, 224, 234, 259,
    260, 266, 270, 271
Memoranda, program. See Program
    memoranda
Merewitz, L., 13, 15, 19, 20, 27, 28,
    48-49, 51, 74, 107, 108, 131,
    141-43, 145, 146, 147, 157,
    169, 170, 172, 180, 222, 223,
    264-65, 271, 276, 281, 282
Midwestern States Educational
    Information Project (MSEIP),
    152, 154-55, 169, 170
Miller, D. W., 52, 70
Mitchell, James, 169, 170
Model, 66-68
Mosher, F. C., 275, 281, 282
Mottley, C. M., 176-78, 180, 181
Multiyear costing, 19, 131-34
Multiyear program and financial
    plan, 264-65
Mushkin, Selma, 21, 219, 223
Muskie, Edmund, 20

National Academy for School
    Executives, 23, 256, 261, 269
Neal, F. W., 107
Nelson, W. C., 38, 223
Newman, W. H., 77-78, 108, 227,
    235
New York City Bureau of Municipal
    Research, 16-17
Novick, David, 5, 14, 16, 17, 18,
    21, 27, 28, 29, 33, 38, 90,
    108, 118, 122, 124-25, 130,
    163, 173, 179, 180, 181
Nowrasteh, D., 205, 207, 223

Object-of-expenditure accounting,
    115, 148, 153, 159
Objectives
    and PPBS, 39-40
    behavioral, 41-43
    criteria for assessment, 60-62,
        63, 66
    criticisms of, 48-49
    hierarchy of, 43-46
    reforms, 40-43
Odiorne, George, 53, 56, 70
Office of Management and
    Budgeting (OMB), 15, 19

Operating costs, 208-209
Operations research, 16, 176
Ovsiew, L., 121, 122
Outcomes, 43-46

Parallel budgets, 259-60
Pareto criterion, 188-89
Partial and evolutionary strategy,
    258-60
Performance budgeting, 18, 123-30,
    136-38
Performance objectives, 43-48, 64-66
PERT, 8, 259
Philosophical criteria in analysis,
    188-89
Pipe, Peter, 41-51
PIPOS, 35-36
Planning
    and programming, 101-102
    and program budgeting, 32-33
    definition, 30-32
    elements, 36
    in PPBS, 29-38
    process, 31-32
    programming and budgeting
        system. *See* PPBS
    purposes, 3-4
    why it doesn't always work,
        35-37
PPA (problems, pressures, and
    aspirations), 63-66
    antecedents, 15
PPBS
    and decision making, 228-30
    and MBO, 52-69
    and politics, 230-34, 274-80
    and program budgeting, 6
    and public expenditures
        economics, 8-10
    and systems analysis, 7-8,
        171-79
    appraisal of, 236-50
    criticisms, 3-5, 273-80
    defined, 215
    described, 1
    fiscal dimensions, 147-67
    history of, 15-23, 252
    implementation evaluation
        instrument, 243-46
    in business, 19-20

PPBS (continued)
    in state and local governments,
        20-21
    phases, 237-41
PPBADERS, 3
PPBES, 2, 22, 248-49
Problem solving, 172
Professional staff development,
    256-57
Programs
    categories, 74-77
    defined, 72-73, 81
    element, 75-77
    levels of, 75-77
    objectives, 94-99
    plan, 77-80
    structure, 73-74
Program accounting, 19, 147, 157-60
Program accounting and budget,
    248-49
Program aggregations, 74-77
Program and budgeting system
    (PABS), 21
Program budgeting, 1, 5, 10, 124,
    130-38
    and education, 10-11
    and PPBS, 6
    history and development, 14-26,
        25-26
Program budget document, 164-66
Programmatic curriculum, 99-101
Programming, 71-107
Program and financial plan (PFP),
    102-103, 131-34
Program formats, illustrations of,
    80-99
Program memoranda, 102-103, 264
Program planning document,
    103-105
Program structure, 73-74, 189-94
Proration, 162
Proxmire, William, 225, 234
Public expenditure economics, 8-9,
    130-31

Quade, E. S., 174, 180, 181, 228,
    235
Quantitative analysis, 194-222

RADS, 4-5

RAND Corporation, 5, 8, 14, 15,
    16, 18, 19, 21, 72
RC-ASBO (Research Corporation of
    the Association of School
    Business Officials), 5, 10,
    22-23, 73, 78, 145
Ringbakk, K. A., 35-37, 38
Ristau, R. A., 267-68, 271
Rouse, A. M., 222, 224, 234, 259,
    260, 266, 270, 271

Schainblatt, A. H., 281
Schelling, T., 273-274
Schick, Allen, 17, 27, 28, 74, 108,
    109, 116, 117, 121, 122, 124,
    130, 131, 135, 145, 146, 276,
    281, 282
Schleh, E. C., 60, 70
Schultz, George B., 15
Simon, H. J., 226-27, 233, 235
Smalter, D. J., 20
Smith, K. W., 173, 180
Sosnick, S. H., 13, 15, 19, 20, 27,
    28, 48-49, 51, 74, 107, 108,
    131, 141-43, 145, 146, 147,
    157, 169, 170, 172, 180, 222,
    223, 264, 265, 271, 276, 281,
    282
Special studies, 182, 265
Staff capabilities, 260-62
Starr, M. K., 52, 70
State-Local Governments Finance
    Project, 20-21, 107, 108
State of the art, 246-50
Stedry, A. C., 115, 121, 122
Systems analysis, 7-8, 16, 172-73,
    174-78

Systems approach, 172-173
Sumner, C. E., Jr., 77-78, 108, 227,
    235

Taba, Hilda, 42, 51
Targeted performance objectives,
    43-46
Taylor, D. W., 227, 235
Thompson, V., 230, 235
Thornton, Charles, 19
TVA, 15, 17
Tyler, R. W., 41, 51

Unit cost analysis, 147, 162-67
U. S. Chamber of Commerce, 20
U. S. Commission on Organization
    of Executive Branch. See
    Hoover Commission
U. S. Department of Agriculture.
    See Department of Agriculture
U. S. Department of Defense (DOD).
    See Department of Defense
U. S. Office of Education, 149-56,
    162, 170

War Production Board, 17
Weisbrod, B., 218, 223
Western Interstate Compact On
    Higher Education (WICHE),
    22-23, 128-30
White, M. J., 281, 282
Wildavsky, A., 139, 140, 141, 145,
    146, 232, 235, 255, 270, 271,
    275, 281, 282

Zero base budgeting, 19, 123, 135-43